a
guide
to workplace
ownership,
participation &
self-management
experiments
in the
United States
& Europe

WORKPLACE DEMOCRACY

Daniel Zwerdling

HARPER TORCHBOOKS
Harper & Row, Publishers
New York, Cambridge, Hagerstown, Philadelphia, San Francisco
London, Mexico City, São Paulo, Singapore, Sydney

CON-TENTS

1 INTRODUCTION

People talk about "workplace democracy," but what do they really mean? There are humanization of work projects, and labor-management committees, and worker-owned companies. There are worker self-managed enterprises too. What are the differences?

9 McCAYSVILLE INDUSTRIES

Former seamstresses at a Levi bluejeans plant struggled to form their own factory. Democratic decision-making didn't work, but they've created a human workplace which cares about people.

19 GENERAL FOODS

Executives designed a dog food plant so worker teams could have carefully defined freedoms and powers. Employees liked it—but now trouble is brewing.

FOREWORD

Daniel Zwerdling has written a timely and useful book. It deserves a wide audience, one going beyond those professionally engaged in debates about either the value or the inevitability of democracy in the workplace. It is timely because of congruent and converging trends in the labor force, in organizational and social values and norms, and in economic and environmental forces. It is useful because it makes clear, as few books have, the range, the complexity, and the dilemmas of organizational and work arrangements attempting to be "more" democratic.

All of the cases described were represented at the Third Annual Conference in Self-Management, yet they are far from identical in philosophy or practice. Their unifying characteristic is, perhaps, dissatisfaction with the status quo ante. Neither the Vermont Asbestos Group (VAG) nor the South Bend Lathe workers were driven by principle—what they sought was continued employment. The solutions they arrived at were the counsel of desperation and would never have been considered otherwise. Indeed, since this book was written, a majority of the stock in VAG has been acquired by an outside investor; the company is, once again, privately owned in the most conventional sense.

Yet the movement for self-management grows. For example, the U.S. Senate has recently passed a bill that would "authorize the Small Business Administration to guarantee loans to employee-owned businesses and to employee organizations seeking to purchase their businesses." The bill is well conceived and backed by an impressive array of members of Congress, armed with a wealth of data supporting their case.

The movement also grows for very practical reasons. The fact that proponents of democracy at work often phrase the "whys" in philosophical or ideological terms, stressing such values as human dignity, should not be allowed to obscure the pragmatic reasons for considering flatter, more participatory, more quality of worklife centered organizational arrangements. For example, the demand for challenging jobs that offer more direct control over working conditions has been growing in recent years, in part as a result of the vast increase in the number of working women and the shift toward a younger, more highly schooled labor force.

The labor force will gradually age over the next twenty years. As one consequence, people will spend more time in certain kinds of jobs, rather than advancing rapidly, because the slots above will already be filled with relatively young people. Therefore, much more will have to be done to enhance the challenge, influence, recognition, and reward available in the jobs that they will occupy.

The impact of education is particularly striking. Over the last ten years the median educational attainment of the entire labor force has increased to 12.6 years, indicating some college. There has been an even more significant increase for blacks, from a median attainment of 10th grade to some college education. Significantly for "experiments" in quality of worklife and worker democracy in factories, this increased education has also reached the blue collar ranks. The proportion of male crafts workers and other blue collar workers with a year or more of college has doubled since 1966; nearly 1/5 of all crafts workers and 1/10 of other blue collar workers have had at least four years of college. Education and age trends reinforce each other: younger workers have the highest rate of expressed dissatisfaction with their jobs, the highest rate of job-seeking, and of unscheduled absence from work.

The state of our labor force signifies more than just new employee demands. It also indicates that more and more workers—including professionals and technical workers as well as lower level employees—will be capable of making intelligent decisions on their own about their work. Think for a moment about the labor force conditions that prevailed when "scientific management"—the model for the new factory system in America and, subsequently, for much of our Western sense of the "best way to organize"—was invented. The economy was growing, with growing markets to satisfy, leading to a growing need for workers and for systems that could make them productive as efficiently as possible.

But the potential labor supply was composed largely of immigrants, both from Europe and the South and largely of rural origin. They were also young, poorly educated, and with only minimum skills; standardized formal or secondary schooling was only coming into being. Thus, organizations faced a labor force without industrial work habits, without strong geographic attachments (therefore potentially temporary) and with different linguistic and cultural backgrounds—all adding up to problems of integration and turnover. This coincided with a general climate of labor unrest and conflict, not yet institutionalized in the relatively polite and structured relationships that now exist between management and unions.

Under such conditions, it is not surprising that there was widespread interest in and acceptance of new work systems that involved: a minute division of labor; work simplification which broke tasks into the smallest component parts; a separation of "thinking" from "doing" work; considerable external discipline; as many impersonal rather than personal controls as possible; an emphasis on standard procedures and rules; and a clear hierarchical distinction between the educated white collar employee and the uneducated factory worker. Today, eighty years later, the situation is quite the opposite: such systems are not even technologically necessary.

It is not at all certain that scientific management and the reduction of workers to cogs was necessary even then. Zwerdling's chapter on Cooperativa Central makes it clear that we do not have to wait for workers to become urbane and educated to exercise effective and significant control over work decisions. In this case, farm workers one step removed from migrants took only a few years to take over most of the key managerial decisions in a substantial enterprise. Since one of the key issues in any discussion of workplace democracy is related to the characteristics necessary for those who participate effectively, this is an important story. Perhaps more people can handle "democracy" than is commonly thought.

Our own work supports this notion. In a number of situations, we have seen workers who were thought to be at—or beyond—the limit of their competence, poorly educated, and even with language problems, show themselves to have considerably greater ability and motivation than anyone had given them credit for.

What *is* workplace democracy anyway? It is clear that it encompasses a wide variety of situations; Zwerdling's examples show us some of the options that exist. Does it mean workers control? Self-management? Labor-management quality of work-life (QWL) committees that analyze jobs and propose and design changes in workplace? Which goals are being met? Which issues should be included? Total management of the enterprise, a chance to shape policy, or those things important to and closely affecting workers?

It is clear, as Zwerdling's examples show, that there are many different goals, and that they are not all met equally well in every new system. In today's discussions of more participatory work systems, it is possible to distinguish three kinds of goals, each of which seems to be independent: economic, political-managerial, and social goals. Who *owns* the organization and is entitled to its proceeds is one question. Who *governs* the organization—what kind of structure, operating, and decision-making vehicles exist—is another. And the question of who has access to either of these—whether organizations are "democratic" in the pluralistic sense of equitable access for women, minorities, and other disadvantaged people—is a third, often quite separate question. Thus, the "democrats" themselves do not always agree on what systems make sense; because their goals and purposes might be very different, they may respond to different constituencies, and they may face different constraints in their own activities. This is one reason why it is so hard to get a consensus on this issue, or why General Foods, the Plywood co-ops, and Cooperativa Central make such strange bedfellows.

By the same token, this is the reason why we can expect to see the drive for workplace democracy—in one or another of these forms—in nearly every organization. It is precisely because these general trends, in the character of the labor force and the economy, are able to manifest themselves in a variety of ways that are increasingly seen as legitimate, if not inevitable, that this book should be so useful. If, as Zwerdling shows, the pressure for democracy at work can be seen in so many varieties, then even the most conservative of organizations might have to respond.

There is a tendency to think of workplace democracy issues as involving primarily blue collar workers. In America we often sharply split "workers" from "managers," in our thinking, forgetting that many people with managerial titles and responsibilities can be themselves relatively powerless in the organization, and that, with respect to the levels above them, they are also "just workers." We also sometimes forget about the vast arrays of white collar and professional workers whose jobs are not bound to machines, but who have as little to say about organizational decision making as the factory or farm worker. Thus, while most of the cases in this book take place in manufacturing firms, there are a few indications that the same principles apply to white collar and professional work—at International Group Plans and American University.

Again, the issue is timely. At the same time that scientific management has been losing ground in manufacturing, its principles have been extending into the service world as pressures for efficiency grow in such diverse settings as hospitals, universities, and franchise retail operations. It would be ironic indeed, if workers in General Motors or other traditional assembly plants are given more flexibility and more job control, and are organized into committees that can make decisions about their plant, while university professors and hospital nurses are faced with more and more rules, job specifications, standard procedures, and exclusion from managerial decisions.

What is the role of unions in all of this (a matter that Zwerdling intelligently takes up at length)? The role of unions must also be considered against the backdrop of labor history in the twentieth century, as we did earlier in discussing organizational structures. As Zwerdling points out, the instinct of economic survival and the need of workers to protect economic livelihood has been the primary function of unions. Some union leaders are now seeing the possibility of taking on other roles, roles that others see as dangerously close to the involvement in the governance of the organization rather than as appropriate responses to new conditions. There are two related questions for the future. First, can new work systems be guaranteed to workers without being written into collective bargaining contracts? (i.e., Are unions necessary?) Second, what role can organized labor play, or should it play, in bringing new work systems into being? (Clearly, if they are not involved, new systems will be seen as management initiatives solely.)

As to the first question, much of the thrust of present union involvement in the issue of workplace democracy or quality of worklife is related to attempts to institutionalize, through traditional collective bargaining, new devices to give union members a chance to participate in decisions related to their own work and environment. Some of this is plainly a response to unions' concerns about being "replaced" but it is also a genuine attempt to differentiate certain ownership or policy related rights of management from shop-floor, job related rights that should arguably involve workers themselves. Whether these can be kept separate is another issue entirely.

As to the second question, it is interesting to note that in Europe, where, as Zwerdling points out, many of the innovations in workplace democracy have been launched and are most fully in place, the unions have been the target driving force for these changes. In the U.S., by contrast, most new ideas about organizations and organizational innovations come from management. There are two major differences: In Europe, unions tend to be much more centralized into the equivalent of a Trades Union Council, and European unions represent the vast majority of workers, whereas in the U.S. unions account for only about a quarter of all workers. Nevertheless, the detailed comparisons and opportunities to learn are instructive.

There is, finally, a question about what it is that makes new organizational systems work, what conditions are necessary, and what learning is needed to support the changes. The sheer variety represented in this book itself makes unequivocal lessons difficult to find. We can conclude that the concept is applicable in a surprisingly large and diverse group of organizations, but we can still argue about why and how, and how much further is possible and desirable. One of the problems is that we do not even know what "working" means. What are the criteria for "success" of more democratic systems? They are clearly more a matter of goals and values than of objective scientific standards. Even in mainstream traditional organizations, the question of the meaning of organizational "effectiveness" is still fuzzy and unclear, even with such straightforward indices as profitability.

But despite this lack of clarity, there are a few lessons that we would like to suggest. One is that the question of change can never be ignored: how to get from here to there and which transition mechanisms to use. The completely worker-owned organizations often started from scratch, developed from a crisis, or were made democratic by autocratic decisions (as at IGP and Cooperativa Central). But for the large established organization, it is important to start slowly and to carve out areas of relative safety in which new systems can be implemented and tested. There is a tendency to see transitional systems as ends in themselves, rather than as vehicles which can help move the organization from one state to another. In all cases, even those of worker ownership, we can also

see that organizational units only become truly self-managed after a period of time. There is always a learning period. Participation requires more than the mere opening of decision making channels; it also involves practice, patience, knowledge and information, all of which take time to acquire.

The cases in this book include some that are relatively new (and running against the tide in their own industry, as in General Foods) and some that are relatively old (and become the industry norm locally, as in the Plywood companies). But in both cases we witness organizational change and drift. It is not only the newer systems, such as Rushton, that go through a period of adjustment, but also the older systems that seem already established. We conclude that it is impossible and unrealistic to seek "one best structure" for life. What is important about democratic structures is not their ends but their means—the very fact that they permit change and adaptation to changing circumstances, that they are flexible and responsive to present needs as they appear.

Workplace democracy, in short, is not merely a means to satisfy new worker demands; it is also a means to assure the most effective response to changing circumstances and times, a capacity that organizations will increasingly need.

Rosabeth Moss Kanter
Barry A. Stein

PREFACE

The women from McCaysville Industries in Georgia—the small garment factory founded and managed by former seamstresses at Levi—had never flown before on a plane. The farmworker from the Cooperativa Central, the $2 million strawberry co-op in California, had to find workers willing to pick his ripe berries before he could come. A representative from the Rushton mine, the Pennsylvania coal mine experimenting with semi-autonomous worker teams, wore his best white patent-leather shoes. The Ford Foundation official who has granted hundreds of thousands of dollars to sponsor workplace democracy projects wore his bluejeans, sandals and necklace.

The event was the Third International Conference on Self-Management, at Washington, D.C.'s American University, in June 1976. Over 500 conferees—hourly workers and academics, union members and students, economists and journalists and union officials—plunged into 60 panels exploring the possibilities for increasing worker participation, ownership and self-management in the United States.

The Conference was organized by the Association for Self-Management, a loose network of several hundred members founded in 1974. The Association Constitution says it is "an open, democratic association for the study of self-management, and the enhancement and development of self-management and organizational democracy." The main efforts of the Association, besides holding occasional regional workshops and publishing a quarterly newsletter on self-management developments, have been focused on holding this series of International Conferences on Self-Management. And the third conference was the biggest and best-attended conference yet.

There were the usual panels so familiar at conferences anywhere, conceived by academics and attended mainly by academics: Psychological and

xii

Sociological Implications of Self-Management, Organizational Culture of Self-Management, Transactional Analysis and Self-Management, and so on. But beyond them, the conference became an important landmark in the fledgling American movement for workers' self-management: for one of the first times, academics and researchers and students met face to face with some of the rank-and-file company employees and unionists they theorize and fantasize about. University of California researchers mingled with coal miners. University of Massachusetts students met assemblers at an automobile mirror plant. The conference provided a rare opportunity for theorists to discard some of their fantasies and confront both the real potential for self-management in the United States, and the obstacles to it.

Workplace Democracy is an outgrowth of that conference. Many of the major sessions at the conference were tape recorded. Using the proceedings of the Third International Conference on Self-Management as a starting foundation, I began to build a guide to workplace ownership, participation and self-management experiments across the nation. Besides the material generated at the conference, I drew on articles in the popular media, academic journals, and books; my own on-site visits to many of the companies; plus dozens of telephone interviews with workers, researchers and managers across the country. The result is a look at some of the major theories of "workplace democracy," a glimpse of what union leaders are saying and doing about increasing democracy in the workplace and—this is the heart of the book—a series of detailed portraits of some of the major experiments across the U.S. and Europe.

Workplace Democracy is by no means an encyclopedia of workplace democracy experiments. There are many projects doing important work, which have not even been mentioned. The companies described here, though, are among the most important—for they represent the major types of "workplace democracy" experiments taking place across the nation. The section on Europe obviously leaves out some of the most important nations promoting workplace democracy, such as Sweden. So much has been written about these nations in the popular press that it seemed needless to repeat it here.

Use the book as a beginning guide—a first visit to companies and institutions and people who are exploring ways of bringing more democracy to the workplace. After your visit, we hope you'll pursue the explorations on your own, using some of the research sources provided in this book as your map.

Some acknowledgements: Financial support for the book was provided in part by The Ford Foundation, Carol B. Ferry and W.H. Ferry. A number of people active in the self-management movement helped produce the book, and made helpful comments about some of the material; they include Larry Bonner, Sharon Grant, Kathy Terzi and Barbara Rothschild Kitsos, as well as Michael Maccoby, Margaret Molinari Duckles and Robert Duckles.

Several times during the past five years I've trekked across the U.S. visiting enterprises that are worker self-managed or worker-owned, or *trying* to become self-managed or worker-owned—or at various stages in between. Whenever I talk with people about their efforts to bring more democracy to their workplace, it is clear that one of the most painful—and also one of the most unnecessary—obstacles has been their isolation. Cut off from similar efforts elsewhere in the nation, the people at these enterprises have none of the hope, experience or sense of power that comes from knowing that thousands of other workers are sharing some of their same visions.

The people at these enterprises are pioneers, struggling to create a new kind of workplace in a vacuum. The Association for Self-Management has accumulated a long list of people in Birmingham, in Salinas, in the Georgia hills and in the Northwest, people who desperately want any articles or books which can tell them, "Is anyone out there doing the same sort of thing we're trying to do?" *Workplace Democracy* is designed to help answer that question.

D.Z.
June 1978

INTRO-DUCTION

When historians in the next century gaze back to the 1970s and the dawning of the last quarter of the Twentieth Century, they may conclude that ours was the era of crucial upheavals in society's most venerated, degraded, and necessary institution. Work.

Work became the obsession of sociologists and psychologists, political activists and economists, academicians and politicians—not to mention workers themselves. People explored the meaning of work, and the lack of meaning of work, the boredom of work and the diseases caused by work. Citizens worried about the crippling shortage of work, and industry worried about the breakdown in the quality of work.

But when you boiled down all the problems and dilemmas in the workplace and extracted a fundamental cause, common to all of them, it was this: in a society which is founded on the ideals of democracy, there is no democracy at work.

This book is about pioneering efforts to create the solution: bringing democracy to the American workplace.

What does "democracy at work" really mean? If you've been following all those newspaper stories on companies that are experimenting with changes in the workplace, it isn't likely that you'll know the answer—you'll be more confused than ever. For the newspapers have bandied about the notion of "worker democracy" so loosely that the terms have lost their meanings.

There are articles about companies like General Foods, which give employees limited powers such as rotating jobs, fixing their own machines or disciplining fellow workers: "Workers Share Helm," one newspaper headline proclaimed. There are articles about companies such as the Vermont Asbestos Group, which the rank and file workers purchased: "Workers Take Over Mine," one headline said.

There are articles about companies like the plywood factories, in which the employees elect the board of directors and vote on major corporate decisions. "Where Workers Run the Show," one newspaper declared. The way the newspapers tell the story, *all* of these dramatically different companies are living and breathing examples of democracy at work.

The case studies in this book, like the examples above, are all about companies that are changing the nature of the workplace—but the *ways* in which they are reshaping the workplace are dramatically different. In some cases, employees have gained limited powers over their day-to-day jobs while in other companies, the workers have acquired enormous power to change the corporation. In still other companies, the workers have gained only the potential to acquire power—perhaps some day in the future. To understand how these experiments fit into the movement toward more democracy at work, it is crucial to view them in the proper perspective. This introduction is a short course on four of the major kinds of workplace changes which often get lumped together under the concept of "workplace democracy": humanization of work, labor-management committees, worker ownership and workers' self-management, or workers' control.

Humanization of work

Drift back to the early 1970s, the years of the "worker blues" and the "worker blahs." Flurries of social research surveys report that American workers are alienated and bored with their jobs. "Significant numbers of American workers are dissatisfied with the quality of their working lives," declared the widely publicized report, *Work In America*, published by the Department of Health, Education and Welfare. "Dull, repetitive, seemingly meaningless tasks . . . are causing discontent among workers at all occupational levels."

Worker dissatisfactions, the report continued, are crippling American productivity in the workplace, "as measured by absenteeism, turnover rates, wildcat strikes, sabotage, poor quality products and a reluctance by workers to commit themselves to work tasks."

To treat these worker woes, a number of major corporations came up with a new kind of cure: social scientists in the field call it humanization of work. As corporate social scientists describe it, the main cause of worker alienation and boredom is the faulty design of jobs. Corporate managers have been preoccupied for decades with the technological design of the workplace—what kinds of machines to use and how to arrange them on the shopfloor—and workers have been considered as living parts to plug into the production machine.

The problem, these corporate researchers say, is that managers have forgotten the *social* design of the workplace: how workers interact with management and with each other, and how they feel about their work. The social qualities of the workplace affect the work process just as much as the technology. Conclusion: if managers "humanize" the workplace—if managers give employees greater autonomy and involvement in the production process—workers will be satisfied and the worker blues will be cured.

And so, major corporations across the country (more than 2,000 of them, according to some estimates) have been "humanizing" their white- and blue-collar factories. A General Motors factory abolished the traditional assembly line, and gave small worker teams the power to assemble entire mobile homes on their own; each worker would no longer be alienated by having to screw on an isolated assembly-line part. Corning Glass encouraged workers to have "coffee with the boss" and weekly rap sessions with the department head; by sharing thoughts and problems about their work, the employees would feel less alienated and more involved in the corporation. At General Foods' Topeka dog food factory, traditional foremen disappeared—and autonomous worker teams took responsibility for directing the day-to-day production process, from deciding who should unload the boxcars to evaluating whether the product is of good enough quality to sell.

Where do the "humanization of work" projects fit into the movement toward more democracy at work? From day-to-day, these reforms do increase workers' autonomy and power over their jobs, and they do boost the workers' morale. In fact, there is scarcely a study in the nation which fails to show that increasing worker participation in the workplace increases worker satisfaction—and productivity as well. But to put the humanization of work projects in perspective, it is important to underscore their limits: While workers gain some power and autonomy over their jobs, they must exercise them within a larger framework which has been dictated by corporate management. At humanized enterprises, the traditional power relationship—management gives the orders, and employees do what they're told—remains essentially unchanged.

Corporations that have humanized the production process have made it clear that increasing worker contentment is not the goal. Increasing worker satisfaction is merely the means to the corporation's primary goal, which is maximizing productivity and profits. The humanization of work experiments at Procter & Gamble have been so successful in boosting productivity, in fact, that corporate executives keep the projects secret, like the recipe for making Pringles New Fangled Potato Chips. A Ralston Purina executive at one corporate conference on humanization of work got hefty applause when he told fellow executives that his company considered its methods of achieving employee satisfaction "as proprietary as new-product R & D [research and development] and potentially as significant."

Labor-management quality of work life committees

As numerous corporations have been "humanizing" the workplace, joint committees of labor and management officials have begun launching similar experiments in unionized companies across the nation. These quality of work life projects, as they're often called, share a basic premise with the "humanized" plants: if workers can exercise more autonomy and power over their jobs, their work life will be more satisfying and the quality of work will improve.

But the labor-management projects take a big step closer to democracy at work. For while corporate managements impose changes on the shopfloor in humanized plants, the unions and shopfloor workers take part with management in controlling and designing the changes under the quality of work life projects. "The *way* in which we do things is as important as *what* we do," participants in the Harman Industries labor-management project write. "This program of work improvement is not one which is designed by concerned managers, with the help of social scientists, and imposed on the plant," but "a *process* of democratic decision-making."

The quality of work life projects come in as many shapes and sizes as the companies and unions which have created them. In some cases, union and management officials launched the project in an effort to achieve specific, tangible goals. As the case study on Rushton Mining Company points out, the management and union hoped to increase safety without hurting productivity, and to smooth troubled labor-management relations. At the American Sterilizer Company in Jamestown, New York, the management and union formed a quality of work life project to

What is a self-managed business?

Jaroslav Vanek, a leading theorist on self-management at Cornell University, and his associate Christopher Gunn, have prepared a guide to self-management for workers in all occupations. Vanek and Gunn believe that written material about workplace democracy is often too complex to be read by some of the people who need it most, and so they have prepared their guide in a sparse, elementary style:

- "The self-managed business is owned and run by the people who work in it—and by no one else. And any money the business makes (after costs and taxes are paid) belong to these workers.

  The self-managed business is *democratic*. That means that all of the workers, no matter what their skill or education, make the decisions on how the business is run. Each worker has a vote, and no one has more than one vote.

  So *only* those who work in a self-managed business own it, vote in it, and get money out of it.

- The self-managed business tries to *teach*. It teaches its workers all of the jobs, and shares what it learns with the community. And it does not discriminate because of race, sex, age, or any other reason.

- The self-managed business does not give up control of its work in exchange for money. Every business needs money to get started and keep running. (This money is called *capital*.) Self-managed businesses need capital, too. And they pay interest for using this capital to anyone who lends it to them—whether it is the government, or a helping agency, or even the workers themselves.

  But it does not give control of the business to anyone just because they loan capital. It gives this power only to those who actually *work* in the business.

  In other words, the self-managed workers "hire" the capital. Most other businesses run the opposite way—the capital hires the workers and controls their work.

- Workers in a self-managed business can loan capital to it. But they do not *have* to. If they do, they are paid interest for it. But again, it does not give them any special rights or powers.

- Every business must keep getting *capital* in order to keep running. The self-managed business does, too—but it must do it very carefully, so the workers keep control.

  A self-managed business can put the money it makes back into the business, or start new self-managed businesses. But if it does, it must pay interest to its workers, who earned that money.

- Because they are a new kind of business, self-managed businesses usually need help to survive. This can come from a *"shelter organization."* Such an organization can help self-managed firms help each other. It can help find money to start new self-managed businesses. It can help self-managed firms to improve themselves and run better. Finally, it can help all of the self-managed firms to unite as part of a national self-managed economy. Such organizations should be developed for each region of the country, and then tied together on the national level.

These are the basic ideas of self-management. They can help working people to take control of their own lives. They can help us learn to work together, in cooperation and democracy. By managing our work ourselves, we can give ourselves more job security and stop being used for the profit of others."

"achieve increased efficiency and productivity" to escape "the threat of layoffs." Other labor-management projects, such as the one at Harman International Industries, have aimed at achieving more philosophical, far-reaching goals—such as stimulating "human growth and development" of the employees.

And, just as the goals of the labor-management projects are different, so are the kinds of influence they actually give employees. At a Nabisco cookie factory in Houston, a top-level committee of top management and union officials has initiated most of the workplace changes; the workers on the production floor have had little voice. But at Harman, committees of shopfloor workers initiate, and carry out, most of the changes on their own.

Labor-management quality of work life committees give employees more influence over the workplace than they had before—far more, at projects such as Harman. And they set in motion a process in which workers can learn to analyze their jobs, think critically about work, and join together with fellow workers to dream up shopfloor improvements and solve problems. But, like the humanization of work projects, they are not aimed at upsetting the traditional balance of power between management and the workers. "A quality of work life effort," says the American Center for the Quality of Work Life, "does not seek or suggest greater worker management control over organizations."

Worker-owned companies

Even five years ago, reading in the morning newspapers that workers had purchased their own multimillion dollar corporation would have been startling news. But today, the headlines come so frequently that they've become familiar. "Miners Buy the Mine to Save Their Jobs." "Employees Acquire Factory." "Workers Buy Textile Mill." Most of the articles suggest that workers *buying* their enterprise is the same as workers' *control*.

But the fact that employees have purchased their workplace is a far cry from saying they control it;

in fact, it doesn't necessarily mean the employees have any voice in making decisions at all. For there are markedly different kinds of worker ownership, and each one gives the workers access to varying degrees of power.

Workers can own their workplace by becoming members of a producer cooperative: witness the workers at the plywood factories in the Northwest or the farmworker ranches in California. In these co-ops, each worker owns one share and casts one vote in corporate affairs from electing the board of directors to voting on how to spend the profits. More than any other enterprises in the United States, these worker-owned enterprises are also worker-controlled.

But workers can also own their own enterprises by buying common stock on the open market. That's how employees purchased the Vermont Asbestos Group, the Herkimer Library Bureau and Saratoga Knitting Mill. In these cases, the workers exert far less power over the company than workers do in the co-ops, because individuals outside the company can also buy stocks. Furthermore, individuals can buy more than one share. The result: managers with high salaries, and financial resources to spare, buy more stocks and cast more votes than hourly workers on the production floor.

There is a third way in which workers have become owners of their firms, one which in practice has given them the least direct control of all—establishing an Employee Stock Ownership Plan, or ESOP. At companies such as South Bend Lathe, for instance, the corporation in effect gave its stocks to the employees, free of charge, by depositing them in an ESOP trust. But as South Bend Lathe and most other companies designed their ESOPs, the number of stocks each employee receives is based on his or her salary—which means, again, that managers get far more shares than the workers tooling the machines on the shopfloor. South Bend Lathe also designed the ESOP so that workers won't have the power to cast the votes on most of their stocks for at least a decade; at most firms that have established ESOPs, the workers will *never* get the power to vote their own stocks. Instead, the stock votes in these worker-owned firms will be controlled by management-appointed committees.

Workers at such companies have the *potential* for controlling their workplace, some day in the future. But it will be years before the potential at these worker-owned firms can possibly be fulfilled.

Workers' self-management

The three kinds of workplace developments we've been discussing—humanization of work, labor-management committees, and worker ownership—have all made the workplace *more* democratic by giving employees more influence over aspects of the corporate structure than they ever had before. Except for the cooperatives, they are *reforms* in the traditional corporate power structure: they leave management's traditional powers intact.

But the fourth major development in the American workplace is dramatically different; it stands the traditional corporate power structure on its head. Under worker's self-management, or workers' control, the management doesn't give the employees some expanded powers on the shopfloor—the rank and file workers control the entire corporation, period.

"Workers' control means that a firm's management should be accountable to its employees," write the editors of *Workers' Control.* "And it means conversely, that the workers—blue- and white-collar alike —should bear responsibility for running the enterprise's operations."

"When we speak of workers' control," writes theorist Andre Gorz, "we speak of the capability of the workers to take control of production and to organize the work process as *they* see best."

Advocates of workers' self-management argue that it is the only long-term solution to the crises of the workplace. Psychologically it's necessary, they argue, as the logical extension of what humanization of work proponents have argued: workers will develop

feelings of self-worth only if they have influence over their own work lives. If workers feel increased satisfaction by gaining *some* power over their day-to-day jobs, then their feelings of self-worth and dignity will mature only if they exert complete control over their work lives.

Self-management advocates also argue it's the only long-term solution to the work crisis on ethical grounds. The philosophical dictum that people are never a "means," but always an "end" is shattered every time an employee "rents" his or her labor out to private corporate owners—sort of a modern version, self-management advocates say, of voluntary servitude.

Self-management is the ultimate solution, advocates argue, because American society is founded on democratic values. "The democratic principle states that

University of California researcher Paul Bernstein lists six crucial characteristics of a self-managed organization—six components which are "minimally necessary" he says, for the workplace democratization process to flourish. If any one of these components is missing, case studies suggest, the self-management structure might break down and even die. The six components:

- Regular participation in decision-making;

- Frequent economic return to participating employees from the surplus they produce, above regular wages and fringe benefits;

- Access to and sharing of management information and management-level expertise;

- Guaranteed individual rights, corresponding to traditional civil liberties;

- An independent board of appeals in case of disputes, composed of peers as far as possible;

- A particular set of democratic attitudes and values compatible with self-management.

Achievements of self-management

"We believe that self-management offers solutions to the major social and economic dilemmas which confront our nation today. Picture the economy: more and more plants are shutting down and workers are losing their jobs. Northern-based factories are moving to the nonunion, low-wage South while many corporations are shifting production—plus jobs, technology and capital—to other nations, such as Taiwan.

"Unions are battling for bigger wage contracts but real wages are still not keeping pace with inflation. Although some corporations have been redesigning work and abolishing the assembly lines, many workers remain alienated and bored. And despite the government's attempt to control pollution, toxic chemicals and other hazards continue to cripple workers, both on the shopfloor and in the community outside the factory walls.

"But now picture a self-managed economy. Workers have ultimate job security because they control the decision to keep operating or shut down the plant. Because employees control their working conditions, they feel more responsible to each other and more committed to the quality of the goods or services they provide. And in fact, experiences across the country show that when employees exert more control over their workplace, productivity, quality and profits usually increase . . .

"Self-management is also likely to increase job satisfaction, since the employees who want to can broaden their experience through job rotation and learning new skills. In a self-managed economy, the employees who control their own workplace are far more likely than private owners to keep it safe and to prevent pollution of the water and air . . . To a community whose economic and environmental health depends on local industry, then, the advantages of worker self-management should be obvious.

"Do many Americans now favor self-management? We believe that national surveys suggest they do. A recent poll by Hart Associates found that 66 percent of the nationwide sample would support some form of employee ownership and control of industry, while 50 percent said employee ownership and control would improve the economy. The survey shows not so much that Americans are consciously advocating self-management, as they are consciously dissatisfied with the existing economic system. Americans, the poll suggests, are open to fundamental economic change."

Federation for Economic Democracy

the people who are to be governed by a government should have an equal vote in electing that government," researcher David Ellerman writes. "Since it is precisely the people who work in a firm who are to be governed or managed by the workplace government or management, the democratic principle implies that it is the workers . . . who should have the voting rights."

But perhaps the most important argument for self-management, advocates say, is more pragmatic. Unless workers control their enterprise—from formulating sick leave policies to setting wage scales, from designing the production process to determining what to do with the profits—they won't have guaranteed protection against the abuses of management. Workers at a humanized factory can ask the management to give them certain concessions; workers in companies with labor-management projects can negotiate for concessions in collective bargaining, or try to blackmail the company—by going on strike—to grant them. But only workers in a self-managed firm have the actual voting power to *shape* the kind of workplace environment and work lives they want.

Self-management advocates argue among themselves over what forms worker self-management should take. Should every worker have a vote on every decision, such as in the collectives? Should workers vote once a year for the board of directors, such as at the plywood cooperatives? Should the workers set up a complex system of representative committees, like at International Group Plans?

But as researcher Paul Bernstein points out, "there is no fixed, single or final state of workplace democracy." The road toward democracy is constantly changing. The companies trying to get there, such as International Group Plans, are constantly in a state of flux. And that, perhaps, is the main message of the book. Some of the companies, such as General Foods, will never even approach a system of worker democracy. Other companies, like IGP, have gone further on the road toward democratic self-management than any corporation in American history. But all of the enterprises described here offer crucial lessons—both positive *and* negative—which can help workers in the future continue on the difficult but rewarding journey toward democracy at work.

McCAYS-VILLE

In the search for signposts toward worker self-management, most participants at the Third International Conference on Self-Management looked for *success* models — companies where the employees play an active role in making fundamental decisions. Some of the most important lessons in the trend toward more self-management, however, can come from the *failures*. One of the most important failures among recent attempts at worker self-management is McCaysville Industries, a women's garment factory in McCaysville, Georgia.

McCaysville Industries is a small factory, with less than 40 workers, all of them women. The factory is inside the cinderblock walls of an old chicken hatchery, around the bend from a river jam of automobile carcasses, at the foot of dirt-red hills scorched by fumes from the local copper smelting plant. Just a dozen years ago many of the women here were yanking 900 seams of denim a day under the needles of a nearby Levi Strauss bluejean factory, trying to meet production demands so they woundn't get fired, sneaking smokes in the toilet stalls so they wouldn't get caught — and taking home $1.25 per hour for the privilege of having any work at all in this depressed part of Appalachia.

Then in 1967 the 400 women of Levi's walked out on what would become a 14-month strike over pay and grievance procedures. They lost. The women had begun looking for work at other garment factories when some labor organizers came to town; as Bernice Ratcliff, one of the strikers and founders of the factory, recalls, "They said to us, 'Well, why not just start your own factory, a co-op?' " With help from the organizers, 60 strikers formed a cooperative garment factory. It was pure co-op. Women rotated the membership on the board of directors to give everyone a chance, and they tried to resolve major issues with a factory-wide vote.

Within a few years, however, the democratic decision-making structure fell apart. The story of *why* it fell apart — why the women could not get adequate financing, forcing co-op members to quit, and why women could not make decisions in a group — makes valuable reading for other employees interested in launching a democratic enterprise.

But while McCaysville failed in its attempt at cooperative self-management, it succeeded at another important goal: working women who had no business expertise and little formal education — most had not even attended high school — were able to overcome enormous economic, political and psychological obstacles and create their own economic base.

The factory has survived. It employs fewer women today, but there is a waiting list of women eager to become employees. Although four women now own and manage the factory, and do not formally include the workforce in their decision-making, they have tried to create a supportive work environment which frees the seamstresses from the controls and pressures of the big corporate plants. Women who would be turned away from conventional mills because they're too "old" or slow are valued at this former co-op,

and allowed to work at their own speed. While McCaysville does not provide a model of worker self-management, the mere fact it survives provides an inspiration for worker and community efforts to create their own economic institutions.

Co-ops in bloom

The late 1960's were a good time for co-ops. The war on poverty was in its heyday; government-funded poor people's cooperatives were sprouting like spring flowers across the impoverished hills of the Appalachians. There were craft co-ops and farming co-ops, and not far from McCaysville some black women had formed two small garment co-ops, too. The young labor organizers who had trekked to McCaysville to observe the strike were confident the seamstresses from the Levi plant could set up their own factory with little trouble at all. The women had already proved they were natural and persevering organizers: Bernice Ratcliff and the others had worked at odd jobs by day and walked the Levi picket lines by night for more than a year, without giving up.

When the organizers called the first meeting of women to talk about the co-op, only 15 showed up. "We didn't even know there was such a thing as a co-op before they told us," said one of the key organizers, Beulah Mull. But the notion that a "co-op" would allow the women to manage their own work lives immediately appealed to them. "After working at Levi, with people breathing down your throat," says Mull, "I thought the idea of people working and building something together was really wonderful. I had this dream: it would be a *people's* thing."

After several more meetings, more than 40 women had joined the co-op group. With the help of a legal counsel to Martin Luther King, Jr., the organizers drafted some fiery bylaws — "to eliminate the paradox of poverty in the midst of plenty," the preamble began, "to endeavor to advance the economic well-being of all the working people." The women scraped up some old sewing machines to rent, and leased an

The co-op structure fell apart because the women tried to be too democratic, to a fault. The entire factory would vote on taking a break

old barn still dusty with hay, which hadn't been used for years. The women began holding potluck suppers to raise some seed money; husbands, children and friends pitched in at night and on the weekends to renovate the barn, install new wiring, and shore up the walls with sheet rock.

The co-op's major hurdle was obtaining sufficient working capital. There are few organizations in the United States willing to finance a group of workers who want to launch their own enterprise and manage it democratically. The Office of Economic Opportunity considered granting $40,000 to the venture but eventually turned it down; efforts to get funds from the Ford Foundation, active in the co-op movement, did not succeed (some of the co-op organizers charged, without evidence, that the president of Levi Strauss, then on the Foundation board of directors, pressured the foundation to ignore the former Levi strikers). The Small Business Administration said it would consider backing a loan, but only if the women would agree to sell control of their fledgling factory to an established corporation.

The women say they never did shop for loans at banks. "Everybody that's supposed to know more than we did told us we couldn't get any loans because we didn't have any collateral," Ratcliff said, "and even if we did, we was told we couldn't get a business loan anyway, because us'ns were a bunch of women."

Finally the women raised small amounts of starting capital from the Southern Federation of Coops and the Southern Christian Leadership Conference. Beulah Mull traveled to New York begging for money, and a philanthropist donated $12,000 in the form of a long term interest-free loan.

Grasping for work

With no economic power to support them and no business acumen to guide them, the women grasped at whatever manufacturing contracts they could find. Most of the early contracts, the women remember, were bad deals. One of their first and longest-term contracts, for instance, not only paid a ridicu-

lously low rate for the garments, but also required the co-op to buy all its zippers, buttons, bags and packing cardboard at extra, and inflated, costs from the contractor's own shop.

For months — years, in some cases — some of the women of McCaysville voluntarily paid themselves only 25 cents an hour. The survival of the business, they say, was more important to them than receiving a regular income. "Some of us could scrape by because our husbands was working in the copper mines," says Ratcliff. "But some of the girls really needed the money, and we paid them, and we paid some of the widow women, or least enough to pay their rent and buy their groceries."

While the factory was limping along financially, the women were trying hard to make democracy work. The membership, which had swelled to 60 women, elected one of the workers as manager, and the rest began rotating on the board of directors. The workers held general meetings on the production floor at least once a week, and often more frequently if important issues came up or if some of the members requested it.

But the co-op structure soon began to fall apart. The members simply did not know how to make a democracy work. For instance, the women did not know when the entire membership should make a decision or when the elected manager could better make the decision on their behalf. Sometimes the co-co-op tried to be *too* democratic, to a fault.

"Beulah insisted on discussing virtually every decision with the membership,"one former member recalls. "We'd stop work and everybody would spend an hour arguing over how long to take a break." And women say the general membership meetings seldom produced a strong and united decision, because few of the workers would voice their opinions openly and honestly.

"When a meeting was called you could do all you could to *try* to get people to talk what was on their minds," Beulah Mull remembers, "but you couldn't get them to say anything that was really bothering them. At the meeting people would agree on anything,

anything — then after the meeting people would break up into groups and start complaining and fighting and whispering behind each other's backs. If people had spoken their minds in the open, they could have understood what was going on and made some real decisions."

But the final blows to the fledgling co-op were economic. The factory was doing so poorly financially that many members were forced to quit and find work at the big corporations such as Levi. They were replaced with women who were not granted co-op membership rights, and so the number of voting members rapidly dwindled. Then the state government, which had no legal guidelines regulating co-op factories, began to put on the squeeze: the government told the factory it was violating state laws by not keeping records of worker overtime and by not paying time and a half for overtime. "I told the state agent 'your wife works 8 - 12 hours a day at home and she's paid nothing,'" Ratcliff said. "'It's my time here and my business and if I want to work here and be paid nothing for it that's my business. And he said, 'We'll find out if it's none of my business. I can send you to prison and fine you $10,000.'"

The state government padlocked the factory shut one week, charging it was illegally not paying taxes; the state had no laws governing producer cooperatives, and so the usual co-op tax exemption which the factory had been claiming was under dispute. State agents told the women they would have to dump the co-op structure and reorganize as a conventional corporation. And so, the 13 original co-op members still hanging on incorporated as a 13-member partnership. Since then the number of partners has dwindled to four, and one of them, Bernice Ratcliff, has been selected as the factory manager. Today, the word "co-op" leaves a bitter taste in their mouths. "I don't believe a co-op can work," says Beulah Mull, who quit the co-op soon after it became a corporation. "There has to be a boss. There has to be someone who makes people do things even if they don't want to, no matter how much they holler and get angry about it. People are followers," Mull says. "They'll grumble and grunt every step of the way, but all they'll do is follow. And as long as they do, nothing in this country will ever change."

A dramatic difference

McCaysville may no longer be a co-op, and the women who work there "don't have any control over the factory or anything," as Lorine Miller, one of the four owners, told participants at the Third International Conference on Self-Management. But still McCaysville offers its employees, and its four owners, a place to work which is dramaticallly different than the conventional garment factories. "I don't think you can talk to any one of the girls out there," Lorine Miller said, "that wouldn't tell you it's the best place in the world to work." Interviews with the employees confirm it.

By traditional American business standards, the McCaysville Industries operation is a joke. "We run this factory like no other factory's ever been run," Bernice Ratcliff laughs. The four owners work the machines on the production floor alongside the other workers they employ, and they pay themselves the same hourly rate—$2.30, except for Bernice Ratcliff, who makes $3.10 as manager, by consensus of the owners, The factory doesn't enjoy the luxury of mechanical conveyors shuttling garments from one machine to the next or mechanical carton packers and forklift trucks; Ratcliff and Miller seal cartons with long swatches of sealing tape moistened with a crumpled paper towel, and they heave them with a grunt into a semi-trailer truck, destined for stores such J.C. Penney, Montgomery Ward, and major garment wholesalers in New York.

Bernice is boss — but in this factory, workers say, that's hardly the word for it. "I was working on the floor, and then Madeline [a co-owner] said, 'I think Bernice is qualified to be manager if she'd try it.'" Ratcliff says, "and the others agreed so I tried it." Decisions are not *made* so much as they evolve by

informal consensus — as the owners get together after work to sip some coffee, to empty garbage and sweep the floor. They often discuss business when they come to the factory on weekends to make repairs, instead of going fishing with their families. The owners have given Ratcliff authority to make decisions on her own, but as one says, "I can't think of anything she does without sitting down with us, and we all talk about how we feel about it and just end up agreeing on something."

But by any measure of worker *satisfaction*, McCaysville Industries is a wonder. The factory has 30 names on its employee waiting list, most of them workers at other garment factories in the area. The most extraordinary quality about McCaysville is the spirit, a relaxed sort of comraderie which is worlds away from the tensions and fears of a factory such as Levi. The women of McCaysville talk about the days working at Levi much like immigrants recall the horrors of the Gestapo in the old country before they fled. At McCaysville, women chat and laugh as they work, joke with the owners, and appear to feel at ease.

One crucial difference between McCaysville and the other garment factories is this: at McCaysville there is no production quota. At factories such as Levi the production quota is a way of life. Time-motion experts gear production rate to the fastest women: if a seamstress fails to meet the production quota a certain number of days in a row she doesn't get full pay, and eventually she gets fired. At a factroy such as Levi, a visitor can watch the women tensed over their machines, ramming denim under the needles like imprisoned speed freaks.

"We've seen production and what it does to a girl," Ratcliff says. "When I was at Levi I wasn't even that slow, but if I lost one minute of work during the day I couldn't gain that minute back and make my production. Sure, we could get out there and set production so high and set a time clock and tell the girls what to do and when to do it but we don't want that. That's why we left Levi."

Caring for factory rejects

At McCaysville, women work at their own speed, and they're given a chance to try out different operations, to find the one they perform best. "At Levi when I was working one operation and not making quota I never got an opportunity to see if I could do another operation better," Ratcliff says. "But here we shift people from one job to another. We try to place the ladies that are a little older on the easiest jobs, so they can come up with a decent amount of work every day, and the younger people who can handle work faster we put on the tougher jobs."

As a result, McCaysville Industries employs many older women who have been tossed out by the big companies — "older women" meaning women in their 40's. "Thirty-nine years old is the age limit at the factories, and after that you can't get work," Lorine Miller told the Third International Conference. "We've got ladies in their 60's. Bernice and I are both over 50. If we couldn't work in the factory," Miller said, "we'd have two choices: go on welfare or work in some cafe washing dishes."

At McCaysville, unlike other garment factories, the workers on the floor enjoy unusual freedoms, perhaps because the owners know well what sewing on a production floor was like. "If someone needs to take off work for some reason or needs a day off at the end of the week," Ratcliff says, "we try to let them have it. One of us, Lorine or I, take over their job for them while they're away." Sometimes Ratcliff and the other owners work late into the night or on weekends, finishing a job which slow workers were unable

to complete during the day. "They're all real good workers and they try real hard," Ratcliff says, "but they can't all work so fast so we try to help them out by finishing the work ourselves."

The factory tries to cater to the women's needs, rather than demand that women cater to the factory's. "The ladies that have children in school, they bring their children with them in the morning when we start work at 7:30," Miller says. "The school buses don't run until about 8, so they just bring their children with them and the bus picks them up at the factory and brings them back to the factory in the afternoon, and the kids wait until their mothers finish work. It sure saves babysitting fees."

"And," Ratcliff added, "if one of the girl's children is sick, why, she can stay home — she don't have to bring us an excuse." Women can leave their machines and take a cigarette break whenever they wish. "And you can go to the restroom when you want to," Ratcliff adds.

"This is a great place to work," says one young woman who sews buttons all day long. "We all really enjoy it here. Why? Because it's so relaxed. I used to work for Sears, and there was lots of tension, three supervisors for every 30 people, breathing down your necks. I'd rather be making $1.65 here (the rate has since climbed 65 cents) than $2 an hour at Levi."

The vicious circle

What's the future at McCaysville? It's something of an economic miracle that the factory has been able to survive the ups and downs of the garment industry. Although the factory is not in imminent danger of folding, it still operates on a fragile financial base. If a major recession hit the industry, McCaysville Industries would probably collapse. If you ask the owners what the latest financial figures are, they can't answer you. "How much did we make last year? That's a figure I don't know," Miller says. "Miss Green, the office girl, we just let her handle everything." According to the factory records which Miss Green fishes from the files, the factory grosses more than

$140,000 in an average year, but seldom ends up with more than several thousand dollars profit. The owners don't take the profits home — they plow them right back into the equipment and plant.

The women of McCaysville are caught in a vicious economic circle. One major problem is their size. With only 30 machines, they can produce only 200 dozen garments a week, and "most people in the business want 500 - 600 dozen a week," Miller says. The women can't expand without more money, but one reason they can't earn more money is that they depend completely on middlemen for their contracts — and so far, the middlemen have dictated meager pay rates.

The women feel powerless to negotiate better contracts. "None of us know anything about how to cost out a garment [to compute how much it will cost the factory to produce an order, and how much the factory should get paid] and you have to know how to do this to make any money on it," Miller told the Third International Conference. "These men will come in — and usually we do work with men — and they'll say, 'We'll pay you $25 a dozen for this blazer,' and they'll take out a pencil and paper, and say 'this is how to break down the cost, you should make 50 cents on this seam and that' and it looks simple, but when we get the [garment] back to the factory it's not as simple as it looked. But we've already said we'll do it, and we're obligated to do it for that amount and we lose money on it.

"The garment we're making right now, we make $20 a *dozen*," Miller told the Conference. "It sells in the store for $9.95 *apiece*. Somebody's making a profit on it, but I don't know where."

The women have also always wanted to learn how to design clothing, and how to sell it directly to the warehouses instead of through middlemen; they want to learn how to organize their business more efficiently. But none of them have ever had management training, and they can't possibly afford to take it.

The women of McCaysville, then, are in a rut — a satisfying rut, perhaps, which at least provides a subsistence living, but still a highly vulnerable rut.

The factory has limped through occasional periods, one of them six weeks long, when the women could get no contracts and had to close down. And the factory can't afford to pay sick leave or health insurance benefits.

Participants at the Third International Conference pressed Bernice Ratcliff and Lorine Miller to describe their long-term visions. Couldn't they find consultants somewhere who could help them become more efficient? Couldn't they find some school which could provide them with business training? Couldn't they design and market their own clothes and build a more secure financial base?

Lorine Miller and Bernice Ratcliff

"Working for yourself, you're not under a strain. You don't have to take nerve pills to stay on the job. And we feel we're helping people and our community, too"

Fear of the unknown

Ratcliff and Miller had only negative answers. They have stopped looking for outside resources to help them; they have become comfortable in their rut. They said they mistrust consultants; "they always say the same thing," Lorine Milller said, "They tell us, 'you're too small, you need 30 more machines, and you have to set a production quota, that's the only way you can stay in business.' Well," Miller said, "we can't afford more machines, and production's what we're trying to get away from. They told us production was the only way we could stay in business nine years ago, yet we're still in business."

The conference session pointed out the crucial need for management consultants who can help workers, such as the women of McCaysville, craft the kind of workstyle *they* want — not impose the same conventional solutions from which these workers are trying to escape. But the conference also pointed out the need for workers, such as the women of McCaysville, to seek outside help and not to accept their historical limitations. The women, for instance, have become convinced that no one can help them, that they cannot learn more advanced business and garment industry skills, even though they have already achieved success where most people predicted they would fail. The women have struggled so hard, against such overwhelming odds, that now they are afraid to take more risks — such as attempting to market their own designs — which could put them on a much more solid economic base. "We're all chicken," Lorine Miller said. "We're too afraid to try anything like that. Because we could lose everything overnight, be out of a job, go back to the factories hunting work. I couldn't even do *that* because I'm past the age limit.

I'd probably end up washing dishes in somebody's cafe."

Participants at the conference pointed out that when the women of McCaysville first dreamed of setting up their own factory, one decade ago, they were taking enormous risks — relying on their own hard work and perseverance to create a factory which scarcely anyone else thought could survive. They took risks, and they succeeded. "When we started," Lorine Miller said, "we did it out of pure meanness and stubborness. If we had known what we would of had to come through, I don't think we ever would have done it in the first place."

Ironically, as the women of McCaysville disparage their own abilities to develop their factory further, they proudly assert their very abilities which made the factory possible in the first place. "I don't think books tell you everything," says one of the owners, "You've got to have common sense and work your way through it. Sometimes I think that's better than all the special training. Experience is the best teacher I know."

"I used to think you needed an education to do things, but we got into this before we ever knew what we was getting into," Bernice Ratcliff says. "And we just did it. You can do a lot of things you never thought you could do without an education. We've shown a thing like this factory can be done. We're under pressure, don't get me wrong. But working for yourself, you're not under a strain," Ratcliff says. "You've not got someone standing on your back, and you don't have to take nerve pills to stay on the job. We aren't making anything, really, but $2.30 an hour is enough money to buy groceries. And we live in just a small place, and on weekends we have a beautiful lake to go to. And we feel that we're helping people, and our community too."

Sources

Transcripts of the Third International Conference on
    Self-Management.
Interviews by the editor with employees and owners
    of McCaysville Industries.

GEN-ERAL FOODS

The first thing you notice when you visit the General Foods Gravy Train plant, set against a backdrop of grain elevators on the outskirts of Topeka, is not the modern decor, not the carpeting, not the single entrance for production workers and managers alike — but the smell. The odor of tallow, cooked and extruded into tons of Gravy Train at a pressure of 120 pounds per square inch, permeates the building, even the workers' skin. But many workers at the General Foods plant say the stink of tallow has been a small price to pay for the benefits of working in one of the first, and most widely publicized "humanized" factories in the nation.

General Foods calls it a "sociotechnical system," a "total system" — more specifically, "the Topeka System." The factory, which started operating in 1971, was designed on the drawing boards to allow employees a considerable degree of freedom in operating the production process. Teams of workers manage the production process day to day, with minimal supervision by management. The teams participate in hiring fellow workers and firing them, and in resolving workplace grievances. Workers at Topeka aren't paid according to their seniority or by a single job they were hired to perform — they're paid according to how many different jobs they learn. The Topeka workers can rotate from unloading a boxcar one day to testing the dog food in the quality control laboratory the next. By traditional corporate measures, the workers have been an unusually productive and satisfied group. "Our data . . . show high levels of satisfaction and involvement in all parts of the organization," a University of Michigan researcher has reported. "In fact they show the highest levels we have found in any organization we have sampled."

The General Foods Topeka System raises important questions about the possibilities and limits of a "humanized" plant in which management unilaterally imposes a "participation" structure on the workers. The workers at Topeka do not own the plant, as the miners at the Vermont Asbestos Group do, and so they have no ultimate control over the structure and direction of the operation. Yet the workers at Topeka have more day-to-day freedom and control over their jobs than the asbestos miners do.

In the long run, the Topeka System is generating potentially serious conflicts. Since the management created the system of workers' freedom and participation, the management can take it away. Observers report that new managers who are not committed to the "system" have been taking charge of the operation, and pursuing profits and production to the detriment of the "quality of work life." The Topeka System, some observers report, is eroding. More and more workers are becoming resentful toward management and dissatisfied with their jobs; the team spirit is breaking down. The entire plant may revert to a traditional autocratic managerial workstyle, observers say, unless management reverses the tide.

Curing labor ills

The Topeka System was created as an antidote to mounting labor and production troubles which had plagued other General Foods plants. In 1969, researcher Michael Brimm writes, General Foods was riding "the crest of a pet food business." National demand exceeded the corporation's capacity to produce. Yet its only pet food plant, in Kankakee, Illinois, was fraught with union-management conflict.

The factory suffered racial conflicts, episodes of worker violence toward supervisors, frequent worker grievances and even sabotage (an entire day's production had to be scrapped after an employee threw green dye into the dog food vat). The manager of the plant, Lyman Ketchum, was assigned by the corporation to a special team of managers to design a new dog food plant. The goal, as Ketchum wrote in December 1969, was to find "a better way to design work and organizations which can utilize the full potential of the workers and managers." The planners would "erase all the 'givens' and begin anew to devise a management system most applicable to today's and tomorrow's environment."

At International Group Plans, the president revamped the traditional management structure upside down to accomplish political and philosophical goals. At Harman International Industries, the management and union devised the joint workplace participation program to improve the "quality of work life" — and emphasized that increasing productivity was *not* a goal. But the General Foods official planning document, Topeka Organization Systems and Development, suggested that increasing profits was a major objective of the new work system. The new system of management, encouraging more worker participation, was more a strategy toward achieving more efficient production than it was a goal in itself. "If business conditions are favorable, then human potential combined with system characteristics will yield cost and quality benefits," the corporate document said. The "objective" of the new system would be "Lowest possible cost of goods with

"An organization which more fully utilizes human potential of employees can pay off in dollars and cents"—General Foods

no sacrifice of product quality, service to the trade, or marketing flexibility."

"To more fully utilize human resources is morally and ethically the right thing to do," the document noted; it also pointed out that "Yesterday's employees that were depersonalized by organizations merely became apathetic, but generally compliant workers or supervisors or managers. But today's employees who become alienated by the organization are more likely to actively challenge or even attack the organization." The corporate document continued: "Humans will best respond (be productive) when there exists a high feeling of self-worth by employee, and employee identification with success of the total organization . . . an organization which more fully utilizes human potential of employees can pay off in dollars and cents."

The General Foods team selected Topeka as home for the new plant, Brimm writes, because the town gave the factory easy access to rail transportation and grain elevators, plenty of room for plant expansion, and a good supply of labor. The executive planners noted that the rural Topeka area was "free of the racial strife and urban-industrial decay" which plagued the Kankakee factory. "No power groups" — meaning no unions — "will exist within the organization that create an anti-management posture," the planning document said. Furthermore, the Topeka location would provide "relatively high physical isolation between Topeka and other parts of the firm." This isolation, the planners felt, would permit the unorthodox new work system to take root and grow, unfettered by the skeptical scrutiny of traditional-style executives in the White Plains, New York headquarters.

Satisfying ego needs

With all this in mind, the planners went about designing their new Topeka System. The layout, the equipment, even the decor would be aimed at satisfying certain human needs. "People have 'ego'

needs," the planners wrote. "They want self-esteem, sense of accomplishment, autonomy, increasing knowledge and skill . . . People have 'social' needs. They enjoy team membership and teamwork . . . People have certain security needs. They want reasonable income and employment security, and want to be assured against arbitrary and unfair treatment." In addition, "People want to be able to identify with products they produce and firms that employ them."

Workers in the new plant, the planners decided, would have "power / voice . . . in things affecting them," such as pay and benefits, hiring and firing, disciplining and counseling fellow workers, training and promotion, job assignments, scheduling production, solving workplace problems, selecting and modifying equipment. In the new plant there would be "fair pay and benefits . . . normal status differentials minimized . . . opportunity to learn, contribute and grow . . . good working conditions . . . pay based on knowledge rather than a special job assignment . . . minimum threat of layoff . . . honest / supportive management . . . elimination of some and sharing of remaining distasteful work . . . willingness to examine anything and change it if it doesn't fit."

The corporate planners took great care selecting employees who they felt could make the system work. Applicants for team leaders — whom the planners intended to become "*not* a foreman or supervisor . . . (but) a kind of coach" — had to pass an intensive regimen of interviews, tests, "role playing exercises" and "criticism-self-criticism" sessions. These psychological exercises, says Brimm, were designed to test the applicants' team spirit, resourcefulness, flexibility, and emotional openness. Once the six team leaders were selected, they spent four months training. More than 600 persons who applied to work on the production lines in the plant were also screened by intensive testing; finalists passed through the same kinds of role-playing techniques used to select the team leaders. The final group of 63 employees "reflected scores on general intelligence, manual dexterity, mechanical and electrical aptitude which placed them above average workers for Kansas industry and other Topeka manufacturing operations," researcher Brimm reports. Twenty percent of the new production workers had held supervisory or higher paying positions at their previous jobs; they had been attracted to General Foods by the promise of a more satisfying work life. The new employees, Brimm reports, considered themselves to be a worker "elite."

Life in the plant

The Topeka System begins at the factory parking lot. The traditional "reserved" parking spaces which gave managers status were eliminated; workers and managers share the same spaces, and enter the plant through the same front door. The carpeting in the workers' locker rooms is the same as the carpeting in the managerial offices. The plant manager's office isn't hidden from the workers, but looks out onto the production floor through large windows — to convey the sense that he works *with* the rank and file employees in the plant, rather than *over* them.

The workers in the factory are divided into two teams of seven to 14 members, on each of three shifts. One team handles the dog food processing: the workers unload the grains, meat by-products, chemical nutrients and organic tallows from the railroad cars, premix chemical dyes and nutrients in large hoppers, transform the ingredients into dog food in enormous high-pressure cookers, and then test it for moisture, density and color in a sophisticated lab. The second team packages the dog food: the workers weigh the proper amount into individual sacks, tie the sacks into large bales, hoist the bales onto pallets, and load the pallets onto boxcars ready for shipping across the country.

When participants at the Third International Conference on Self-Management asked workers from the Topeka factory, "Who really runs the plant?" one employee answered, "As far as operation and running of the plant, the people do. The day-to-day decisions are made by the people in the plant." The corporate planners designed the factory to give workers control over production processes which could actually have been automated. For instance, the factory could have been designed so that engineers could control the mixing and cooking process from a central command center. Instead, individual operators who have never had formal training operate enormous and complex machines, varying moisture, fat content, density, heat and other critical variables on their own initiative.

The factory could have hired special lab technicians to perform quality control evaluations. Instead, rank and file workers are trained to work in the "large, well-equipped modern laboratory, dazzling in its sophistication," as Brimm describes it. Workers weigh dog food samples, titrate solutions, extract and measure moisture, and determine on their own, without a supervisor's direction, whether the day's production of dog food is good enough to be shipped to market. Rank and file workers have the power to condemn whole batches of the dog food. "The team leader said to ship the product like this," one worker told Brimm, pointing to what he and fellow workers had analyzed to be inferior product. "I just waited till he left and scrapped until we got a good product."

In a conventional factory, workers would be classified as process operators, mechanics, quality control technicians, cleaners, boiler operators, grain unloaders — but the Topeka plant workers rotate from job to job as they wish, with their fellow team members' approval. "One day I came in and worked the 10-pound line," bagging 10-pound sacks of dog food, a worker told Brimm. "The next day I worked in the lab." Workers are hired at a base starting rate, regardless of their previous job experience or expertise; once they master their first job, usually the most grueling and boring, such as hoisting bales on wooden pallets, they earn the "first-job" rate. When a worker wants to learn a new job, he or she applies to the fellow team mates. If the team members feel the member is ready to move on — the worker is judged not only by technical proficiency but by whether he or she is "willing to assist others and work hard toward the improvement of his team," according to the plant manual — they vote to "promote" the applicant to a new job. Each job takes about four to seven months to master. When a worker learns all the jobs within a team, he or she earns the "team" rate.

Workers who wish can learn all the jobs in the plant, and earn the "plant rate," about 50 percent more money per hour than the base pay. No matter what the job, workers perform most of their own maintenance work — in fact, workers can shut down the entire production line on their own initiative, if they feel the machines need work. The workers start up production on their own, too. One observer reported arriving at the factory one night at midnight. The graveyard shift was starting production — there were no managers, not even a team leader, in the plant.

Hiring and firing

The workers also play an important role in hiring fellow workers. When a team has a job opening — which occurs seldom according to employees, since the turnover has remained at 10 percent per year or lower — the entire team, or perhaps a subcommittee of the team, interviews and screens the applicants and votes on a final choice. Technically, the team leaders have the final say, but workers at Topeka say the team's vote usually stands. "Team elections of individuals were normally made on the criterion, 'Would you want to have a beer with this guy?'" Brimm reports. Applicants who didn't meet the test were considered "a bad system fit."

The teams also have handled discipline, including firing fellow employees. In some cases, observers report, the teams try to resolve disciplinary problems outside the team meetings, through informal talks with "problem" workers or through other kinds of peer pressure. If a worker arrived late to work, Brimm reports, "The unstated question, 'Where were you?' followed the offender until he had exonerated himself." Or, when workers feel one of their teammates has not been performing well, they may bring it up at the meeting before or after the shift.

"We have a regularly scheduled team meeting once a week," employee Karen Cooper told the Third International Conference on Self-Management. "Most of the time we just express the fact that we think it's a concern, to the person, and see what his reaction is. That makes a big difference on where you go. If his reaction is 'So what?' then the response might be, 'We think you need to take some time off [without pay] to think about your attitude.'"

The General Foods employees at the Third International Conference stressed that the teams, not the team leaders, usually impose the disciplinary sanctions on the workers. "What really works the best," Karen Cooper told the conference, "is when we ask a person what *he* thinks we should do with him. You'd be surprised how strict they are on themselves. We had one guy who was very, very bad about coming in late. The problem with coming in late is that we work with a minimum amount of people, and if we're one person short that doubles the work of the people working with him. We had a couple of meetings with him and we finally had all we could take, and we asked him what he would do in our situation. He said,

'If it was me, one more time and that would be it.' He set that restriction on himself." Another worker who chronically came to work late, the employees at the conference said, told his team members they should demand him to bring a doctor's excuse next time he was late to work — or fire him.

Few workers have been fired; the first two employees who were fired were also black, which generated considerable tension in the plant and charges of racism. Although the system of discipline by peers is democratic at the team level, the system gives workers no structural appeal — no grievance process, no hearing by peers. Workers at the conference said that fellow employees who feel they have been unfairly disciplined can complain informally to their team leader and then to the manufacturing operations manager: "If that doesn't make you feel any better you can go to the plant manager," one employee told the conference, "and if that doesn't satisfy you, well, you can go get a lawyer." The Topeka employees at the conference dismissed the possibility that a team punishment might not be justified. "Chances are if you get punished or fired, you deserve it," one worker said.

According to Brimm, production workers not only focus their energies on disciplining each other, but also are bold in hashing out dissatisfactions with their team leaders. "Team members saw the most pressing disciplinary issues as those concerning team leaders," Brimm writes. "Over a two-week period, three team leaders were confronted by their groups regarding the frenzied competition which had developed within the management group" over which team could produce more dog food. One worker, says Brimm, reprimanded his team leader, "We don't make any more dog food when you pace up and down."

Although worker powers at Topeka have been limited mainly to the day-to-day production process, workers have been given some input in *plant*-level decisions. For instance, when equipment salesmen visit the plant they don't do business with the plant manager but with the workers who will actually be using the machines. The workers have access to pro-duction information such as sales, output, and communications from product receivers. Each year the management asks the worker teams what level production they think they can achieve, and what equipment they might need to achieve it. The workers draft proposals for pay raises from year to year, although as one worker told the Third International Conference on Self-Management, "the final say is with the corporate people in White Plains."

Getting satisfaction

Most observers agree that the Topeka System has had positive effects, both on the workers and on plant profits. According to General Foods consultant Richard Walton, who helped design the factory, the factory operated for almost four years without a single lost-time accident; only 70 workers have been producing the levels of output which corporate engineers had expected 110 workers would be needed to produce. Absenteeism has remained below 1.5 percent, and the factory has achieved unit costs about 5 percent less than at General Foods' conventional plants, saving about $1 million per year.

Many observers say the economical achievements stem from the fact that Topeka System workers are "satisfied" — at least, considerably more satisfied than workers at most General Foods plants. When Ford Foundation researcher Robert Schrank visited the factory in 1973 he found "high levels of worker participation, freedom to communicate, expressions of warmth, minimization of status distinction, human dignity, commitment and individual self-esteem."

One effect of the plant structure, many workers say, is increased worker cooperation and comraderie. When a boxcar of heavy sacks rolled in, Brimm reports, all the members of the processing team including team leader pitched in to help with the exhausting chore. Employees walking by the packaging line would usually help out tying some bales before moving on to their own jobs. When a worker accidentally spilled dog food or raw ingredients,

Brimm says, the mess was "seldom cleaned up without the development of an ad hoc team of volunteers."

Workers at Topeka, observers say, seem to care about each other. Since there is no formal job training program, for example, a worker who wants to learn a new job must be trained by a more experienced worker. "I have encountered few teachers and colleagues," says Harvard-educated Brimm, "who exhibit the patience, skill and sensitivity which I observed and experienced among this work force." Brimm and other researchers have noted there is a high level of emotional interaction among workers at the plant: workers counsel each other, or confront each other openly, in the lunchroom, at the lounge pool table, or perhaps in a team meeting. Occasionally, Brimm reports, team meetings developed into intense, emotional sessions "which paralleled the most intense encounters which I have seen emerge from training [T] groups."

Outside lives

This atmosphere has reportedly affected the workers' personal lives outside the factory doors. "Something is wrong," one worker told Brimm, "when I can talk openly here at work in front of 14 other people and I get home and can't be open with my wife." "I began to be more open at home talking about my feelings and things like that," another employee told Brimm. "My wife would look at me like I was crazy."

Under the Topeka System, observers report, workers who had been tied to a single machine most of their work lives, at another factory, began learning new skills as they rotated from one job to another. It elevated their expectations, and enabled them to look at their work with a broader perspective. "Individuals who now complain openly about the content of a job design are those who passively accepted a more narrow, repetitive task in previous employment," according to Brimm.

The rotation and cross-training among jobs also has helped to break down the hierarchy of seniority and job ratings which separates one worker from another at conventional plants. In this atmosphere, Brimm observes, the workers talk about "my machine" and "our plant" with a sense of pride. "Ninety-five percent of the employees are sold on the system," employee Jim Weaver told researcher David Jenkins. "We've had our problems, but we can sit down and work them out. I like General Foods. It's the only job I ever had where I felt I was part of the company. General Foods put responsibility on me and I accept it . . . I feel wanted." Before the Topeka System came along," Weaver said, "I wouldn't have thought it possible to find this many people who took such pride in their job."

A good thing goes bad

For the first several years, according to most accounts, the Topeka System flourished. Team decision-making was an important focus of the plant's operation, workers exercised a high degree of autonomy on their jobs, and the vast majority of workers enthusiastically supported the system, their jobs and the corporation.

In the past several years, however, the plant operations and the employees' mood have started to change. The "positive work culture," reports Richard Walton, describing a November 1976 visit, "had declined. Not a steep decline, rather a moderate erosion. By general agreement it is still a very productive plant, and a superior place to work, but the 'quality of work life' had slipped. And while the majority still supported — by their own behavior — the unique strengths of the 'Topeka System,' an increasing minority did not."

Walton reports that some of the important qualities of the Topeka System — including openness and candor among workers and managers; team decision-making and team cooperation; the workers' perceived influence on plant policy; confidence in the corporation and cooperation among shifts — have begun to crumble.

One of the most important changes, both Walton

and Brimm have reported, is that worker teams are controlling and influencing fewer and fewer decisions as the plant is becoming more conventionally hierarchical. During the first few years the teams usually met at least once per week, sometimes several times a week, to discuss issues ranging from hiring new members to confronting interpersonal conflicts, to voting on changes in the production line. Although General Foods workers at the Third International Conference on Self-Management reported that some teams still meet weekly, often the meetings are "as simple as to say what we're expected to be doing next week or the fact there's going to be a company picnic," one employee told the conference — management says they don't have time to spend in the luxury of meetings. The major reason: the corporate headquarters launched a "prolonged push for maximum production," says Walton, which "had a dramatically negative effect." The teams increasingly suppress discussions of controversial and emotion-laden issues, in order to "get to work."

According to Brimm, "decisions were surrendered less frequently to equipment operators and some previous decentralization was reversed.... Shifts which had once begun with 'Who's going to work the 25-pound (bagging) line?' were now hastened along with 'Why don't John, Fred and Bill start up the 25-pound line?' " Brimm reports that team leaders have assumed an increasingly autocratic, managerial role — cancelling workers' coffee breaks, docking a worker's pay when he returned late from a company softball game, ordering workers in the quality control lab to approve dog food which they believed was not good enough quality to be shipped — all in the name of increased production. Quality has sometimes suffered, Walton agrees, "undermining one source of (workers') pride."

Observers report that other important changes have soured the "quality of work life" at the Topeka plant. For instance, between 1973 and 1976, according to Walton, three of the four managers who had been most responsible for launching the Topeka System left General Foods. One of them was the popular plant manager, whom workers trusted and felt would "go to bat" for them, as Walton describes it; he was replaced by a manager "seen as philosophically unsympathetic to Topeka, raising doubts about the hierarchy's understanding or commitment to the Topeka innovation."

Another development which soured worker attitudes was the construction of a new canned dog food plant next door. During the first year, the canned product sold far worse than corporate planners had expected, and there were two large layoffs. In 1976, sales zoomed, however, and in an effort to maximize production, Walton writes, "management chose to defer the introduction of many aspects of the work structure." Management's seemingly harsh and conventional methods of handling the new plant convinced many workers in the dry food plant that the management commitment to the "Topeka System" was quickly waning. This deepened the workers' already growing insecurity and mistrust.

"They have a very tight schedule producing nationwide," team leader Warren Lynch told the Third International Conference on Self-Management. "So business gets in the way of taking time to stop and deal with things."

What's to blame?

Some of the changes in the Topeka System have been the product of personality changes: new managers, new team leaders and new employees who don't share the enthusiasm of the original "pioneers" have moved into the plant, dampening the system's spirit. Other changes which are souring the climate, according to some observers, seem to be rooted in the very nature of the General Foods experiment.

From the beginning, Brimm argues, it was a unilateral *management* experiment: management granted to the employees certain carefully planned and limited freedoms and powers. These freedoms and powers gave the employees more autonomy while performing their jobs from day-to-day, but they did not change the fundamental nature of the manage-

Workers have enjoyed the power to make their own decisions, but only if they mimic what management would have decided on its own

ment-worker relationship. When workers have exercised the power to make decisions, Brimm argues, the kinds of decisions they make are often "meaningless." "The manager who asks 'How will we divide the work today to reach our goals of 100 tons of output?' yields a meaningless choice to the team," argues Brimm. "The question has not opened meaningful choices as to quantity of product, nature of product or possible technology." Furthermore, workers have enjoyed the power to make their own decisions, Brimm points out, only as long as those decisions mimic what management would have decided on its own. Warren Lynch, team leader at Topeka, told the Third International Conference on Self-Management: "If any time in my judgment I feel the team is not handling an issue correctly, I can make the decision over and above the team." In one instance, one employee told the Conference, "A guy [on the team] was up for a higher [pay] rate and the team voted to give it to him. But Warren overruled us and said 'no way.' We got together again and decided Warren was correct."

"You get right down to the fact that they [management] can do whatever they want," said employee Tom Zappa. "They run it. They own it. What's to stop them? They can do whatever they want. I can't stop them. What right do I have? I mean, they didn't even have to let us do this whole thing [the experiment] in the first place," Zappa told the conference. "That plant is there for one reason — to make money."

The gap between what many workers expected the Topeka System to be, and the reality of what the System actually is, had caused some of the tensions, according to Brimm. The organization was misleadingly defined as "self-management," Brimm says: "The concept of self-management was . . . developed in the promise of a future without team leaders. A later epoch was envisioned, where the total and responsible assumption of supervisory roles by team members would make their former leaders obsolete." Yet workers began to feel, according to Brimm, that they were "free to make decisions [only] so long as these yielded the same outcomes that the higher level

authority would have chosen." Topeka employees unrealistically began to expect that a system which encourages rotation and training in all the jobs in the plant would never become dull or routine; when the system became not a novelty but a way of life, the vision crashed. "One individual faced the challenge of operating a fork-lift truck . . . one worker achieves the autonomy of choosing among activities in the bulk unloading areas," says Brimm. "Another worker, the autonomy of moving from his job as 'humper' [hoisting bales onto pallets] after two hours." "We were all in the clouds for a long time," one employee told Brimm. "But 300 tons of dog food a day, every day, can bring you down to earth in a hurry."

These limitations have been aggravated by the fact that the job training and rotation system no longer function as well as they did during the first few years the factory was operating. "The prolonged push for maximum production," Walton writes, "also caused a deferral of the movement from one team to another which could occur after an operator had earned 'team rate.' This delay in opportunity to learn jobs on the other team postponed the date at which one could earn 'plant rate.' This tended to undermine commitment."

Some of the growing problems at Topeka stem from the way production employees interact with each other on the teams. While team decision-making has in many ways helped bring workers together in a new cooperative spirit, in some ways it has pulled workers apart. Under the pressure of increased production, teams which once went out of their way to help each other now compete for the "glory" of the highest output.

Probably the most divisive issue in the plant, according to observers, is pay. For one thing, workers who have applied to their teams for — but been denied — the plant rate, resent workers who *have* received it. They also resent the teammates who voted against them. Knowing that fellow workers will help decide their future in the plant, many employees are afraid to be open and honest, one of the original tenets of the Topeka System. "One worker explained that the tenuous basis of his security makes him continuously mindful of his relations with the many people who could help or hurt him in the future," Walton writes.

Worker fears

Some workers, according to Brimm, feel that the Topeka System exploits them in the long run. For instance, while pay rates in the plant are far higher than the average rates which semiskilled or unskilled workers earn at other companies in the Topeka area, they are far lower — perhaps two thirds lower — than the rates which skilled maintenance workers or industrial mechanics earn at other plants. The General Foods workers are not classified as mechanics or maintenance workers, yet many of them have learned and performed those tasks, and they feel they should receive higher pay. Furthermore, since they have not been classified as "maintenance" workers under the General Foods scheme, they may not even be able to take their new skills with them if they move to a new company.

This dilemma leads some workers to charge that working under the Topeka System is not a passport to a better job, but a sentence to remain in the General Foods corporation forever. "What do you say to a worker who has only a high school education but whose resume says he can run a [quality control] chemistry lab?" one researcher asked rhetorically at the Third International Conference on Self-Management. "That doesn't cut it in the outside world. You've got to have a chemistry degree." The Topeka System, the critics charge, enables General Foods to run a plant with many highly trained and skilled workers, while paying only a fraction of the wages they deserve.

Some workers at the Topeka plant have become discontent because they say the system has not been working well enough. But to some extent, the Topeka System is in trouble precisely because it was working too well — as far as some corporate executives were

concerned. They think workers were exercising *too much* power. "It became a power struggle," one former employee told *Business Week*. "It was too threatening to too many people." Personnel managers objected to workers guiding decisions about firing and hiring. Quality control managers in the corporation resented the fact that rank and file workers were controlling quality control decisions in the plant lab. Engineers felt disturbed by production employees handling machine maintenance and other engineering work. The corporation has recently added seven new management positions to the plant, according to *Business Week*. The management says the new managers are necessary to handle plant expansion, but many workers feel they have arrived to scuttle worker powers and shore up the once minimal management autocracy.

In some ways, observers say, one of the early strengths of the experiment — its isolation from the corporate headquarters — became one of its most important handicaps. Planners of the Topeka System deliberately isolated the plant so that skeptical corporate executives could not tamper with the system so easily, and attempt to thwart the unorthodox methods of team decision-making and other worker powers. The fact that the executives at headquarters did not heartily support the project was not a good omen to begin with; the fact that Topeka managers tried to remain so distant from them — arousing resentments and suspicions at White Plains — made the situation even worse. Corporate evaluations, according to Brimm, gave Topeka managers low marks, and "condemned" hiring practices at the Topeka plant.

At the Topeka plant, "managers themselves," according to Walton, "felt that as a result of their pioneering work they had lost rather than gained in career progression within GF." Their feelings seemed confirmed: almost none of the top managers or team leaders at the Topeka plant were promoted inside the General Foods system. Instead, "Openings in the chain of command which linked Topeka to White Plains had been filled by managers viewed as 'hardliners' opposed to advocates of more humanistic managerial programs of the Topeka type," according to Brimm.

Whither Topeka?

Today, some observers say, the Topeka System struggles against a combination of indifference and outright hostility from General Foods headquarters. As *Business Week* notes, "General Foods, which once encouraged publicity about the Topeka plant, now refuses to let reporters inside."

The former plant manager who helped plan and give birth to the Topeka System used to say that the system must "diffuse or die": that is, the system must spread throughout the entire corporation or, isolated and adrift, it will wither. If he is right, the prognosis for the Topeka System seems grim.

The "negative drift of the work culture" at Topeka has been important, Walton wrote after his November 1976 visit, but "more signigicant . . . was the absence of potent corrective devices, of a self-renewal capacity." While the work teams have not grappled effectively enough or often enough with issues at the team level, there has been virtually no system at all to grapple with issues at the *plant* level. "There have been no regular plant-wide forums in which issues can be raised and addressed," Walton writes. So while more and more employees have been feeling dissatisfied about the drift of the Topeka System, there is no structure to flush out this dissatisfaction in a constructive way — no structure which enables production workers and managers to work together to hammer out some solutions and improvements. This forbids workers and managers "to continually assess the work system and take initiatives to evolve its form," writes Walton.

Despite the growing problems at the General Foods plant in Topeka, observers and employees there agree, work under the Topeka System has been more satisfying and enriching than work at other area factories. Compared to an ideal of worker self-management, the System may not have achieved that much for its employees. Compared to a conventional, highly structured factory, however, the System has made some important advances. The major question which confronts the Topeka System is whether the corporate management will permit it to continue and to evolve — and whether any workplace participation project, controlled unilaterally by management, can survive for long.

Sources

Ian Michael Brimm, *Analytical Perspectives in Organizational Behavior: A Study of an Organizational Innovation*, 1975 Dissertation, Xerox University Microfilms, Ann Arbor, Michigan.

Richard Walton, "Work Innovations at Topeka: Six Years After," draft manuscript for the *Journal of Applied Behavioral Science*, dated December 12, 1976.

"Topeka Organization and Systems Development," document by the General Foods Corporation, December 30, 1969. Quoted in Brimm.

Lyman Ketchum, paper presented at "Humanizing of Work Symposium," American Association for the Advancement of Science Annual Meeting, December 27, 1971.

Ketchum, statement before the Senate Subcommittee on Employment, Manpower and Poverty, July 26, 1972.

"Workers Share Helm," by Alta Huff, *Topeka Capital-Journal*, August 6, 1972.

David Jenkins, *Job Power*, 1973, Doubleday.

"'Worker Freedom' Experiments Appear Successful," by Jack Houston, *Chicago Tribune*, October 21, 1973.

"Stonewalling Plant Democracy," *Business Week*, March 28, 1977.

Personal interviews by the editor with employees of the General Foods Topeka plant, at the Third International Conference on Self-Management.

RUSH- TON

Most of the worker participation projects across the country have taken place in factories. But one of the most widely publicized experiments with semi-autonomous worker teams was launched more than 600 feet deep in the ground, in the dark and dusty netherworld of an eastern Pennsylvania coal mine. The Rushton Mining Co., in Occola Mills, Pennsylvania, joined the United Mine Workers in launching the nation's first worker participation project — a "quality of work life" project — inside a coal mine.

The changes the project brought to the coal mine were less dramatic and pervasive than at some other projects around the nation. The coal miners didn't buy the mine from its private owners, as the Vermont Asbestos Group employees did. Workers at the mine didn't get off work three hours early and attend school, as many employees do at Harman International in Tennessee. The project did not abolish the foremen, as the General Foods Topeka plant did. But the

Rushton-UMW experiment did give miners, who used to be controlled minute to minute by a boss, freedom and power to organize and control mining operations underground, day by day. It trained miners, as no mine has trained miners before, to understand the rudiments of federal safety laws; it also trained them to perform different jobs — miners on each participating crew can rotate from one job to another if they wish, and all of them earn the highest possible union pay. While most miners descend into the coal mine literally every day they work, the Rushton miners involved in the experiment spent occasional days, at full pay, discussing problems and learning about the job in a classroom with representatives from other shifts and with management. In the process, the miners may have increased their safety record. The experiment suggests there are possibilities for increasing worker participation in other coal mines across the country — an industry which has one of the bloodiest labor organizing histories of any industry in the United States, an industry which will become increasingly important as the nation increases dependence on coal as industrial fuel. And the project has demonstrated that coal miners can improve safety conditions without decreasing their production, shattering the coal industry myth that if safety improves, profits must suffer. The project also shows that a veteran U.S. labor union can use the kind of worker participation projects which many union leaders have opposed, to improve the working life and earnings of its members.

But the Rushton project is also a case study of the obstacles and mistakes which can destroy a worker participation project; witness the union local vote to abandon the experiment in 1975. A look at *why* the union members opposed the project in the final showdown can provide valuable lessons for unions that contemplate bringing the same kind of project to their own workplace in the future.

Roots

The first notions of a quality of work life project in Rushton were born in the United Mine Workers na-

tional office, in Washington, D.C. Union officials became interested in worker participation not as a strategy for improving worker "satisfaction," but, according to former UMW staff member Davitt McAteer, "primarily because of our concern over mine safety." McAteer had read psychologist Eric Trist's accounts of his worker participation experiments in the British coal mines after World War I; Trist had found that increasing worker autonomy in the mines achieved impressive gains in safety. "The union had been dissatisfied for some time with the slow pace of improvements in mine safety," McAteer said, "and was willing to examine the potential of a new program." Trist told the UMW officials that he would be willing to work with them on an American mine project.

The union, Trist and a group of psychology and management consultants from Pennsylvania State University decided to try to launch the workplace participation experiments in two mines, one small, one large. If the project worked in vastly different operations, they reasoned, union leaders and management officials across the nation would be convinced that such a project could work in *their* own operations, too. Efforts to launch a program in a large mine collapsed after the union local at one target mine voted to reject it. But efforts to launch the experiment at the modest-sized Rushton Mining Co., with its 150 workers, proceeded as the union and the consultants had planned.

Why was the Rushton management interested in pursuing a worker participation experiment? Warren Hinks, then owner and president of the mine (he later sold the mine to Pittsburgh Power and Light Co., but remained as president) saw the project partly as a strategy for smoothing Rushton's stormy labor history. Hinks had opened the mine in 1965 as a non-union shop. It took the UMW two years and a five-week strike to organize the mine, and even then Rushton was often shut down by wildcat strikes.

Hinks was concerned "about a new generation of miners who were younger, better educated and more militant than past generations," according to consultant Trist and his colleagues. "Management was will-

The foreman, once an autocratic boss, would be responsible for maximizing safety. The miners would control their own jobs

ing to explore any organizational innovations that would curb the increasing number of wildcat strikes." As Hinks saw it, a worker participation project also might help the union and management forge a better working relationship.

Hinks was also interested in the project because, he told the press, "it appealed to me as the only humanly practical way of achieving the productivity and accident rates we would like to achieve." "I think it is ridiculous for just 15 percent of our working population (management) to be concerned with productivity and the service we perform. Inasmuch as everyone's economic welfare is at stake," Hinks told another reporter, "I think we all have to be involved."

With the help of the consultants, UMW president Arnold Miller and mine president Hinks signed a letter of agreement pledging to seek "new job designs so that all people in the company can experience increased satisfaction and increased quality of work and working life."

Next they formed an *advisory committee* with eight union representatives, seven management officials and three consultants, to forge the general direction and structure of the project. The advisory committee formed a joint union-management *steering committee* — six representatives from each side, including the mine president, superintendent and president of the UMW local — to develop the working details of the experiment and to govern the project from day to day. The equal representation on the steering committee guaranteed that both union and management would retain "joint ownership of the project," according to Trist and his colleagues.

It took the steering committee four months of meetings to hammer out the final proposal. In October 1973, the local union membership voted narrowly to launch the experiment, 25-21.

What the agreement said

As the agreement spelled it out, the project began in only one section of the mine, involving three shifts of nine workers each—the operator of the continuous mining machine, 34 tons which slams against the rock and tears out a ton of coal each minute; his helper; roof bolters; shuttle car operators and a mechanic. According to the agreement:

- Every worker in the section would earn top union pay, a boost for some workers of $12.50 per day.

- Every worker in the section would be trained not just in one task, as usual, but in every task inside the mine. For the first time, workers would be trained in state and federal mine and safety laws, and they would learn precisely what mine practices constitute a violation.

- The foremen would no longer be the bosses of the mine, responsible for directing the miners in every task and maximizing production. Instead, the foremen would be responsible for maximizing safety and the miners themselves would take charge of the underground work process. As one project document said, the foreman "may suggest corrective action but not direct the work force to carry it out. He must bring the matter to the attention of the group or shift, who will decide what action it will take." The new arrangement, say the project organizers, eliminated the traditional and dangerous contradiction in which the foreman was responsible for both safety *and* production.

- The mine management and the union made a trade-off. While the management agreed to suspend some of its prerogatives to direct the work force — guaranteed to management in the National Bituminous Coal Wage Agreement of 1971 — the union would agree to attempt to resolve grievances by peer discipline outside the normal contract grievance procedure. Only if the work crew and the steering committee could not settle the dispute on their own would the union resort to the lengthy official grievance process.

Once the plan was accepted, the steering committee posted bids for the special section, selecting volunteers on the basis of seniority and qualifications.

In case any of the volunteers didn't like the new style of working, they could switch back to their previous jobs during the first 60 days (only one opted to switch). And either the management or the union could scuttle the entire experiment at any moment, with merely a phone call. No one would be trapped in an experiment they did not like.

The miners actually began working under the project in December 1973, when they began meeting every Friday and Monday for three weeks in a classroom above ground. With Trist and the other consultants as instructors, all 27 miners plus three foremen from the shifts studied the experiment guidelines, discussed the principle of autonomous work teams, and studied mine safety laws. The miners also studied each work task in detail — at least, in as much detail as possible in a classroom — dissecting every step of each job as it is practiced underground.

Then in February 1974, each of the three crews in the experimental section selected one representative to serve on a joint union-management *section steering committee*. The 10-member committee, which included two local union representatives, would be the grassroots-level governing body for the experimental project. By the end of the month, the orientation sessions were complete, the miners had received their training, the decision-making structure was in place — and the workers began working underground in the new "autonomous" way.

For the miners, and foremen, it was a significant change. "It is not unusual for a foreman (in a traditional mine) to tell the men where to cut, when to make gas checks, where to lay power cables, where to place the roof posts and bolts, when to eat lunch," as a *Business Week* article said. "The foreman," one miner told the Third International Conference on Self-Management, "has assumed an almost 100 percent authoritarian role in the industry." But now the workers were making these decisions. For the first time, miners and foremen began to emphasize cooperation among the three shifts in the section rather than competition; in the past, production was measured

shift to shift, and one shift would leave the machinery and supplies in a mess in order to thwart the next shift's production. But now that production was measured on a 24-hour basis, researchers report, the shifts went out of their way to help the miners who followed them.

As the new way of working became less of an experiment and more of a routine, the members of each section, including the foremen, continued to meet in a classroom for one all-day session every six weeks, to review special problems which had cropped up during the last six weeks and to prepare for the next. Members of management, including the foremen, and the steering committee held meetings at irregular intervals, in order to discuss occasional disputes, talk about possible gains sharing plans and other issues. In October 1974 the Rushton management announced it was opening an entirely new section in the mine. It said the experiment was going so well that it would apply the experimental structure, top pay rates and all, to the new section too. Eighteen months after the project was first conceived, half the mine was operating under the "autonomous" work team approach.

Satisfaction in the mine

Miners who participated in the experimental sections reportedly were enthusiastic about the changes. "Interviews with participating miners made it abundantly clear that most of them enjoyed the experience," according to McAteer. "Over and over again, we heard miners say that they would continue to work autonomously even if the pay differential were taken away, and that they needed no incentive outside the additional satisfactions they received to continue working autonomously."

Widespread press accounts seem to confirm it. One aspect of the project miners especially appreciated was the training. "It's a good thing," miner John Albert told a reporter for the *Philadelphia Inquirer*.

"You learn stuff in the classroom that you wouldn't get under the old way. Like I was in water treatment and I was afraid to go on a front-end loader for fear of getting fired by the union. Now it's like being in business for myself. I can do every job out there."

Miners told the press, as they told the project researchers, that they felt they were truly making some important work decisions, and felt proud about it.

Miner Mark Naylor, for instance, told *The Washington Post* he had volunteered for the experimental section only "because I was going to get paid a higher rate." But after he started working in the section "that was the last thing I thought of. The work got a lot easier. We were making all the decisions ourselves about how the work should be done. . . . The men got a little pride in their work now," Naylor said. "It used to be before they wouldn't talk to anybody. They'd just come out, hang up their light, shower and go home. They could care less. They didn't worry about the section and the way it was left. Now they try to leave it in good shape. Now they tell you about problems when they come out. Before they wouldn't tell you a goddam thing."

Before the project got underway, Naylor told a labor-management conference on quality of work life projects, "It used to be when a machine got busted, we'd just sit around, happy like, until the foreman spotted it and called in a mechanic. But when a machine breaks down nowadays, whenever we can . . . we just fix it ourselves."

The new sense of pride, miners told researchers, made them less tired on the job. "Suddenly, we felt we mattered to somebody. Somebody trusted us," one miner told a labor-management conference in Buffalo. "The funny thing is, in the new system, the crew, we don't really get tired anymore. We probably work twice as hard as we did before, but we don't get tired . . . . It's like you feel you're somebody, like you feel you're a professional, like you got a profession you're proud of." The new spirit, some miners claim, even extended into their homes. "I'm not as tired when I go home anymore," miner Lem Hollen told *The Washington Post*. "My wife . . . told me just

the other day that I was a lot easier to get along with."

The quotes in the press and at labor-management conferences have tended to be a bit euphoric, perhaps unrealistically so. For in spite of the miners' enthusiasm for the project, the autonomous sections did not accomplish the union's or the management's major purposes — to improve safety significantly, or, as management had hoped, to boost productivity. The disappointing results contrasted sharply with widespread press accounts, which proclaimed that the project "resulted in a dramatic drop in the frequency of accidents in the mine" (*Business Week*) and "dramatic reductions in . . . absences, safety violations" (*Philadelphia Inquirer*).

Hazy results

Actually, UMW official Davitt McAteer and a colleague wrote, "Very little can be said in the way of authoritative conclusions about the relationship between autonomous working and mine safety." At best, McAteer and John Esposito reported to the Ford Foundation, there may have been "some safety gains for the experiment"; for instance, while the number of accidents in the traditional sections increased slightly in 1975, the number of accidents in the autonomous sections increased by less. The number of violations cited by government inspectors were spread evenly among the autonomous and nonautonomous sections — and while the absentee rate in one of the autonomous sections was better than in the traditional sections, absenteeism in the other experimental section was virtually the same.

As for costs and production: while some sets of statistics suggest that costs in one of the autonomous sections dropped dramatically, other sets of statistics show there was not much difference. The UMW researchers themselves say, "We confess to a certain confusion concerning reported cost figures." While the figures don't show that coal production increased as a result of the experiment, they clearly show that production had *not decreased*. And that suggests, the

One of the major mistakes in the project was the failure to involve middle management, so they could feel a part of things, too

consultants report, that "production was not adversely affected by the shift to autonomy." It proves that when miners begin taking their own work under control, neither safety nor production will suffer.

To a considerable extent, then, the quality of work life project was a success. Miners in the autonomous section said they were enthusiastic about the changes in their work. Safety may not have improved significantly but it did not suffer. All the miners in the autonomous sections had boosted their income to the top pay rates. Yet on August 20, 1975, when the miners assembled to decide whether or not to extend the autonomous structure to the entire mine, they voted no. The entire project was tossed out. Why?

Management officials, union officers and consultants stress that the vote to end the project was a narrow one, 79 - 75. Interviews with the miners after the vote, according to consultants, suggest that most of the miners who had been working in the autonomous sections voted to continue and expand the project; it was the miners who had been left out who voted to abandon it. Looking back, management and union officials and the consultants say they can trace the collapse of the project to the way they launched it at the beginning.

They had decided to start the experiment in 1973 in only one section, rather than impose it on the entire mine overnight. "There was virtually no previous experience in the mining industry with an innovation of such far-reaching implications," Trist wrote. The union and management leadership agreed it would be best to proceed slowly.

But the decision to have two different styles of work, side by side in the mine — some of the miners working autonomously, getting special training and receiving top pay, the rest of them working conventionally — guaranteed that rumors, resentments and suspicions would simmer. For instance, "quite a number of union members, including some of the most influential older workers, expressed the view that the autonomous experiment was a plot to break the local union," Trist wrote. Many union members shared a view, widespread in the United States labor move-

ment, that worker participation projects would coopt the workers to management's side — even though it was the UMW's national leaders who had first suggested the idea.

Many miners were suspicious about management's willingness to pay top rates across the board. It reminded them of attempts by other mines in the region to undercut union organizing attempts, by "buying off" workers with wages above UMW contract levels. The Rushton mine is one of the few unionized mines in eastern Pennsylvania, and what's more, miners recalled that president Hinks "had bitterly opposed the successful union organizing effort" in the late 1960's, as the consultants wrote. "Many of the older miners who had taken part in the organizing effort had little faith" that the president had changed his anti-union views. "They're just trying to bust this union," a 27-year mining veteran told the *Philadelphia Inquirer*. "I worked these goddam scab places before. I can see it."

The poison of envy

Paying top rate to every worker not only seemed like union-busting to many miners, it made the older miners with seniority jealous. Some miners had worked for 20 years or more to earn top pay, and now "greenhorns" with scarcely any experience were earning exactly the same pay, overnight. Miners in the autonomous sections also enjoyed other privileges which made miners in the conventional sections furious, according to the consultants. They would spend entire days out of the dust and dark of the mine, lolling, as the other miners saw it, in the comfort of a classroom. They were paid to attend committee meetings at a restaurant in town, complete with drinks and roast beef. Some of them traveled to other cities, all expenses paid, to speak about the Rushton mine at special conferences, as though they were some special elite. "Super-miners" they were called in the miners' scornful locker room lingo. With all this envy and hostility building up, the consultants speculate, the miners who had been shut out of the experiment put a stop to it with their "no" vote.

The project was plagued with other problems, however. Within the autonomous sections, the project was not always working smoothly. Mine president Hinks says one of the major problems was the stiff resistance to the autonomous work methods among many managers. Hinks seemed to throw full support behind the experiment, but he actually visited the mine only once or twice a week, during special helicopter visits. Most of the time lower management ran the show, and many of them were "dead set against change, (and) lapsed into old, authoritarian habits," according to *Business Week*. There was a constant tension between some of the management and the autonomous worker teams, the consultants say; managers, threatened by some of the workers' increased autonomy, treated miners with "disdain" when they asked for better scheduling of tools, better maintenance, and other services which only foremen could have requested in the past. Hinks says one of the major mistakes in the project was the failure to take special efforts to involve middle managers — to hold special training sessions for them, to involve them on steering committees, to help them feel they would gain something from the project too. Instead, most of the attention was lavished on the underground workers, the union and the top management. Middle management felt left out.

Hindsights

Consultants, union officials and management agree now that they could have avoided some key mistakes. They could have expanded the experiment to the entire mine sooner, they could have communicated with miners who were not yet in the autonomous sections better, they could have held special training for middle management. In some ways, all of these failures spotlight some of the inherent limits in a workplace participation project which is conceived and directed by top officials, whether in the management, the union or both. The miners never asked for the project in the first place, at least until the idea had already been presented to them, and once they voted to go ahead with it, the miners were scarcely involved in the planning. In effect, the miners were merely plugged into a worker participation project after top union and management officials had already dictated it.

The rhetoric of the project, with all the talk of "autonomy" and "participation," may actually have contributed to the deep mistrust which many miners felt, for in some ways this rhetoric was dishonest. "In the context of the Rushton experiment, autonomy is a severe misnomer," the United Mine Workers evaluators wrote. "It implies a full range of responsibility on the part of each and every worker. In practice, however, what it meant was a limited amount of training in productivity and safety and some regular exposure to group activity sessions. All this was in quite limited contexts."

McAteer and Esposito say management's unilateral decision to open a brand new section, particularly under the "autonomous" system, without first consulting the union rankled many union officials and workers. It seemed to make a mockery of the basic principles of the project — participation. "The decision to open the section, when to open it, what machinery to use — all of this was strictly a management decision announced to other participants by management. Planning by the autonomous group came after all fundamental decisions had been made. In other words, management still decided where and when, indeed whether to go autonomous," the former UMW staff members wrote. "The workers were left with how it should be done. In this sense, the term autonomy disguises management's continued authority but did not modify it."

Inside the mines, the workers' degree of "autonomy" was not always what it was proclaimed to be. Although the workers were supposed to be in charge of production under the project, some foremen refused to relinquish ultimate authority. "If a man wants to try something, as long as it's legal I'll let him try it," one foremen told the Third International Conference on Self-Management. "They can express their ideas. But I have the final say-so over everything."

Some union officials have criticized the project because they say it focused on giving the miners modest powers to participate in problem solving, while ignoring some of the more basic working conditions which can make life underground so difficult. "There was no attempt at all to change the essential physical and psychological environment of the workplace," McAteer and Esposito said. "Lunches were still eaten underground. There were no opportunities for breaks away from the mine. The use of time clocks continued. There was no place in the mine for hot meals, nor were refreshments brought to the mine. In short, there were almost no attempts to make difficult and unpleasant work more comfortable by giving the men access to some basic amenities." Looking back on the project, McAteer says he feels simple physical improvements inside the mine, such as better lighting, may well have had more impact on mine safety than the "autonomous" system did.

Limits of change

The Rushton project, then, suggests one important characteristic of many union-management workplace participation projects: while they reform the way in which workers, foremen, and management interact from day to day, they may do little or nothing to alter the fundamental power relationships between workers and management. "All of this is not to say that the autonomous experiment is a failure," McAteer and Esposito conclude, "but simply to say that it should be viewed for what it is . . . a relatively limited experiment designed to expose the miner to some additional information about coal mining and coal mining safety and to loosen up to a certain degree on the traditional management control."

Although the local union members have voted to abandon the experiment, the "autonomous" way of working is not entirely dead. Rushton president Hinks has continued the program in a modified way, on his own initiative, throughout the entire mine. The union no longer participates officially, however, and there is no question that management makes the ultimate decisions. The old steering committee continues to meet, under a new name, but less frequently than before. Miners still hold training sessions above ground, but far less often than they did during the union-management experiment.

But today, both workers and management officials agree that the spirit of the mine has soured and that the "autonomous" way of working is barely limping along. Some foremen have reverted to their old autocratic ways, management officials concede, and middle managers scarcely make a pretense of supporting the right of workers to order supplies, schedule maintenance and perform other semi-managerial tasks. Most important of all, top management and workers say in private, the mine is pervaded by a deep mistrust among the miners. "I'd say we believe Hinks, oh, maybe 50 percent of the time," says one miner who has served on the steering committee. Many miners are still bitter about the management's decision to fire 10 workers for instituting a strike in the spring of 1976.

And many miners are bitter that after years of discussions with the union, the mine management still has not agreed to institute a gains sharing program which would give the miners profit sharing or cost-cutting bonuses in addition to their normal pay.

The top management says it still has not been able to hammer out an equitable system with the union. The miners feel differently. "Hell, we've been talking about this four years now," one says. "All we can figure is the management has never intended to give us gains sharing and they're still trying to string us along."

Sources

John Esposito and J. Davitt McAteer, "Evaluation of the Autonomous Work Experiment at the Rushton Mine," a report to the Ford Foundation, January 1977.

Eric Trist et al, "An Experiment in Autonomous Working in an American Underground Coal Mine," *Human Relations*, February 1977.

Ted Mills, "Altering the Social Structure in Coal Mining: A Case Study," manuscript, no date

"Here's where the worker can be his own boss," by Ray Holton, *The Philadelphia Inquirer*, January 11, 1976.

"When miners try to boss themselves," *Business Week*, February 2, 1976.

Transcripts of the Third International Conference on Self-Management.

Interviews by the editor with employees and management of the Rushton mine.

HAR-MAN

You'll find Harman International Industries on the edge of the sleepy town of Bolivar, Tennessee, population 7,000. Bolivar still has a monument to the Confederacy, only one movie theater, one radio station, two restaurants and no bars. Aside from the old-time southern courthouse, the biggest buildings in town are the agricultural supply stores where farmers pull up in their coveralls and pickups and chat about the crops and the weather.

Harman Industries, which makes most of the auto rearview mirrors in the U.S., is a crucial force in Bolivar and surrounding Hardeman County, for it is the second largest employer in the region next to the state mental hospital. But Harman has another distinction which gives it a more important niche in United States labor history: Harman is home for what was the first and perhaps most important management-union experiment in worker participation in the nation. The experiment—launched in 1972 by the

United Auto Workers, the Harman management, and consultants from the Harvard Project on Technology, Work and Character—has involved virtually every worker in the factory.

The working core of the Work Improvement Program is a network of more than 30 shopfloor committees, in which employees initiate changes from painting the walls to redesigning an assembly line. Some changes have been unusual: workers who achieve their production quota in less than the normal eight hours can leave their job and even go home if they like. But the most significant feature of the project isn't so much the specific changes that have taken place inside the factory—it's the fact that unlike other workplace participation projects, none of the changes have been imposed by top union officials or management. The shopfloor employees have initiated virtually all of the changes on their own.

While most work participation projects stop at the factory gates, the Harman-UAW Work Improvement Program is reaching into the community. Workers have used their new influence to form a community child care center and a credit union, and even a school open to families and fellow residents in the community.

The organizers of the Work Improvement Program have deliberately attempted to make the Harman-UAW experiment a living model for corporations and unions across the nation. "The goal of the Bolivar project," writes former project director Michael Maccoby, "is to create an American model of industrial democracy: a model that is acceptable to unions and that might stimulate further union efforts. The project is based on the view that a national movement to improve the quality of work is unlikely to succeed without union support."

Inauspicious origins

The Work Improvement Program did not come to Harman Industries in Bolivar because it was a comfortable, model plant. Far from it. The approximately 1,000 workers were housed in three huge Quonset huts left over from World War II. When the project was getting underway, one of the consultants, Robert Duckles, wrote this candid account:

"The production floor is dirty and disorderly, compared to many large factories belonging to richer companies. Like most engaged in this kind of work, it is noisy. A shortage of storage space and the pace of production which overworks the luggers and towmotor operators result in parts and materials being pushed into every available corner and sometimes strewing out into the aisles. No time is allowed for anyone to keep his work area clean and orderly. Many machines are kept in poor repair due to lack of replacement parts and a lot of ad hoc repairs with wire and roughly cut pieces of metal.

"The atmosphere is stuffy and irritating to some because of fumes from die cast, plating and paint, and the towmotors, even though efforts have been made to blow away the most noxious fumes. There are holes in the roof and pools of water on the floor. In winter there is inadequate heating; in the summer no air conditioning. Comfort and sometimes safety have been ignored in the all-out effort to maximize production and profits. Only recently has management started to improve the physical conditions of the plant . . . The offices of the managers, engineers and clerical workers are in the front of the building, sealed off from the production area. They are cleaner, quieter and air-conditioned."

The Harman factory had been built in the Bolivar region because there were few unions and labor was cheap. The United Auto Workers didn't organize the plant until 1969. Historically, management and union officials agreed, labor relations had been strained.

"At the start of the project . . . the spirit was one of hostility, resistance and open conflict between management and workers," Maccoby writes. "The economics of the auto parts industry, fierce competition, price squeezing by the four customers, and fluctuating demand for cars, intensified insecurity and the dehumanizing conditions of work which fed this spirit." Workers, Maccoby says, were treated as

A key strategy in the experiment was never to bypass conventional union-management structures, but to make them stronger than ever

a "standardized replaceable part of the process," which bred "anger, hostility, depression and stifled creativity."

Some workers still talk about the notorious "buzzer incident" in 1972, as a symbol of management's once autocratic spirit: one day the factory's 10 a.m. buzzer, which signaled that workers could take their coffee break, failed. The management ordered workers to delay their cherished break half an hour, until the 10:30 buzzer, which still worked. Angry workers took their breaks at 10 a.m. anyway, timing themselves with watches and clocks. Top executives lashed back at this display of "autonomy" and independence, by suspending some of the workers for three days without pay.

As Michael Maccoby remembers, the Work Improvement Project began when UAW vice president Irving Bluestone, a longtime advocate of industrial democracy, met then company president and owner Sidney Harman at a conference on workplace democracy. Like most union officials, Bluestone had strongly opposed workplace participation projects controlled unilaterally by management; unlike many union officials, he was eager to experiment with shop-floor democracy projects controlled jointly by management and the union. Harman had earned a reputation as a progressive businessman who insisted management "must have the courage to run risks." Before taking over Harman Industries, he had been president of the experimental Friends World College on Long Island. Harman had a "sense of mission," as Maccoby told the press. Harman and Bluestone agreed to launch the first management-union workplace participation project in the nation.

The project began during the summer of 1973. The management, union and their consultants—a third party team led by Maccoby, who insisted the consultants would remain neutral—decided to take the experiment one step at a time, making sure they had a strong base before moving on to the next development. The first step was to gather accurate information about employee attitudes, so that researchers

conducting future studies would have base data to which they could compare. The study, conducted with the help of the W.E. Upjohn Institute for Employment Research, was based on in-depth, four hour interviews with 60 workers, plus shorter interviews with about 300 more employees and 50 managers.

What workers said

The results confirmed in detail what most people already knew: the employees were intensely dissatisfied with their work. As the researchers reported, "most workers don't trust the company": 55 percent disagreed that "when management says something, you can really believe it is true." Most workers felt management ignored them: 77 percent agreed, "It is hard to get people higher up in the organization to listen to people at my level." And the majority of the workers, 77 percent, asserted that, "This company cares more about money and machines than people."

It was a factory where workers did their jobs silently—"don't speak unless spoken to"—and where almost half the employees had ideas for improving work which they never told anyone. The majority complained that their share of the company's earnings was not fair, and many blacks and women, who accounted for 40 percent and 30 percent of the workplace, respectively, charged there was widespread discrimination.

Workers at Harman were so hostile toward management, in fact, that many went out of their way to be destructive: 57 percent said they or fellow workers had occasionally performed work "badly, slowly or incorrectly on purpose" to strike back at management. Employees seemed so turned off to the company, in fact, that when the consultants held some seminars to discuss the results of their study with any workers who wanted to attend, only three or four out of 1,000 workers showed up.

The next step in the experiment was to set up a management-union structure which would screen and approve all project developments. First, the project organizers created a top-level management-union "advisory" committee, including the corporation executives, members of the UAW International, and nationally known experts in the quality of work field. In the fall of 1973, the Working Committee was born, comprised of five representatives from the union and five from local management. One of the key strategies of the project structure, Maccoby stressed, was never to bypass the conventional management-union structures but to strengthen them, to "respect the existing authorities and try to improve them." If any part of the experiment, no matter how small, was initiated without the management and union playing an equal role, Maccoby emphasized, it would be sure to generate "opposition"—and the project would collapse.

Next the management and union agreed to pursue a common set of principles. "The purpose of the joint management-labor Work Improvement Program is to make work better and more satisfying for all employees, salaried and hourly, while maintaining the necessary productivity for job security," the agreement began. But while many worker participation projects in the U.S. have aimed at boosting productivity, the Harman project declared pointedly, "The purpose is *not* to increase productivity." Project participants worried that if they increased plant production, especially given the stagnant economic climate, the management might lay off workers, ensuring the project's collapse.

Steps toward change

The project's goals were "ambitious," as Maccoby has described them. While many previous worker participation programs have been motivated by management desires to reduce absenteeism, turnover,

---

Four sacred principles

The Harvard Project on Technology, Work and Character insists that labor-management projects can flourish, and help workers to grow, only if they are committed to a set of "principles of human development." Labor-management projects which pursue only specific goals such as increased productivity, or nebulous goals such as "improved quality of work life," tend to be gimmicks, project director Michael Maccoby says, with little impact and a brief lifespan.

Maccoby and Neal Herrick, formerly with the Department of Labor, conceived four principles which are considered sacred at the Harman plant. All workplace changes initiated by the Work Improvement Program, labor and management agree, must fulfill these principles:

- *security*—creating conditions which free workers from the fear of losing their jobs, and which maximize their financial income;

- *equity*—guaranteeing fairness in hiring, promotions and pay; an end to discrimination against women and minorities, and profit sharing if productivity increases;

- *individuation*—understanding that each worker is different. Individuation, as the participants define it, means that changes in the workplace should be structured to allow each worker to satisfy her or his individual development. The employee must not be forced to participate in a prescribed way that executives and social scientists have deemed is "satisfying" for them. Changes in the workplace should accomodate everyone as much as possible, and permit workers to get the job done at their own pace;

- *democracy*—making free speech, due process, and workers' participation in decisions which directly affect them a way of life in the corporation.

sabotage and other symptoms of worker malaise, the Harman-UAW Work Improvement Program set out "to reorganize the way the company itself operates." The union and management officials pledged to pursue four specific goals (see box).

Once the management and union participants had agreed on the four principles, they began to solve actual problems in the workplace. At first they concentrated on issues which the workers themselves had identified, in the survey interviews, as the most pressing—environmental problems such as the temperature extremes in the plant, the irritating air pollution, and traffic jams in the parking lots. Workers had been infuriated by the company policy permitting bill collectors to track down debtors inside the factory; now, the Working Committee notified bill collectors, the factory was off-limits.

Early in 1974, the project organized a three-day seminar led by Einor Thorsrud, director of the Norwegian Industrial Democracy Project, to help spark some ideas for shopfloor experiments. By spring, the Working Committee had launched its first experimental groups, in three different departments.

The Working Committee decided to launch its first experiment in the assembly department, where the rearview mirrors are put together. They selected assembly partly because it was a large department with a large workforce, which would be likely to supply a good number of volunteers for the experiment. The factory had accumulated a surplus stock of finished mirrors, which could be used as a sales cushion in case the experiment caused substantial production losses, as it struggled to get off the ground. And the department did not operate for more than one shift, which meant the workers could redesign the work process if they wished without worrying how it might affect the workers on a shift after them.

The key to the experiment, as the principles of individuation and democracy implied, was that the workers themselves would analyze problems with their jobs and propose their own solutions; the work changes would not be imposed by either the consultants or the management. But the first day of the experiment, the project organizers discovered how much worker mistrust and apathy they would have to confront. The foreman asked for a few volunteers; none stepped forward. When the foreman hand-picked some employees and assigned them to the experimental team, two insisted they did not want to participate, and backed out. Workers were suspicious, project consultants say, that management would use the experiment to boost their production—in spite of assurances from the union that production rates would not change. And furthermore, as project consultant Robert Duckles and manager John Lyle wrote, "Many people are not ready to plunge into something new, abandoning old customs . . . "

But enough volunteers finally stepped forward, and the experimental group finally got off the ground; shopfloor employees met with their foreman, the department supervisor and Lyle. "The first and subsequent two meetings were rather low-key, with an undercurrent of anxiety," Duckles and Lyle recalled. Nevertheless, workers began to hash out some of the goals they wanted to achieve. They wanted to improve the pace of production, for instance, by eliminating the frequent and annoying starts and stops and breakdowns—or "downtime"—which made the workday drag. Employees said they wanted to improve the "housekeeping" or cleanliness in their work areas, much of it cluttered and filthy, and they wanted to achieve the scheduled production quotas. The group agreed it would approach these goals in four stages: analysis and planning; getting everyone involved; action; and finally, evaluation.

First efforts

Despite the early tensions and anxieties, participants recall, the first meetings were productive. Workers soon began to propose, and then carry out, some small but effective changes. For instance, they decided to equip the production line with a backup screwdriver so the line wouldn't have to stop, as it normally did, every time the bit in the main screwdriver broke. They decided to teach the woman who operated the screwdriver to change bits herself so she wouldn't have to wait for another worker, who specialized in changing the bits, to be called from another part of the plant. And the employees decided they would install a special light which would signal the materials handler whenever extra parts were needed. Traditionally, workers would have to search for him all over the plant, wasting time.

After two months, the experimental group in the assembly department devised an even more ambitious plan: if the workers could achieve the production quota before quitting time on any given day, they would continue working anyway—and accumulate the extra hours as "bonus" hours, which they could take off some day in the future. Before, workers would sit idly around their machines and knit and chat whenever they reached production in less than eight hours; they were bored and it didn't do the company any good. Now, workers who finished their quota early could go home a couple hours before quitting time or save up their bonus hours over a few weeks and then take a couple days off.

As the assembly department project was getting underway, other experimental groups were struggling to a start in other parts of the plant. A group of six workers in the polish and buff department collapsed when an employee grievance generated management-worker tensions—"worker members of the group informed us they did not have enough trust in management to continue with the experiment," Duckles and Lyle wrote. Undaunted, the Working Committee circulated a memo to workers describing the purpose of the experiment in detail, assuaging some of the employees' fears, and seven workers volunteered to join the experiment. After a few meetings, they decided to experiment with some workplace changes: the members of the group would decide work assignments as a team, rather than merely obey the directives of a foreman; workers who finished their jobs early would help out teammates who took more time; and the worker team would keep its own records of parts produced, efficiency, and the number of bonus hours the team members were accumulating.

A third experimental group was born spontaneously when women on the pre-assembly line, where the mirror shell is bracketed and screwed to its base, asked their foreman if they could join the project. The foreman passed their request to the Working Committee, which agreed, and the women began to organize their own meetings. They hammered out eight goals, including: helping each other achieve production quotas; gaining free time to learn new skills, and go home early; making their workplace more attractive; improving the quality of their work; reducing "downtime," and installing better tools and fixtures at their work stations.

Within a few months the women had increased their production speed so much that they began accumulating substantial chunks of bonus time. One week they threw a party during work hours while another week they used their bonus hours to tour the factory—something few employees had ever done before. A week later, the women chose to use their bonus hours to go home a few hours before quitting time. The project began to nurture cooperation among the workers, cooperation they said had never existed before. When one of the women on the line offered to quit because she couldn't work as fast as the others, and "held them back," for instance, the team "told her not to worry about it as they were all in this to help each other," according to Duckles and Lyle. The workers began tagging their work so they could be held accountable, and recognized, for its quality. Within two weeks, Duckles and Lyle report, the value of wasted, carelessly stripped screws plunged from almost $40 a day to zero.

Shopfloor highs

Morale in the experimental departments seemed high; "the work stations have been painted in colors chosen by the workers," Duckles and Lyle wrote. One of the Harman workers told the Third International Conference on Self-Management how her mood changed when employees became involved with the experiments. Before the project, she said, "it was just work, work, work, from 7 a.m. to 3:30 p.m. Sometimes we would finish earlier and we would be bored. Some of the ladies would bring cards, needlework. When the program first came, we were apprehensive but we decided that it couldn't be any worse. We would do anything so that we could go home earlier when our work was finished. We didn't know what we were volunteering for but we figured it couldn't be any worse. Now working there I feel just like it's a big family."

By late 1974 the experimental groups had become so successful that the factory was no longer plagued by worker resistance to the project. Instead, most workers in the plant, who were not participating in experimental groups, were becoming envious and hostile—hostile that they couldn't benefit too. Workers began to complain that their colleagues in the project groups enjoyed "more freedom, and they seemed to be elite or special," Duckles and Lyle said. Workers protested that they would have volunteered for the experimental groups long ago if only the company had explained more carefully what the groups would actually be doing; they charged that the company had failed to communicate carefully with the employees [today, both company officials and the consultants agree]. But more than anything else, the workers not participating in the experiment resented the "bonus" hours which project participants were enjoying. They saw fellow workers like Oscar Rivers, a polisher, leaving work after only five hours every day — yet getting paid for eight. And so in January 1975, one year after the Work Improvement Program had begun, the Working Committee voted to expand the project throughout the entire factory — that is, if the employees said they wanted it. In a special referendum, the workers voted that they did want to participate in the project, by a majority of 81 percent.

The guts of the factory-wide program is a network of more than 30 shopfloor committees, called core groups. Each department has at least one core group, some larger departments have several. Each core group operates like a grassroots-level, mini-working committee: a typical group includes at least one man-

agement representative (usually the foreman), one representative from the local union (the steward), and from one to four employee representatives elected by fellow employees in the department.

Most suggestions for work changes and new ideas in the factory are born in these core groups — all workers are free to attend the meetings, or to send their ideas through their representative. When a core group approves an idea, it sends it to the company Working Committee for final approval, or criticism. Sometimes the working committee and the core groups pass proposals back and forth several times, before everyone agreees on its final form.

The core groups have become the gears of the Work Improvement Program. Visit the Harman factory, and you'll probably be able to attend several different core group meetings in less than a day. The core group in polish and buff, for example, spent several months meeting once a week to discuss problems with the ventilation system, production methods in the department, quality control problems and departmental budget matters. The core group which represented workers producing the American Motors line of mirrors held numerous meetings to discuss the growing problem of work stoppages and "downtime," and, as one worker told the Third International Conference on Self-Management, the group decided to keep careful production records on the assembly line. Every time the line stopped, the employees

would jot down the information in a log—why the line stopped, for how long—and then the workers on the line would analyze the information. When the workers took their report to their supervisor, "he just flipped over this information because he had never seen it all together before," the employee told participants at the conference. The data showed that one machine was causing most of the problems; the workers got a new machine, and the work stoppages were almost eliminated.

Bonus hour debate

One of the most critical issues confronting virtually all the core groups has been the growing controversy over bonus hours, or "earned idle time," as the company calls it. It's a popular benefit which not all the workers can enjoy equally; in fact, some workers cannot accumulate earned idle time at all. For instance, the four workers who *polish* zinc die castings can finish their eight hour production quota in only five hours, and go home if they wish, while workers who *make* the die castings can accumulate only an average 4.5 hours of earned idle time each *month*. Some employees are trapped by the technologies of their jobs to a full eight-hour day, with no chance for gaining earned idle time. The discrepancies, many workers say, violate the WIP principle of "equity," and create employee discontent.

The Working Committee and the core groups have been tossing around various proposals to make the system more equitable. One possibility would be a cost-savings sharing plan: workers who could cut costs in their department would earn extra income, which would somehow be computed to equal the benefits workers receive when they get earned idle time. Where possible, workers might be able to choose between the two plans, extra income, or time off. The Working Committee flatly rejected a proposal by some employees to earn financial bonuses by increasing production above the quota. As Maccoby writes, "this would lead to loss of jobs."

Consultants Robert and Margaret Duckles have stressed that "the functioning of the core groups has not always been as smooth" as it might seem. "While in some cases core groups have taken initiatives in areas other than earned time, in others the questioning of earned time has been just about the only topic on which the core group has met." In some cases, according to the Duckles, core group members have worked smoothly together and with their fellow workers, while the meetings in other core groups have "been difficult and at times tempestuous."

But one important sign that the project is altering the way employees perceive their work, consultants say, is that the roles of the core groups and behaviors of the employees are continually changing. Early in the project, for instance, core group meetings "had to be initiated by the staff almost entirely," the Duckles report. "Now meetings are initiated by the core groups themselves" most often.

These changing roles and behaviors, consultants say, are the most important achievements of the experiment. Since the Work Improvement Program was first launched, the consultants and the Working Committee have agreed that the specific changes carried out in the factory are not as important as the *way* those changes were initiated and carried out. For the most part, the changes have been initiated and carried out by the workers.

"The *way* in which we do things is as important as what we do," Duckles and Lyle wrote. "This program of work improvement is not one which is designed by concerned managers, with the help of social scientists, and imposed on the plant, but a program that is owned by everyone that it affects from the beginning . . . This process is quite different from job enrichment, in which experts may enlarge a job for workers. The workers at Harman may decide to make changes similar to job enrichment . . . but *they* have made the changes and reserve the right to modify them. The goal is to institute a *process* of democratic decision-making and evaluation rather than any specific changes in tasks."

Workers in the factory can attend a variety of classes from hydraulics to guitar. They set up a community child care center, too

So when some critics of the program have argued that it has not achieved many dramatic benefits for the workers—that many of the changes at Harman are little more than incentive plans such as bonus hours and the chance to go home early—Duckles and Lyle argue that "it is worth noting that these are the goals that the groups have chosen for themselves."

Live-in consultants

One of the most important—and unusual—features of the Harman program has been the work of the third party consultants. From the beginning of the program, the consultants have seen their roles not as experts who impose or even propose projects for the workers to follow, but as instructors who teach the Harman workers to analyze their jobs and job environments and make changes on their own. The consultants have tried to maintain complete neutrality since the project began, and most workers and managers say they have succeeded and earned their complete trust.

Unlike consultants at any other work participation project in the nation, the Harman consultants live in the community and work fulltime in the Harman plant. They have become a crucial resource for both shopfloor workers and managers in the factory, asking some of the tough questions which workers or managers are afraid to ask, proposing possible solutions (without advocating one more than the other) which workers and managers don't think to suggest, prodding workers and managers alike to speak freely and honestly at core group and working committee meetings. Unlike the consultants at most projects, who visit the factory once or twice a week, or less, the Harman consultants have become intimately familiar with the plant, the business and the personalities—which encourages workers and managers alike to trust their judgments and advice.

Most of the work participation projects in the United States have been limited to changes in the way work is performed on the factory floor. But the Bolivar Work Improvement Program has attempted to go beyond these projects by attempting to bridge the gap which separates most workers' lives inside the factory from their lives outside the gates. Perhaps the most unusual innovation is the in-plant school. Workers, their families, and even residents in the community can attend a rich variety of classes, which are held before the shift, after the shift, sometimes even during the shift, at lunch. "Improvement in the workplace and education go hand in hand," as one worker told the Third International Conference on Self-Management.

The school began early in 1975 when the experimental core groups began discussing different ways they could use earned idle time. Many employees said they would like to use their bonus hours not just for going home early—although that is an important benefit for workers with families and workers with part-time farms—and not just for socializing. Instead, many said they wanted the chance to learn new work skills or crafts which had always intrigued them. Others had never finished high school and wanted to get a degree. So a management-union committee was formed to draft an educational program for the working committee.

Today, more than 40 classes have been formed, with well over two hundred students. Teachers are paid by the union-management project fund, although some teachers are funded by the county under its vocational education budget. It's a little like the "free schools" which have sprouted in college towns across the country, except the Harman school is housed in a mirror factory.

Classes in the school are formed "when employees express an interest in them," according to the Duckles. "The first mention of a particular class or activity could come from anywhere. Some have arisen in core groups, others in the working committee, most are ideas that come up informally . . . Typically, an employee consults the program staff, and with our encouragement sets out to discover who else is interested in participating." A handful of employees in the paint department organized a course in paint technology, and tool room workers launched a class in die technology. Courses have included computer language, leadership skills, hydraulics, introduction to data processing, metric measurement, square dancing, theater group, ceramics, precision measurement instruments for quality control, typing, car care for women, and a class which earns its students a high school diploma.

Some workers study guitar during their lunch hour every Wednesday; others go to Bible class on Thursday afternoons, after their shift. One of the most popular courses has taught employees first aid, while another favorite has been art appreciation. This class, Robert Duckles writes, has "put pencils, pastels and brushes into the hands of people who 'came to watch' and 'can't even write good' and helped them come up with something they can feel some pride in."

Cultural renaissance

The dingy Harman factory has been blooming with a cultural renaissance of sorts: there have been free concerts in the cafeteria, with gospel singing and country music by workers and community musicians, and an arts and crafts fair. "We have . . . been struck by the fact that certain special interest classes, particularly those in art and Art Appreciation, have demonstrated an awakening of critical awareness and critical thinking," Duckles reports. "The fact that there are classes is a result of people expressing an interest and getting assistance in implementing them."

One expression of this critical "awakening" is the new factory newspaper, the Harman *Mirror*. Before WIP, there had long been a newsletter published by the personnel department, one of those typical corporate newssheets—a tepid collection of interviews with employees, items about a potluck supper and other innocuous information. As the Work Improvement Program got underway, employees began talking about the need for some real communication about issues. The result: the Harman *Mirror*, edited by employees. An editorial board composed of man-

agement, union and workers reviews the contents of each issue, not to censor any articles but to make sure that controversial views are paired with opposing arguments. The result, workers say, is a lively paper full of heated debates. Typical issues include articles proposing a four-day work week, a petition signed by about 60 employees, asserting "We Want To Keep Second Shift ! ! ! !" and an attack on a recent U.S. presidential veto. One issue of the *Mirror* contained a heated letter from an employee, criticizing a quote by Harman president Sidney Harman in *Business Week*; the same issue carried a response by Harman. The paper also has a lighter side to it, such as poetry by employees, sports news, and even religious articles.

The paper has become so honest and often controversial, the Duckles report, that it has "been an irritant to a number of people."

"Some people say things used to be calmer and people got along better before the *Mirror* and this whole project started stirring things up," one Bolivar worker said. "That's what happens when you encourage people to bring their feelings to the surface, tensions burst out in the open. But I think it's a lot better for everyone in the long run."

The Work Improvement Program is nourishing other changes in the employees' lives outside the plant, in the community. Some workers who had discussed the need for a day-care center in their core groups helped organize a community center; both workers from the plant and others in town now have a place to take their children during the day. Workers in the plant also organized a credit union, which gives loans at low interest rates the workers could not obtain from a commercial bank. A group of prominent Bolivar citizens, impressed by the Bolivar Harman project, have formed a Community Improvement Foundation to explore ways the entire community could adopt the Harman WIP principles "to facilitate new discoveries of the uniqueness of human worth" and "stimulate growth toward a fuller degree of human potential." The factory has urged the county to fund a $650,000 Work Research Improvement Center, although the county is balking.

Now the flaws

The achievements of the Work Improvement Project do not mean that the project is without its critics and faults. Some workers have charged that the changes in the "quality of work life" in the factory have actually been meager. "We cannot get a fan. We cannot get anything but a patchup job done on our dust system," a 12-year veteran of the plant told a local newspaper. "The program is in reality nothing but a scheme to get more work out of the employees, but it's done nothing to improve the quality of life for most of us in the plant." Some employees charge that they have little or no power, despite the core groups; "everything that works out seems to be the company's idea," one told the local press.

Part of the discontent seems to result from the gap between inflated worker expectations and the reality of what the project has delivered. Some workers expected the core groups and working committee to give the employees decision-making powers. But as project consultant Michael Maccoby has stressed, the project was nothing of the kind.

"The principle of democracy was interpreted as establishing the right of each individual to have a say in decisions directly affecting him. In fact, the factory was and is in many ways not democratic. Managerial authority is handed from the top down and workers have no say over who will be their supervisors, much less who runs the company. Decisions about investments and pricing are not usually discussed (although the company did consult with the union about pricing in order to save jobs). What the program has done is to create new areas of democracy and participation in analysis and decision-making which can grow as participants develop greater understanding about the business."

Other problems stem from the resistance among some managerial-level employees to the Work Improvement Program. When middle-line managers, such as foremen and supervisors, have endorsed the program, the core groups have often worked well. But when middle-level managers have resented the program, employees have confronted major obstacles to carrying out changes in their workplace. Some managers at Harman say the foremen are the most neglected employees in the plant.

"The foremen at our company don't know what the hell to do. They feel like no one's supporting them," a middle-level manager says. "We haven't had any training for them, and they don't really know what the program's supposed to be about or how far they can go with it. The workers want one thing from them but they aren't sure whether they have the authority to give it. And some of them are scared, they feel like they're being squeezed out of a job if the shopfloor employees and core groups get too much influence. How do we make the program a growth experience for them too?"

Still another problem which weakens the Work Improvement Program, according to some employees, is that many workers don't participate actively enough. "We sometimes get irritated and frustrated at griping without initiative," write the Duckles, who say that many employees complain about the way things are at Harman, without actively trying to create some alternatives. But they add, "When we get impatient in this way we are usually forgetting that the American industrial tradition is one in which energetic managers determine what needs to be done . . . The tradition is *not* to listen to employees and join with them in the search for alternatives . . . The Bolivar employee, like most others, is thoroughly socialized to expect this as 'the way things are done.'"

In late 1977, Sidney Harman sold the company to the Beatrice Corporation, a $5 billion multinational conglomerate. Beatrice has maintained that it supports the Work Improvement Program and will encourage the project to continue. And while there have been no major new initiatives, the WIP does seem to be going strong. Core groups are meeting, and workers are initiating occasional changes on the shopfloor; the Harvard consultants have been replaced by an in-house staff; old courses at the factory school are coming to an end and new courses are taking their place.

Employees, observers say, have learned much about analyzing problems and proposing solutions on their own initiative, and making decisions in groups—and they have learned that changes are possible. These skills, more than any single change, are perhaps the main accomplishments of the Harman management-union experiment.

Sources

Robert Duckles and John Lyle, "Work Improvement Program, Harman International, Progress Report, June 1974," manuscript.

Robert Duckles and Margaret Molinari Duckles, "Progress Report; The Work Improvement Program at Harman International, June 1976," transcript.

Michael Maccoby, "Changing Work—The Bolivar Project," *Working Papers fro a New Society*, Summer 1975.

Maccoby, "The Quality of Working Life—Lessons from Bolivar," September 13, 1976, manuscript.

"The Bolivar Project, October 1972-April 1975," manuscript from the Work Improvement Program, Harman Industries.

Baseline Study at Harman, by the Harvard Project on Technology, Work and Character.

"Plant is experimenting with changing work on line," by Agis Salpukas, *New York Times*, Arpil 9, 1975.

"Backward-looking product fails to mirror Harman's clear vision," *The Commercial Appeal* (Memphis, Tennessee), September 1, 1975.

"Experiment: Industrial democracy," by Bill Roberts, *The Jackson Sun* (Tennessee), April 18, 1976.

"How workers can get eight hours pay for five," *Business Week*, May 19, 1975.

Transcripts of the Third International Conference on Self-Management.

VAG You'll find the Vermont Asbestos Group mine in the foothills of the Lowell Mountains in northern Vermont. Drive down the unmarked dirt road, which branches off from Eden Mills—a town of two general stores, a gasoline station, a banquet hall and a clump of clapboard homes. The mine, 2,300 acres of it, has gouged a scar out of Belvidere Mountain. The landscape is jumbled with diesel trucks, conveyor shafts, massive shovels and drilling cranes, giant steel-jawed crushers, and a huge plant which crushes the gray ore and extracts the precious asbestos fibers.

This mine, with its more than 175 employees and annual sales of $7 million, has become one of the largest worker-owned corporations in the United States. It is the nation's only worker-owned mine. VAG has also become one of the most widely publicized examples of how workers threatened by a plant closure can use the strategy of worker ownership to save their jobs.

Until the workers took control of ownership of the mine in March 1975, the asbestos mine had been a marginal subsidiary of the GAF Corporation, a conglomerate then ranked number 214 on the *Fortune 500* list of industrial corporations. To the conglomerate, the mine was merely "a small division that we acquired 10 years ago in a merger," as one GAF executive described it. But to the people of north central Vermont, the mine had been for years the biggest and best-paying employer. It's an economically depressed region, with spectacular mountain landscapes and an unemployment rate of about 12-15 percent. GAF shocked the entire region when its New York City headquarters announced, in January 1974, that it planned to liquidate the plant within the following year.

But the workers in the mine organized a community campaign to buy their company, scraping up savings, chipping in $50 each, knocking on the doors of banks, soliciting contributions from town merchants and neighbors. They succeeded. The workers now own a controlling share of the mine, and they elect the majority of the board of directors. In their first two years as owners of the mine, the workers earned the biggest profits in the company's history. And since the takeover in 1975, the worker-elected union officers have negotiated—with the worker-elected board of directors—an almost 50 percent boost in wages.

The experience at Vermont Asbestos Group proves that workers can organize a campaign to purchase a factory in trouble, make a profit, and build themselves and their community a secure economic base. But VAG is not a model of worker self-management—far from it. Day to day, the plant operates as traditionally as it did under conglomerate ownership. A handful of managers make the fundamental decisions about how to run the corporation, and the rank-and-file owners out in the quarry and processing mill follow their orders. This gap between ownership and control, in fact, ignited a crisis at VAG which threatened to destroy worker ownership.

Today, worker ownership remains intact. But the story of the asbestos miners—what went right and what didn't—teaches valuable lessons to any worker and community groups who attempt to take control of their own corporation.

Economic death knell

Workers at the asbestos mine remember the day they heard the mine was going to close like a prisoner recalls the day he heard the death sentence. "Eliminating 178 jobs in an urban area sounds like a nominal sum," says Richard Hamilton, manpower representative for the economic development department of the Vermont Agency for Economic Development. "But in that rural area the effect of a shutdown would be a disaster. People would have two alternatives—go on welfare or move."

Besides the mine, there is virtually no regular employment possible. The 120 farms which once operated in the area have dwindled to 18. The ski industry offers temporary employment during the winter, depending on the weather, but the main resorts are farther south.

The plant closing would have exerted a devastating effect on the economy of the entire Northeast Kingdom, as the region is called. The annual payroll of more than $1.7 million supports dozens of area merchants. The mine property tax provides 50 percent of the total tax income in the town of Lowell, and almost $100,000 in taxes for the two counties which the mine straddles. If the mine closed it would sap 30-50 percent of the annual business from the St. Johnsbury and Lamoille County Railroad, perhaps jeopardizing the rail operations and damaging other shippers, too. And the mine closing would cut deep into the income—$300,000 worth—of the Central Vermont Public Service Corp., the regional power company.

With such drastic potential social and economic repercussions as a backdrop, the GAF announcement to shut the mine sounded oddly detached. "We're a big plant and this is a small division that we acquired 10 years ago in a merger," a vice president told a Vermont newspaper. "The price of our continued investment in the plant . . . was higher than the worth of the asbestos."

The maintenance supervisor said to fellow workers one day, "Why don't we buy the place?" Says a friend: "I thought he was a nut"

Corporate officials also blamed the coming closure on the Environmental Protection Agency, which had declared the mine must install about $1 million worth of pollution control equipment to stay in business. "Tremendous increase in costs," as a GAF vice-president said, "makes further operations unfeasible."

Political observers who argue that small town Americans are powerless and apathetic should look to the citizens of the villages of northern Vermont to change their minds. Within a few days after GAF had announced the plant shutdown, more than 200 mine workers and townspeople gathered for a night meeting at Lowell's major landmark, a combination dance hall and bowling alley, to hash out a solution to the crisis. One of the first orders of business was to form a worker-community committee to spearhead the public campaign.

"We elected members just like you do at a fraternity," one worker said. "We had open nominations, the whole bit. The only ground rule was we had to have five management people on the committee, five hourly people and five outsiders." The board in turn elected a five-member executive committee to draft strategies, but the board would be required to vote on all decisions.

Futile tactics

Led by the committee, the town tried various tactics to save the mine. First they held a series of public "hearings"—one of them drew a crowd of 400 including the state governor—presenting witnesses who testified that the asbestos fibers at the GAF mine weren't as hazardous as other asbestos fibers are; therefore, the workers said, EPA should drop its pollution control demands and GAF should find it profitable to stay. National asbestos experts dismissed the claims, and in any case, the tactic didn't work.

Next the townspeople hoped they could persuade the U.S. President to halt the closing of the mine on grounds that asbestos, used widely in the defense industry, was essential to national security. That didn't work either. In the meantime, the worker-community committee approached the governor's office and the state Agency for Development and Community Affairs, hoping they could put some muscle on EPA and persuade the agency to back off—another tactic ending in failure. The state agency did draft an economic feasibility study, which besides documenting the economic upheaval a plant closure would cause, concluded that there was enough asbestos left in the mine to make the operation profitable for at least six more years.

Armed with the feasibility study, the workers shopped for a corporation which might want to buy the mine from GAF. But "no one wanted to touch us now that GAF had taken a stand," mine employee John Lupien told a local reporter. "A couple of companies showed some interest but their proposals would have put us right back into the predicament we had with GAF. We couldn't risk letting another GAF come in here and clean out the rest of the asbestos and leave us high and dry." The townspeople had offered all their support—at one typical meeting, the local newspaper reported, "a large attendance of workers and townspeople were on hand despite the harsh weather conditions." But nothing seemed to work.

That's when mine maintenance supervisor John Lupien said to some fellow workers one day, "Why don't *we* buy the place?" "Personally," says a friend, "I thought he was a nut. The idea was nice, but where in hell were we going to get the money to buy the plant?"

But "John got permission (from the mine management) to put up a notice on the bulletin board, calling for a meeting of all the interested employees at the bowling alley that night," says Merle Lanpher, a veteran worker in the mine. The workers voted to attempt to buy the mine themselves.

The workers' long and painful struggle to obtain financing to buy the mine offers valuable lessons to workers elsewhere in the United States who have contemplated purchasing their own plant. It's possible, and the experiences of the miners show *how* it's possible—but it also takes enormous patience and perseverance.

The only positive encouragement the asbestos

miners received in the early days of their campaigning was a cut-rate sales offer from GAF. The corporation agreed to sell the mine, which produced $7 million in sales last year, for a salvage price of only $650,000 (the price was later reduced to $450,000). But then the miners approached some big New York and Boston banks to obtain financing, and started getting used to failure. "Mr. Lupien got in touch with a dozen or so eastern banks, without success," the *Wall Street Journal* reported. "The bankers were reluctant mainly because mine workers had no liquid assets of their own; they had to borrow everything." A consultant put it less gracefully. "When we went to the big lenders," says investment consultant Andrew Field, "their first reaction was, 'Jesus Christ, the monkeys are going to run the zoo?'"

"If you run through your mind what the economic and political situation has been in this country, you can understand this [effort to buy the mine] has been an interesting crusade," state official Hamilton said, as the workers shopped for some loans. "Here bankers have been turning down blue chip investments for lack of money, and here's a bunch of mine workers going in and saying 'Put us at the top of your investment list.'" The miners' early approaches to government lending organizations, such as the Small Business Administration and the Commerce Department's Economic Development Administration, were also rebuffed. "What we need," Hamilton told a reporter, "is a nice federal program to take on a high risk program like this."

Selling the stocks

But gradually, the miners started making progress. State officials and investment consultant Field drafted a new economic feasibility report, concluding that the mine would have a guaranteed market for at least half a dozen years as other asbestos mines shut down across the country. The new worker-owned mine would have captive customers who needed asbestos and had no other sources to turn to.

Next, the miners decided to sell corporate stock in the mine, to finance the takeover. They agreed to sell at least 51 percent to fellow workers, so they could retain ultimate financial control. "We got some offers for stock by developers who were willing to buy half a million dollars worth of stock," says employee Dennis Eldred, "but we refused them because we wanted to run the company. That was our basic principle from the day John [Lupien] got his crazy idea that we were going to buy the company, and run it: it would be *our* company."

As a result, the organizing committee voted not to sell more than $5,000 of stock to any single person or interest. One of the toughest tasks, Lupien has told reporters, was to persuade workers earning less than $9,000 a year to invest money in uncertain $50 shares of stock. The mine workers fanned out in the community and sold stocks like Fuller brushes. "Each of us on the board got a territory and we went house to house like traveling salesmen, trying to sell stocks," says Merle Lanpher. "Our pitch was, we can all either go down the road on March 15 [the projected closing date] or we can buy it."

The townspeople pitched in with enthusiasm. Local grocery stores bought shares, and Rotary Club members responded to the workers' pitch. The student council at the local junior high raised $200 and bought four shares. "Did I buy stock? Of course I did," says Ed Wilson, owner of the popular Charlmont Restaurant. "The closing hit close to home. I mean, everybody's family or friend or relative works up there in the mine. If that place closed down . . ." he laughed grimly. "Everybody in this town wants to see this thing work, and wants to help out if they can. The miners up there have helped me out too, coming here for banquets and parties and things like that." The sales campaign raised $78,000 cash among the mine workers and others in the community.

The workers' campaign achieved a breakthrough when the Vermont Agency for Development and Community Affairs agreed to guarantee 80 percent of any bank loan to the VAG. Even then, the banks now negotiating with the workers, mostly smaller, regional banks, balked at the thought of lending money to a workers' group without tight strings attached. "I really didn't think it was worth the risk," said Norman Rolband, president of the Sterling Trust Co. in Johnson, Vermont. Rolband was credited with eventually putting together a financial package—but at first, he recalls "There was no management track record, no guarantee that the EPA wouldn't mess things up again."

Finally, another state agency—the Vermont Industrial Development Authority—issued a special 100 percent loan guarantee, meaning that the banks could make virtually a risk-free investment. "Even when the state guaranteed the loan we still had doubts," Rolband said. "No bank wants to be forced to foreclose on a loan, especially if it's the state you're foreclosing on."

But the consortium of seven banks finally agreed to lend the workers $1.5 million toward the purchase of the mine and the pollution control euqipment. The loan technically was granted not to the workers but to a local community development corporation, the Association to Boost Lamoille Enterprises, which "bought" the mine for a symbolic $1. Title would be transferred to the workers when the loan was repaid.

Last minute success

Even after the consortium had worked out the loan agreement, the financial package was so precariously pasted together that it seemed on the verge of coming unglued almost minute to minute. The deal was so fragile that workers were privately betting the whole thing would fall through. Several times the banks threatened to pull out—once when EPA issued some new dust emission standards for asbestos tailings; once when a dispute erupted over the loan interest rate; another time when the banks insisted that they should control the workers' choice of management; and yet another time when a planned $200,000 debenture plan, which an investment consultant had worked out, collapsed. At the last minute, however, the SBA—which had shut the door on the miners early in their struggle—granted a 90 percent guarantee

on a $400,000 working capital loan from a local bank, and the fragile financial package remained intact.

Then suddenly, before the final touches had been put on the financial plan, GAF announced it would begin shutdown procedures unless the deal were consummated almost immediately. Only when the state squeezed a two week extension out of EPA was the deal finally made. It made front page news across the country. On March 13, 1975, Lupien signed the sales agreement in the governor's office in Montpelier. The workers had raised $2 million, all but $100,000 of it —the community's and the workers' own shares—in loans. Workers controlled 78 percent of the company's stock.

The worker-owned mine has prospered even more than the optimists dreamed. In less than a year, John Lupien told the Third International Conference on Self-Management, the mine had returned a 100 percent dividend to its stockholders. After only one month of operation, VAG had repaid the SBA-backed $400,000 loan, "about four years ahead of schedule," Lupien said. So far, the mine had needed to draw on only about 30 percent of the $1.5 million loan from the bank consortium, and it had already paid back a $250,000 note from GAF which hadn't been due for five years.

Business was so good the first year, in fact, that the production employees received a 19.4 percent wage and benefit increase.

What accounted for the startling commercial success? One reason, some workers said, was that the rank and file members were committing themselves to their work with greater spirit, now that they owned the mine. "When we first took it over the biggest majority of fellas, after seeing what they done, they got quite a bit different attitude toward the whole thing," says one worker-owner. "They had more interest in their work, they come to work every day, they treated machines better." But Lupien told participants at the Third International Conference on Self-Management that the main reason for the mine's financial success was the fact the price of asbestos surged

65 percent during the first year VAG was in operation.

It's not workers control

Widespread media accounts of the Vermont Asbestos Group story have tended to equate the workers' *purchase* of the mine with workers' *control* of the mine. An Associated Press account of the purchase ceremony in the governor's office proclaimed that now the miners were "running the show"; the article closed with the dramatic observation that John Lupien was "only an employee himself this morning. Now he is chairman of the board," as if most of the workers had suddenly been boosted in power and stature.

It's not so. While the VAG experience is an important case study of the rewards and difficulties of worker ownership of a firm, it is by no means an example of worker control or worker self-management—at least, not yet. The shareholders, including the employees, do elect the 15-member board of directors (at first the board included seven hourly workers, seven white hats, plus a state politician, but now there are only four blue-collar workers on the board). And the worker-elected board does vote on general policies and any corporate expenditures over around $7,000.

But most of the key decisions are made by a five-member executive board, essentially the same top managers who ran the firm under GAF conglomerate. In fact, when workers bought the plant, a state official stressed that "The management and administration of the mine will continue just about as it has in the past." As John Lupien told participants at the Third International Conference on Self-Management, buying the company "was a desperate move to save the jobs" —not a political strategy to build workplace democracy. When Lupien was asked if self-management might come to the company eventually, he answered without hesitation: "I don't think that it will ever come about here."

From the first day the workers went shopping for financing, bank officials, state agencies, investment counselors and others made a concerted effort to make sure that the workers would *not* become involved in managing their own mine. "Something we *don't* want to see," investment counselor Andrew Field said while he was trying to piece together a financial package, "is an employee-owned corporation ending up with decisions being made on the floor of the stockholders' meetings. It would be a horrendous situation if decisions were dumped on the stockholders to make a nice democratic vote. If any lender suspected that, you wouldn't get a dime. And *I* would not be a party to it," Field said, "if it would degenerate into a situation where all the employees got to elect the board of directors from within the plant."

This philosophy at VAG—that electing the board of directors from workers inside the plant would be a degeneration—contrasts sharply with the philosophy at other worker-owned firms. The boards of directors of the northwest plywood cooperatives are entirely elected from worker-members inside the mills and so is the board of the Cooperativa Central in California. While the worker-owners of International Group Plans insurance company are not required to elect the board of directors from among themselves, they have the power to do so if they wish.

And while companies such as IGP carry out important decision-making in worker committees, managers at VAG shrink at the thought of such a practice. "It's not a large company, and we [management] can talk and discuss things with the employees, and question them about what they want, so we can make decisions for the best of everyone," Lupien told participants at the Third International Conference. "Employees are always free to discuss anything they want with the foremen or with any member of the board of directors. Sure, we've made some work changes at the employees' suggestions." For instance, Lupien said, one employee suggested paying dividends just before Christmas instead of afterward, as had been planned, so that workers could use the cash to buy presents for their families. Management agreed. The board of directors also instituted a new plan, at one employee's suggestion, to pay a worker 10 percent of any cost savings achieved as a result of his or her idea about how to improve the work process.

Closing management doors

But beyond informal discussions, the manager-owners at VAG have given the rank and file employee-owners little voice. Meetings of the board of directors are usually closed to the workers who elected them. The company does not make an effort to share managerial and financial information with the employees who own the company; in fact, managers have often made an effort to withhold it. As Lupien said at the Third International Conference on Self-Management, "The only problem is that employees, being employees of their own plant, they want to know everything. There's a lot of things that have to be kept confidential at the executive level." For instance, Lupien said, the board of directors and the managers were secretly discussing the possibility of buying a new parcel of land. But word leaked out to the newspapers, speculators bought the parcel, and the asking price soared. Lupien blamed the incident on production employees, who he surmised "spread it all around town"—although he has no concrete evidence. And Lupien said employees want to know too many financial "details" about their own corporation. "Workers want to know, for example, 'What do you do with the money? What's the president's salary? What's the vice president's salary? Where do you spend your expense accounts?'"All this is information, Lupien contended, which employees do not understand in a proper context.

Simmerings of change

As workers at VAG have been getting used to the idea that they actually own their multimillion dollar corporation, they have gradually been making it clear they want more equal treatment in corporate affairs, and that they want to share bigger chunks of management power. The change in the attitude of the rank and file has come slowly. At first, employees at VAG started grumbling. Some complained that management seemed to forget the plant is worker-owned, not run by a corporate dictatorship. "People didn't know who was getting how much money," one worker told *The Washington Post*. "And then there were the managers who gave very little credit to anyone else like it was a one-man show, and it wasn't." Workers started chipping away at managerial prerogatives by attacking somewhat superficial but symbolic issues, such as managerial privileges. Under the GAF regime, for example, managers enjoyed an annual lobster dinner—paid for out of company funds and sales at the workers' canteen. After the workers bought the mine, they strenuously objected to the managers-only banquet and the dinner was cancelled—to the outrage of some managers.

Over the past few years, rank and file workers have started demanding more equal treatment in more substantive issues. Ever since employees in the mine could remember, managers received paid sick leave, while production workers did not. But during recent contract negotiations, the rank and file workers demanded sick leave—and got it. "Now we can take off a couple days sick, and still get paid, for the first time in history," an electrician in the plant said proudly.

But as the miners continued to raise more and more separate issues that troubled them, serious tensions started brewing. When the miners bought the corporation they never established—never even *thought* about establishing—special shopfloor committees or other formal channels that would address issues not covered under normal collective bargaining machinery. "The workers never had any understanding, never had any discussion, of what the meaning of worker ownership was or what their rights were," says Janette Johannessen, a Cornell University researcher who has spent months studying VAG.

Employees became disgruntled as they watched

Most of the miners have asserted that they intend to keep ownership of the company. And they want control over crucial decisions

Jobs vs. cancer

One interesting footnote to the story of the Vermont Asbestos Group shows how a desperate economic plight can blind employees to the severe hazards of their jobs. The GAF corporation blamed the plant closing on the EPA, for demanding costly pollution controls—and the employees, rather than endorsing stiff controls to protect their health, said they agreed with the conglomerate. "EPA is to blame for it all," John Lupien told one reporter.

While medical experts across the country had firmly documented the relationship between asbestos fibers and cancer and other lung diseases, few of the workers at the asbestos mine said they believed it. They cited statistics, later discounted by asbestos researchers, suggesting that the average life expectancy of VAG workers was greater than the national average, and that therefore, the asbestos fibers were proved safe. Workers frequently told the tale of a VAG quarry foreman who retired, apparently in good health after 43 years with the mine — more proof, they said.

"Hell, we all got friends and relatives who've worked for years in the mine, and I don't know any who've ever died from asbestos," one worker said—although he acknowledged that several of his relatives, veterans at the mine, "can't walk up the stairs too good without losing their breath." Workers quoted various studies supposedly showing that VAG's brand of rock, serpentine rock, "is harmless," as John Lupien told a reporter—even though officials at EPA and other national health officials said the VAG fibers can cause cancer like any other astestos fibers.

In the final analysis, however, it wasn't scientific studies which workers cited as they downplayed their pollution problems, but the desperate realities of their economic struggle. "They say you can die of cancer from asbestos after 30 years," miners often said in interviews with reporters. "But you can starve to death in a year."

"their" board of directors retreat behind closed doors and vote on key decisions in secrecy—but they had no forum to protest it. Workers became angry as they watched managers ignore their suggestions for improving the workplace—but had no forum to complain about it. With no way of translating discontent into positive action, employees turned their discontent inward, provoking "bitching and backbiting," as one worker called it, and poisoning employee spirit.

The tension finally exploded in the Spring of 1978. Some months earlier, members of the board of directors had proposed using corporate profits to build a subsidiary wallboard company. The new factory would use waste rocks left over after the asbestos fibers had been squeezed out of them. On the face of it, most employees thought the new factory seemed like a good idea: it would generate long-term profits for the company, and provide more employment in this depressed mountain region. Plus, the subsidiary would get rid of asbestos wastes, which were becoming literally a mounting problem.

But most workers also feared that pouring company funds into a brand new venture might leave the company stranded for cash, just as major expenses were coming up. "We're going to have a lot of expenses up here to keep the mine going," Andre LeBlanc, a driller in the quarry, told *Dollars & Sense* magazine—expenses such as "stripping to expose new rock, new equipment, a new dust standard." Furthermore, many workers—who earn only around $10,000 per year—wanted to plow some of the company's surplus cash into higher take-home pay. So when the board of directors called a special meeting of the stockholders, to vote on the proposed subsidiary, the workers voted overwhelmingly *against* it. They would be willing to build the new plant, shareholders told the board, *only* if the management raised at least 50 percent financing from sources outside the company's own coffers.

The board of directors bluntly ignored the shareholders' vote. And as this book goes to press, VAG is launching operations at its new wallboard subsidiary, financed 100 percent by the workers' profits.

Employees at the mine were furious—and they demonstrated their outrage in two ways. At the peak of the controversy, a wealthy local building contractor, named Howard Manosh, offered to buy workers' shares in the mine for almost $2,000 a share, 40 times what the miners had paid for them three years before. Some miners, enraged at the way "management has sold us out," as one employee put it, gladly sold their shares. "People was just fed up, what with the board ignoring them and all," one employee said recently. "They figured if things kept operating the way they was, why, the stocks wouldn't be worth much in a few years anyway."

At the same time, the corporation held its annual board of directors elections. In a raw protest of the board's abuse of power, the workers booted off all but one of the incumbent directors and replaced them with a brand new slate, including Manosh and several Manosh allies. "If I'd been sitting on the board, and called a special meeting and everything, and the boys had elected me, and that was their choice not to put that money in there, I wouldn't have gone ahead and invested all that money," one employee said angrily. "Those fellas on the board are there to represent us, not shut their ears to what we say."

The national media gave big play to the drama at the asbestos mine; virtually all of the popular press accounts have played the story as the demise of worker control, as the inability of rank-and-file workers to keep control of their own corporation when the going gets rough. "Horatio Alger in the Pits," *The Washington Post* headline proclaimed, "Workers Buy, Run, Sell Mine." "All signs now point to the demise of worker ownership," the article declared, adding that "the headiness of financial success was apparently harder to wield than a 15-pound miners' pick . . . the experiment had turned into a sort of Frankenstein monster."

Actually, the truth was far more complex. For one thing, the workers did not sell the "workers' dream," as the *Boston Globe* put it—rank-and-file employees

---

What does the union do in a worker-owned plant?

Labor leaders often worry that unions would be obsolete in worker-owned firms. But so far, as the history of the Vermont Asbestos Group and other worker-owned companies show, unions continue to play their traditional role when the workers take control. When the miners bought their mine, their union—Local 338 of the Cement, Lime, Gypsum and Allied Workers—remained.

The first year after the worker purchase, relations between the union and the worker-elected board of directors were smooth. The board and union agreed on a contract after only six hours of negotiations, compared to the previous year's three-week negotiating bout between the union and GAF. The worker-elected board agreed to boost paychecks 15 percent, and add company-paid life and medical insurance for the first time in the mine's history. The workers also won a 50 percent boost in pension payments. Negotiations and the final contract package, researcher Dick Cluster reported, were "the best anyone can remember."

As the rank and file workers and the VAG management have grown apart, however, the union has continued to play its traditional adversarial role. Two years ago, when the board refused to meet worker demands for a wage increase, the union came within hours of launching a strike until the board met the employees' demands. "The union's just as important as it ever was," says one member. "I always belonged to the union, and I reckon I always will."

still own a majority of the corporate stock. The miners *did* hand Manosh effective *control* over their corporation, however—with 30 percent of the stock and his hand-picked slate sitting on the board of directors, Manosh has gained effective control over fundamental corporate decisions. Says Cornell researcher Johannesen: "There's no organized opposition against him at all."

But in a curious and confused way, many miners say they turned to Manosh not to scuttle the ideal of worker ownership, but to *assert* their right to control the corporation. To an outsider, giving the reins of power to an outsider scarcely seems the way to assert worker control. But the events at VAG must be interpreted according to the miners' own experience. Manosh enjoys a popular image as a "rough-hewn, self-made businessman," as *Dollars & Sense* describes it, a local boy who made good. Many employee-owners at the mine firmly believe, however naively, that Manosh will manage the corporation in *their* best interests, unlike the previous regime. "If Manosh's board gets in," truck driver Ken Huntley told *Dollars & Sense* just before the explosive board of directors election, "the white hats will be just workers, like you and me."

"The workers knew they didn't like the [former] board and management," says researcher Johannesen, "and they didn't like the way they were being treated. But they had no well-formed alternatives, no one whom they could have more confidence in, whom they could turn to." So when Manosh stepped in, Johannesen says, "that seemed like the perfect out for them."

If you talk to the miners today, you'll hear the philosophy of worker ownership proclaimed strongly. "To me this is *our* company," says an electrician in the mill. "I still would like to see it employee-owned, which it is right now. I never bought my shares to sell them and make a lot of money. I bought them to maintain the operation of the mine by the boys. After you work 30 years for another company, if you can work for your own company, and be proud of it, why, that's quite a thing."

But the future of the Vermont Asbestos Group is uncertain now. Some workers predict most of the shares will eventually be sold to the private investor, and the mine will revert to private ownership. Others see a different future, and talk of increasing employee participation in decision-making. "Some of the guys think they should have more say over how things are run," one employee-owner says. "They think they should have a say over how to run the general operations, like how to manage day-to-day stuff."

However the worker-owned company evolves in the future, one point should be underscored: it will be the rank and file who decide just what to do with this corporation. Taking control of the mine ownership has guaranteed workers in this depressed mountain region a more secure future than any of them had ever dreamed. If the miners sell out, at least they'll make a substantial profit; if they hold onto their plant, they'll have the ownership power to diversify or make other changes as they wish. Only five years ago, the miners were hired labor under a multinational conglomerate; today, unlike most workers in the United States, the miner-owners of the Vermont Asbestos Group have the potential power to change their workplace.

Sources

"VAG Rates a Salute," *The Transcript*, February 3, 1975.

"Prospect of Losing Mine Hangs Heavy Over Lowell," by Katherine Gregg, *Burlington Free Press*, May 16, 1974.

"Lowell Miners' Dream Becomes Reality Today," by Sam Hemingway, *Burlington Free Press*, March 12, 1975.

"Asbestos Miners Switch to New Roles as Bosses," AP, *New York Times*, March 13, 1975.

"Asbestos Workers Take Over GAF Mine," by David Tornquist, *The Chronicle*, March 20, 1975.

"Vermont Miners Are Bosses Now, Vow to Save Jobs, Make Profit," by Tom Slayton, *The Boston Globe*, March 16, 1975.

"Miners Buy the Mine to Save Their Jobs: Then Business Booms," by David Gumpert, *Wall Street Journal*, August 25, 1975.

"Asbestos Workers Buy Out GAF's Mine," *Business Week*, March 31, 1975.

"Working Capital," by Ben Achtenberg, *Working Papers for a New Society*, Winter 1975.

"What Makes Them Think They Can Run the Mine?" by Sam Hemingway, *The New Englander*, June 1975.

"Workers' Mine a Success," by Susan Geffey, *The Washington Post*, April 15, 1978.

Personal interviews by the editor with employees of the Vermont Asbestos Group and others.

Transcripts from the Third International Conference on Self-Management.

THREE MORE

Even five years ago, the notion that workers across the country could buy their own multimillion dollar businesses seemed ludicrous. Today, as conglomerates discard unwanted factories, worker-owned or worker-community owned enterprises are mushrooming across the landscape. The Vermont Asbestos Group is only one example. In January, 1977 the 1,000 workers of Bates Fabrics, Inc., in Lewiston, Maine became owners of their own mill. The same month, 1,300 employees at two plants in Georgia and Texas purchased the Sea-Pak Corporation, a manufacturer of frozen foods. Later the same year, more than 800 workers in California and Oregon bought two factories from the Fibreboard Corporation, and formed their own Pacific Paperboard Products, Inc.

Case studies of three more adventures in worker and worker-community ownership follow. A common thread of experience runs through all three: a conglomerate was discarding a subsidiary and threatening to devaste a local economy, but the workers and community banded together and saved it. But while the workers now own their corporations—profitably so—they do not yet control them. And the gap between ownership and control is starting to cause employee discontents.

South Bend Lathe, Inc.

"The workers take over a factory, and the government backs them to the hilt," the *Wall Street Journal* began. "Moscow, 1917? No, South Bend, 1975, but don't worry. The revolution hasn't come."

That's the way the nation's leading business newspaper described how 500 rank and file workers bought their own South Bend Lathe, Inc., in the shady college town of South Bend, Indiana, for a cool $10 million. The company, founded in 1906, had been a family-owned operation until Chicago-based Amsted Industries snapped it up in 1959. With its 500 skilled operators manufacturing $20 million worth of lathes, drills and punch presses each year, South Bend Lathe ranked as one of the nation's top machine tool shops. You'll find a South Bend lathe on virtually every vessel in the U.S. Navy. But as the machine tool industry slid into a recession in the early Seventies, according to press reports, Amsted announced it wanted to sell the plant.

The city of South Bend has confronted troubling economic problems ever since 1963, when Studebaker, the auto manufacturer, shut down its massive, sprawling factory, which at one time had employed 10 percent of the local workforce. Since then other companies had closed their doors, gradually whittling away the city's manufacturing base. In 1950, according to the *Wall Street Journal*, 60 percent of the town's workers were employed in manufacturing industries, compared to less than half that many in 1976. And while Amsted wanted to sell its plant to a new corporate parent, no takers could be found—except a corporate liquidator. That's the corporate version of a scrap dealer: the company specializes in

taking over ailing companies, stripping them down and selling their salvagable parts, then shutting them down for tax write-offs.

But then the president of the plant, J. Richard Boulis, called in attorney Louis Kelso, one of the nation's leading proponents of employee stock ownership plans (ESOPs—see box). Boulis and other plant managers joined together with local union leaders, city bankers, government officials, and representatives of the U.S. Economic Development Administration —and pieced together an ESOP strategy which would enable the rank and file workers and salaried managers to buy their own plant.

Here's how the plan worked:

- EDA gave a $5 million grant to the city of South Bend, which immediately lent the money to a newly created employee trust. The terms of the loan were easy: 25 years to repay, with three percent interest.

- The employee trust also borrowed another $5 million from three commercial financial institutions, at commercial interest rates which will float with the market.

- Meanwhile, the managers and employees created a new corporate entity, which issued 10,000 shares of stock; with the $10 million in cash, the employee trust bought the stock; in turn, the new corporate entity paid the $10 million to Amsted Industries and bought South Bend Lathe.

- Each year, the company will distribute a portion of its profits to the employee trust, which will in turn use the profits to pay back its long-term loans. The profits deposited in the trust are tax deductible—which gives the South Bend Lathe company a hefty tax break. As the loans are paid off, the stocks will be released to the employees. Each employee will receive a certain number of shares, based on how long they have worked in the company and how much money they earn. The average employee received 2.3 shares the first year after the purchase, worth more than $1,000 each.

Mixed fruits of ownership

What effects has the employee purchase had on the corporation and the workers themselves? Financially, observers report, the company has prospered since the employees took control of ownership. While the corporation had lost money between 1970 and 1975, according to a report by the University of Michigan Institute for Social Research, the company moved into the black after the workers took over. Pre-tax profits the first year of worker ownership were 20 percent on invested capital. Orders boomed: Within a year after the employee purchase, according to the *Wall Street Journal*, the company "landed the biggest job in its 70-year history . . . to supply 236 lathes to Tennessee schools for use in industrial arts classes."

The researchers also reported—based on data collected 18 months after the workers had bought the

What's an ESOP?

In recent years hundreds of corporations, from Mobil and Weyerhaeuser to Atlantic Richfield and Hallmark Cards, have been proclaiming they are partly employee-owned. The reason: they have set up Employee Stock Ownership Plans, or ESOPs. Under ESOPs, employees receive corporate stock, without having to pay any money out of their own pockets. Some companies, such as South Bend Lathe, have used ESOPs to give control of ownership to the employees in order to save the plant. But in most corporations, the main purpose of forming an ESOP isn't to foster workers' control—it's a gimmick to raise investment capital for the corporate management at cheaper rates than they'd have to pay at a bank.

Here's how an ESOP works: Let's say the company wants to raise $2 million for expansion. It could get a bank loan for $2 million, of course, but then it would have to pay back the loan and the interest out of its after-tax profits. Since the corporation is roughly in the 50 percent tax bracket, it would take $4 million in pre-tax profits to pay back the $2 million loan.

Instead, the company sets up an employee trust. The trust borrows $2 million from a bank, and then gives the $2 million to the corporation; in return, the corporation gives the trust the corporate stocks. Every year the corporation will give part of its profits to the employee trust, which will send the profits to the bank to repay its loan.

Here's the gimmick: under U.S. tax laws, the corporate profits placed in the ESOP trust are tax-deductible. And that means the corporation has raised $2 million in capital, virtually for free. The employees now own the stocks, which they can cash in instead of a pension or retirement plan when they leave.

Don't the employees control the corporation now that they own the stocks? Not necessarily —and not usually. When a corporation sets up an ESOP, it can specify in the contract that management-appointed trustees will cast the stock votes on behalf of the employees—which means the employees gain no power at all. But the employees could demand, under the contract, to have the voting power "passed on" to them— which would give them voting control over the corporation.

So far, then, ESOPs have been used mainly as corporate financial gimmicks. But they have the potential to become a powerful tool in the movement toward workers' ownership and control.

factory—that productivity "appears also to have increased since the change in ownership," while quality has also improved. The rate of rejects and customer returns has dropped, and the rate of grievances has also "changed for the better," the researchers say.

The researchers caution that the data don't prove the worker purchase has caused the financial and workplace improvements, although they do suggest some relationship. Whatever the causes and effects, both employees and the survey data agree on one change: morale of the employees and managers surged for the first year or two after the purchase.

Before the purchase, many workers have said, people regarded working at South Bend Lathe as "just another job." But after the workers took control of ownership, people took more interest and care in their work. "It's, 'Hey, you've got your hand in my pocket if you don't do your job,'" June Molnar, a tool and cutting grinder, told *Time* magazine. Many employees felt buoyed by the notion that they own corporate stocks. "By the time I get out of here," Jim Kospa, a gearbox worker told the *Washington Post*, "I should have a bundle of money in stock." According to the Institute for Social Research survey, 58 percent of the production workers said there were better communications and relationships between people and departments, while 45 percent of the employees said that most workers have "better attitudes and morale," in their work. "I've never had it so good," one employee told the University of Michigan researchers. "We get raises more often and bonuses; we get turkeys at Thanksgiving and things like that we never had before." Since the employees purchased the firm, wages have increased from an average $5 to almost $5.75 per hour.

The glow fades

But recent reports from inside the factory suggest that the initial glow of ownership has begun to fade. The reason, insiders say, is that workers had nebulous expectations when they became owners of the factory

that "things would change." "We thought things would be different," says Robert Newton, a 30-year-old machinist who grinds out gear blanks. "For a while all the guys here were going around saying, 'Yeah, it feels good to be an owner. Now I can tell them what I *really* feel.'" But except for the bonuses and turkeys, workers say, things haven't changed at all. The decision-making structure is as autocratic as it was when the Amsted conglomerate owned the firm. The traditional power relationship between managers and rank and file remains exactly the same—even the top managers running the firm are the same. "People say the ESOP is not what they thought," says Gerald Vogel, operator of an automatic screw machine, who also serves as vice president of the United Steelworkers local. "People are asking, 'What do we have different now than what we had before?' When you get down to the real meat of it," Vogel says, "there really isn't much difference."

Today, when the afternoon shift ends, you can join Robert Newton and fellow workers at a tavern down the street, sipping beers and mulling over how their dream has soured. They recite a long list of charges and complaints: managers keep information secret, managers waste corporate finances, managers treat workers with disrespect, managers spend corporate money—"*our* money," workers say—buying subsidiary without even consulting the workforce. The major theme, no matter what the anecdote, is that the work-owners at South Bend Lathe feel forgotten and ignored. "You wouldn't believe all the dumb things management does to waste money around here," one worker says. "But when you come up with an idea about how to make things better, you feel like they're saying, 'Oh, don't listen to him, he's just an hourly.' Hell," the machinist says, "there are a lot of intelligent guys out there on the floor been working five, ten years. There's nobody who can run that shop better than they can."

And workers say they bristle as management exhorts them to work harder and earn more profits for "their" company—only to distribute the profit bonuses according to salary, so that managers in the

Some workers are starting to demand concrete powers over corporate decisions. Recently employees sent petitions to the president asking for 50% power on the board of directors

air-conditioned administration building walk off with the biggest chunk. "We should all be cutting equal sized pieces out of a pie we all more or less baked," Newton says. "They're trying to make ESOP slaves out of us. They tell us, 'It's *your* company, you're the owners—now do as we tell you.'"

Many employees at South Bend Lathe will tell you they never expected power over day-to-day managerial decisions, and in fact don't want it. But they expect that when management formulates crucial corporate policies or makes major financial investments, "at least they'd be discussed with us," says union leader Vogel. "I think people were led to believe that ESOPs would make have-ees out of have-nots. A lot of people felt now that it's theirs, they'd be in the driver's seat, they'd be the boss—they'd have a bigger voice in management decisions."

As ferment spreads among the employee-owners of South Bend Lathe, a growing number of workers are starting to demand a share of corporate power. More than half the hourly workers have sent a petition to the plant president demanding control over half the

board of directors a board that management hand picked, originally with the United Steelworkers' blessings, to include only two token employee representatives (one resigned from the board, so only one worker representative remains). And some employees argue that controlling half the board should be just the beginning. "The whole board should be elected by the employees," insists Gerald Vogel, the lone remaining worker representative on the board. "After all, this company's employee owned. We should elect the people who run it, just like we elect the people who run our union, and the people who run the country."

So far, managers at South Bend Lathe seem to be handling the growing discontent mainly by ignoring it. The management called three company meetings—each for a different third of the employees—to encourage the rank and file to ask questions of top managers and air grievances. But the forums were a one-shot affair which employees say cannot give them meaningful input to corporate affairs. When asked about the power imbalance between hourly employees and

---

Shattering the corporate myth

"People commonly assumed that a big company would never shut down a subsidiary if it were making a profit and that further, if a big company could not operate the local plant at a profit, then the plant was inevitably doomed to failure and could only survive through an endless infusion of government funds.

"Furthermore, it was assumed that plant shutdowns were a painful but necessary part of the natural processes of economic life. We live in a competitive world in which only the fit survive. Old and inefficient plants go out of operation while old but efficient plants expand and new plants are built to provide further employment. It would be wrong to violate this 'economic law' by trying to keep inefficient plants in operation.

The government should only seek to deal with the *effects* of plant shutdowns. Thus we find widespread support for measures that provide unemployment compensation, retraining for workers and so on. Saving jobs through a shift to employee-community ownership was seldom considered because of widespread belief that this was not a practical alternative.

"The cases we have been studying . . . should destroy two common myths: that a big company can always do better for the local plant than employee-community owners and that a big company would not abandon a plant if it were making profits."

William Foote Whyte,
"In Support of the Voluntary
Employee Ownership and
Community Stabilization Act" 1978

managers, corporate Vice President William York refused to discuss the issue. "This kind of discussion could cause a rift in our company," he said. "There are people in the [United] Steelworkers who would like to drive the wedge deeper and deeper until they destroy us." But some employees feel the wedge between managers and hourly workers has already been driven. Scores of frustrated employees boycotted the recent board of directors election, when they picked up the ballots and discovered they had only two possible votes—yes or no for a slate of candidates handpicked by company executives. "Frankly," one formerly enthusiastic advocate of the ESOP says, "morale stinks."

So far, the employee-owners of South Bend Lathe don't have the power to translate their mounting discontent into constructive action. Like the employee-owners in most corporate ESOPs, the workers at South Bend Lathe do not have actual voting control over most of their stocks—at least, not yet. Instead, trustees appointed by management do. As the employee trust pays off its $10 million loans, shares of voting stock are being released gradually to each employee's control. At the end of 1978, the third year of worker ownership, one third of the shares were released, or "vested"; most of the stocks will have been vested by 1985.

This means that by the mid-1980s, the workers will have the *potential* power to take control of the corporation if they want to. For while managerial-level employees will each control considerably more shares than the average production worker, since shares are apportioned according to salary, the production workers as a bloc will control about 66 percent of the stocks. The key question is whether the rank and file will have the desire, the knowledge, and the unity required to assert their potential power—potential power which the worker-owners at firms such as Vermont Asbestos Group have never learned how to use.

The union's role

Union leaders across the country often criticize the concept of workers owning their own workplace,

and they criticize the notion of having union officers serve on the boards of directors, too. Workers and union leaders who take any part in making managerial decisions, the typical union line goes, will "get sold out to management" (see *What labor thinks*). From the outset at South Bend, however, the local United Steelworkers leaders supported the idea of worker ownership, not out of philosophical reasons but out of pure survival instinct. "We were very much for it," Vogel says. "It meant saving our jobs."

At first, the two top officials in the union local sat on the board of directors; one resigned because he said he couldn't adequately represent both his union members and management at the same time. But Gerald Vogel, the other union representative on the board, says he does not feel a conflict of interest. "I think it's a good idea (serving on the board)," Vogel says. "It makes me able to do a better job (as a union leader), having a broader understanding of finances and how the company works.

Meanwhile, top officials at United Steelworkers international headquarters in Pittsburgh have taken a dim view of the ESOP at South Bend Lathe—indeed, at any corporation. Their major point of contention is this: when the ESOP was negotiated between the plant managers and the union, management persuaded the union to give up the workers' old pension plan, which they had received under Amsted Industries. The company, top managers insisted, couldn't afford both the ESOP and a pension. Theoretically, many workers at South Bend Lathe should retire with as good or better a financial nest egg with the ESOP as they would have under a pension—for if the corporate stocks keep increasing in value they could become worth tens of thousands of dollars. When workers retire, they can sell their shares back to the ESOP trust at a value set by an independent consultant. But there's a catch: as the *Wall Street Journal* notes, "current older employees can't accumulate enough equity [through ESOP stocks] to match their lost Amsted [pension] rights." Furthermore, if company finances tumble, the workers stocks could be practically worthless when they retire, leaving them nothing after decades of work. "Three bad years in a row," says Robert Newton, "and we could all really be wiped out." But most employees say theirs was a choice of the lesser of two evils. "It was either give up the pension," one union member says, "or give up the job."

Spreading the gospel

One of the major obstacles to worker-controlled and worker-owned companies has always been their isolation. Individual firms thrive, but don't regenerate. Asbestos miners may have saved their asbestos mine in Vermont, but their experience will not give birth to other worker-owned firms across Vermont. The employees at the Herkimer Library Bureau and Saratoga Knitting Mill have helped buy their companies and save their communities' economic base—but neither event will multiply and nourish other worker-owned firms in New York State. That is one of the most unusual features of the South Bend Lathe experience: what the workers have achieved in this factory, taking control of ownership, should directly cause other worker-owned firms in the community to grow. That's because as South Bend Lathe pays back the $5 million plus interest to the city government, the city will in turn "lend it out again to other industries interested in employee ownership programs," South Bend's mayor told the *Washington Post*. Now that workers in this noisy machine tooling factory have saved a crucial economic resource by buying their own jobs, city officials will never think the same way about worker ownership again. "I think employee ownership is the coming thing," he said. "It's the only way middle- and lower-income people can accumulate capital."

Saratoga Knitting Mill

Saratoga Springs, New York, is best known to the rest of the nation as home of a famous racetrack which attracted the rich and powerful during the 1930s. But to the 17,000 residents of this town in rural, upstate New York, the local name which is even more important today is Saratoga Knitting Mill. For years, this manufacturer of fine quality women's lingerie has been an important economic force in the region, employing up to 150 workers. For four decades after its founding in 1932, the factory, one of 16 plants in the Van Raalte textiles corporation, had never failed to earn a profit.

But then Van Raalte was gobbled up by the Cluett, Peabody conglomerate, and the fortunes of the factory began to change. Under conglomerate ownership, reports researcher William Foote Whyte at Cornell University, "a whole series of bad decisions" caused a "precipitous drop in volume of business and profits." The major mistake, Whyte suggests, is that Cluett, Peabody dismembered Van Raalte's own sales force and turned over sales to the distant conglomerate's sales staff—and as a result, a product which had received specialized sales care became just one more item in a vast conglomerate line. "While this saved selling expense it had a drastic impact on Van Raalte sales," Whyte reports. "(T)he Cluett, Peabody salesmen did not know the Van Raalte merchandise . . . and so the whole selling campaign broke down."

Under the conglomerate's mismanagement, according to Whyte, Van Raalte's business plummeted from $72 million in 1968 to only $20 million in 1974; the Saratoga Knitting Mill itself suffered badly during this period. In February 1975, the beleaguered mill laid off half its 140 employees, and soon after, Cluett, Peabody announced that Saratoga Knitting Mill and seven other plants in the Van Raalte chain would be sold.

"When the announcement came out from Cluett," plant manager Donald Cox told the *New York Times*, "several people came to me—some people on the plant floor—and they said, 'Let's buy this and run it ourselves'."

With the help of Saratoga's major bank and a local assemblyman, Cox and 40 other employees, ranging from loom operators to top managers, pieced together a financial package and purchased more than 60 percent of the company's stocks. Most of the workers

Workers: beware of stage 2

"Our research suggests that many employee- or community-owned firms are likely to go through at least two distinct stages in their early history. Stage 1 includes the period from the announcement of the closing of the plant through to the saving of jobs by establishing the new firm, and continues into the early weeks or months following this momentous event. In this stage, workers, union officials, management people, local officials and community leaders are all working together to save the plant. This is a period of intense activity and interactions among those serving together in the common cause. When victory is won, the event is celebrated throughout the community, and worker and management representatives give public testimony on how highly they regard each other. A spirit of brotherhood prevails.

"In stage 1 workers and union leaders lack any clear expectations as to how the plant will be run in the future, but involvement in the campaign to save the jobs leads them to feel that in the future they will be treated more as the social equals of management people, that their ideas will be valued, and that they will be respected and trusted. Management people are likely to be so preoccupied with their new business responsibilities that they devote all their attention to financial, engineering and marketing problems. If they give any thought to union-management or worker-management relations, they are likely to assume that workers, now being co-owners of the firm, will appreciate the wisdom of management decisions and will comply more effectively with management orders.

"Such failure on both sides to recognize the social requirements of the new form of ownership leads the parties into stage 2, which is marked by the deterioration of hopes, trust, and mutual confidence as labor and management slide back into the same old frictions and misunderstandings that prevailed before the change in ownership."

William Foote Whyte,
"In Support of the Voluntary
Employee Ownership and
Community Stabilization Act," 1978

borrowed from friends and relatives and chipped in their own savings. "The employees in that plant mortgaged their homes, borrowed on their life insurance, and I don't know what all, but raised enough money," Cox told the Third International Conference on Self-management. Outside investors bought the remaining 15 percent. Organizers of the stock sales limited any single purchase to only 100 of 3,000 shares, so no one investor could take control of the company. While some employees bought only one share, worth $100, plant manager Cox bought the maximum amount. Today, about half the employee-held stock is in the hands of 16 managers, while approximately 25 production employees control the other 50 percent. Employees vote according to how many shares they own, so high-salaried managers wield the most voting power in the corporation. The seven-person board of directors, elected by the shareholders, is dominated by four mill employees including president Cox, a former vice-president, and two rank-and-file workers. Three outside representatives include a banker and a corporate attorney.

Knitting back to prosperity

Financially, the new worker-community owned mill has been a dramatic success. After the worker purchase, Cox launched an aggressive marketing campaign and business boomed. Today the factory is operating near peak capacity, with a workforce back to 140 employees; just recently the company bought new knitting machines and other costly equipment. Unlike some competitors in the textile business, the new Saratoga Knitting Mill has not had to lay off any employees. Waste and rejects have decreased, and the number of customer returns have dropped, too. In 1976 and 1977, the company earned substantial profits.

The factory has launched an employee stock ownership plan (ESOP) so that even employees who didn't purchase the original stock to save the corporation will now receive shares, essentially for free. Eventually, the production workers will control a majority of the corporate stock.

While the Saratoga Knitting Mill is worker-*owned*, the mill is not worker-*controlled*. The day-to-day decision-making inside the factory is no different than it was under conglomerate ownership; rank-and-file workers don't exert any more influence over shopfloor or corporate decisions than they ever did. "We have been able to make this employee-owner conversion," Cox said, "without making any changes in the management group."

From the beginning, factory manager and president Cox stressed that the factory would not be an experiment in "collective control" or worker self-management. Cox caused a stir at the Third International Conference on Self-Management, in fact, when he appeared before a panel session called "Starting Self-Managed Enterprises." Members of the audience obviously expected, and hoped, that Cox would announce some bold experiments in worker decision-making inside the knitting mill.

"This session is about 'Starting Self-Managed Enterprises'?" Cox began. "I consider that a misnomer because my company was not and is not a self-managed enterprise. I make all the decisions." Participants in the audience asked Cox when he planned to begin bringing workers into the decision-making process. "In my lifetime," Cox replied, "the factory will never be run in a democratic way by the workforce. I can overrule anything." Some of the

participants in the audience began to laugh derisively. "What's this guy doing here?" one participant whispered, to no one in particular.

Cox understood the laughter, and answered: "I have quite a different approach in this than most of the academic people," he said, referring to the large number of academics attending the conference. "And I think it springs from the simple fact that I'm sitting in the middle of a situation where I have to write $150,000 worth of checks every week just to make sure that the doors stay open. I have . . . people to take care of and keep in line and keep operating and keep interested. I have creditors that I owe three quarters of a million dollars. So the situation I'm in," Cox said, "I can't afford to experiment. Whatever I do has *got* to be right."

A vague discontent

Since the workers and managers of Saratoga Knitting Mill purchased their factory, the mood inside the plant has undergone some dramatic shifts. In 1976, just after the takeover, Cornell University researcher Michael Gurdon reports, worker morale and enthusiasm were high. But since then, Gurdon's surveys show, "there has been quite a change on the part of the rank and file. There's more cynicism now, and more mistrust among employees toward management," Gurdon says.

Part of the discontent, Gurdon reports, comes from production workers' feeling that "the top managers are the ones making all the money," as Gurdon describes it; "workers say, 'we're not getting anything out of it (ownership).' " It's true that managers are making more money from their share of the mill's ownership than production workers are, since the average manager owns more than twice as many shares.

But pinpointing the other source of the workers' souring mood is more difficult. On the one hand, Gurdon's attitude surveys show, most employees do not have concrete complaints about the decision-making structure or any specific demands for more

After the thrill of their purchase begins to fade, the workers feel discontented that they have little more power than before

power. "People are happy their jobs were saved and the company is doing well," Gurdon reports, "and there's no great drive for change." "I find no fault with the company," as one 30-year veteran says. "The place is doing very well, which is good—on account of my age, I knew I couldn't go out and get a job any other place."

On the other hand, insiders say, many workers *do* have a vague if inarticulated desire for more involvement in decision-making—and they feel frustrated that they've been denied it. "People expected a little more in the decision-making process than there's been," knitting foreman Hugh Hibbert observes. "They were of the idea they'd have a little more say at the managerial level." Ask employees just what kind of say they expected, and they aren't likely to give a specific answer. But some talk angrily about the first shareholders' meeting, when they saw how managers with more shares could steamroll decisions—no matter what the rest of the employees thought.

Murmurs of change

Since Cox attended the Third International Conference on Self-Management, observers say, he has been talking about gradually introducing some limited forms of worker participation. For instance, Cox has called meetings with small groups of employees, just to chat informally about their work, on Saturday mornings at the local Holiday Inn. But, according to one observer, "there has not been a tremendous amount of interest" on the part of either the rank and file workers or the top management. Managers, including Cox, feel cautious about making any substantive changes in the decision-making structure—they fear that any change, no matter how small, could backfire and hurt production. In the volatile world of textiles, the company's managers are perhaps even more sensitive to production levels than most.

Managers also talk despairingly about some of the workers' low level of education. "We get employees who don't even have a high school education," one production manager says. "They even have difficulty advancing to become a mechanic because they don't have the necessary education to do mathematical problems like fractions, or reading different gauges. I don't see how these people could be trained to make management decisions, or to be in a position to veto some plan they may not understand."

The production workers, on the other hand, don't show much interest in Cox's informal meetings "because of their ingrained pattern of subservience and suspicion toward management," Gurdon observes.

The souring mood at Saratoga Knitting Mill exemplifies the vicious circle which seems to be snaring workers and managers alike at the growing number of worker-owned firms. Workers have vague expectations that "something will change" after they take control of ownership—yet neither the production employees nor the managers even broach the subject while united in the heat of purchasing the plant. After the thrill of their achievement begins to fade, the production workers begin to feel discontented that nothing has changed, and that they have no more influence or power than before—yet, the production workers aren't even certain what kind of influence or power they want.

Managers fear giving workers any significant responsibilities in making decisions, since the workers don't have the training or experience to meet the task—yet the workers will never gain that crucial training or experience as long as managers refuse to give it to them. "If the initial goodwill had been immediately followed by discussions on how to manage the company," one Cornell University researcher says, "there would have been a momentum for more worker participation. People would have been ready for change." Today, at Saratoga Knitting Mill, the momentum is against it.

Mohawk Valley Community Corporation

(Editor's note: the following case study is based largely on information provided by researcher Robert Stern of the New York State School of Industrial and Labor Relations.)

When the Sperry Rand conglomerate announced on March 29, 1976 that it planned to liquidate its three-story library furniture factory in Herkimer, New York, at the foot of the Adirondacks, the news hit the region "like a bombshell," according to the Utica *Observer Dispatch*.

True, the announcement did not come to some city officials as a complete surprise; the conglomerate, whose major products include sophisticated electronics for U.S. warplanes, had been murmuring about closing this odd child among its conglomerate offspring for several years. The Library Bureau, which had been founded in 1876 by Melvil Dewey of Dewey Decimal fame, was out of place in the conglomerate, executives said. And while the highly reputed factory was earning a considerable profit, executives said, it was not making *enough*—22 percent on invested capital, "the standard used by this conglomerate's management in determining an acceptable rate of return on its investments," says researcher William Foote Whyte at Cornell University. "If Sperry Rand could make more money elsewhere by shifting its investment out of the Herkimer plant," Whyte writes, "then the shutdown decision made good economic sense to the top management of the conglomerate."

But when the news finally hit this depressed area, where boarded-up companies litter the landscape like crumpled beer cans, and unemployment hovers at 13.7 percent, nothing could soften the shock. The factory, which sold $10 million worth of goods per year, employed 270 workers, including a 55-person marketing staff. Most of them were middle-aged, and most had worked in the factory an average of 17 years. The total payroll exceeded $3 million, making the factory a vital economic force in the small towns of Ilion, Mohawk and Herkimer, total population 22,000.

Closing the factory would devastate not only the immediate workforce and their families; almost 200 farmers in the area sold hardwood logs to the factory, more than $875,000 worth each year, to be debarked, cut, planed, and fashioned into the library furnishings found at prestigious institutions from Notre Dame and Princeton colleges to U.S. embassies around the world. Local congressmen and other political figures tried to persuade Sperry Rand not to close the plant, but corporate executives insisted their decision was final.

Within days after Sperry announced its planned shutdown, scheduled within the coming year, two separate groups of businessmen expressed interest in buying the plant. One group, dominated by managers at the factory, "knew the business well but had little grasp of the financing problems involved in the proposed purchase," Robert Stern reports. The other group, led by local investors, "had a better grasp of the financing problems but knew little of the routine operation and business" of the factory. The result, says Stern: "Each was too weak to act alone."

Through the efforts of the Mohawk Valley Economic Development District, the local conduit for U.S. Economic Development Administration programs, the two groups merged. They formed the Mohawk Valley Community Corporation, the corporate entity which would attempt to buy the Library Bureau plant.

Who has $6 million?

From the beginning, observers report, Sperry Rand resisted negotiating with the community, as if it preferred not to sell the plant. Sperry had a good financial reason: the conglomerate figured it could earn $7 million merely by liquidating the factory, selling off its valuable European-made machinery, and writing off the shutdown factory as a tax loss. The estimated sales value of the operating plant, on the other hand, was less than $6 million.

Finally, though, Sperry Rand agreed to negotiate a deal. Local organizers devised a three part strategy for raising the necessary cash:

- $2 million, they hoped, would come in the form of a loan from EDA;

- local banks would lend another $2 million;

- the community and workers would raise up to $2 million more by selling common stocks.

EDA soon approved the $2 million loan, as organizers hoped, but with strings attached: the Mohawk Valley Community Corporation would have to raise the community's share of the cash first.

Organizers called a town meeting at the Herkimer Community College, the town's biggest meeting hall, and hundreds of citizens showed up—workers and their relatives, concerned citizens, town merchants and businesspeople. "Feelings ran high," Stern says. The citizens formed a Concerned Citizens Committee to launch a community stock sales campaign—and within 24 hours, they had already raised $11,000 in seed money to help fund the drive.

The story of the community's efforts to buy the plant is the story of overcoming one difficult hurdle after the next—many of them tossed in the way, observers say, by Sperry Rand. Just as the community stock campaign was getting underway, the conglomerate announced from its Philadelphia offices that it would require a $250,000 cash downpayment before entering further negotiations—"one which would not be refundable even in the event that the proposed sale did not succeed," says Stern.

Local organizers called major political figures in state politics, including the U.S. Senators' and governor's offices, and apparently in response to the pressure, the conglomerate executives dropped their down payment demand to $200,000.

When union leaders and workers first heard the plant was going to be shut down, they had been shocked. "We never thought Sperry Rand would get rid of it, seeing as how we were making money," says Carl Vogel, president of Local 344 of the International Union of Electrical, Radio and Machine Workers. "I really didn't believe it would be possible to buy it." But then, Vogel says, the workers knew they had no choice. "We got a bunch of people here who don't want to quit," Vogel says. "They're at an age when they can't retire. They have to work. Where are they going to go? It was either go out and draw unemployment, and then go on welfare, or go and purchase the plant."

Observers credit union leader Vogel and his membership for saving the community by raising the crucial downpayment. "I went right through the plant, floor by floor and man by man," Carl Vogel recalls today, "and I told them, 'We got to come up with the money and I don't care where you get it. Draw it out of the bank or out of your mattresses.' The manager of a local finance company told me he made $50,000 in small loans in a single day. And we come up with $193,000 in cash in just a few days," Vogel says proudly. "The employees alone."

Next, the community had to raise the $1.8 million more in cash from stock sales—within 90 days, Sperry Rand demanded. It was a herculean effort. "We started to sell stock," John Ladd, director of the Economic Development District, told Stern, "and if you have never tried to sell $2 million worth of stock in 45 days in an area like ours, a depressed area, try it sometime. We brought in experts . . . and they advised us that we should concentrate on the little guy in the street. What we call street financing."

The takeover may have been launched by businessmen, but the workers and townspeople ran with it. Workers from the factory and Jaycees and submarine shop owners and others fanned out through the small towns sprinkled down the valley, knocking on doors and selling stock coupons like raffle tickets. The Conservative Party congressman bought stock (and donated it to the Herkimer Boy Scouts) and local businessmen chipped in, from the local funeral home to the local beer brewery. Retired school teachers brought in shoeboxes and dumped hundreds of dollar

"We got a bunch of people who don't want to quit. Where are they going to go? It was either go on welfare or go and purchase the plant"

bills, musty from years cached in their basements, on the formica folding table in John Ladd's office (the minimum purchase possible was 100 shares at $2 each). The Concerned Citizens for Library Bureau Committee mailed thousands of letters to librarians across the state—and local TV and radio talk shows turned over huge chunks of airtime to publicize the worker-community takeover ("I counted 65 different shows I was on myself," Ladd remembers).

In fact, it's difficult to find someone in Herkimer today who did not take part in the community effort. "Sure I bought stock, $800 worth," says Vincent Chirico, wiping tomato sauce on his apron in the kitchen of Chirico's Italian restaurant. "It's my community, and it's a good firm, and the guys working in the factory are my customers. If they hurt, I hurt. You see that man over there?" Chirico said, pointing to the bar counter where a clump of men were swapping prank stories. "He lent money to the fire department so they could buy stocks, too."

Ironically, while workers and community forces in Herkimer were struggling to save their factory by buying it, local, state and federal officials were trying to save a second Sperry Rand plant just 70 miles away in Utica—but with a different tactic. When Sperry announced it was going to shut down the Utica factory, officials in effect bribed the conglomerate with land and tax incentives worth millions of dollars. The incentives were so generous that one Sperry executive called them "perhaps the most attractive offer I've seen in all my years of business." But the offer wasn't good enough. In August 1976 Sperry shut the Utica plant and put 1,100 employees out of work—and shifted production to the Sunbelt.

Three weeks later, the Herkimer strategy worked. Hours before Sperry Rand's deadline, the community raised its $1.8 million in cash. On September 28, 1976, the Mohawk Valley Community Corporation—representing 3,500 workers, managers, town citizens and others within a 50-mile radius—took control of ownership of their own plant. Ninety-five percent of the plant's workers were part-owners. Managers and production employees together controlled a third of the corporation's stocks.

Ownership, but not control

Since the community bought the factory, it has been doing well financially, despite a few downturns in the market. The plant recently bought out two major competitors and a subsidiary in New Jersey, and now is negotiating to buy a fourth factory which makes the metal fittings for its library cabinets. The company's marketing team, which Sperry Rand had previously forbidden to launch sales campaigns abroad, is actively pursuing foreign markets including several Arab nations.

Worker benefits—the average wages are $11,000 per year—have increased, and the company recently established an Employee Stock Ownership Plan. Eventually, through the ESOP, the production workers will own the majority of the corporation stock.

But while ownership of the factory has changed hands, there has been virtually no change in the factory's *control*. The union locals and their members have no representatives on the board of directors, which is dominated by local businessmen and plant executives. The internal decision-making structure is virtually the same as it was under the Sperry Rand conglomerate.

When the workers bought and saved their factory, that's the way they wanted it—at the beginning, anyway. "I never thought I was buying a piece of management," a young employee named Ron Kuzniak says. "I was just buying a piece of paper to stick in the drawer—and saving my job."

But the act of becoming part-owners of the plant seems to have ignited a subtle chemical reaction among the employees—a vague but growing sense that now that they've saved their factory and become part-owners, something between managers and shop-floor workers should have changed. "We expected things would be different," says Carl Vogel, echoing the worker-owners at South Bend Lathe and the other worker-owned firms. "You know, everything would be more equal, more brotherly love, everybody working hand in hand. We expected to be treated like part-owners, with respect—not just as employees. But they've just kind of pushed us to the side," Vogel says, "and said, 'We're the boss.'"

As a result, workers say, the initial jubilation among production workers—that "we saved our jobs" euphoria—has begun to sour, just as it has at Vermont Asbestos Group, South Bend Lathe, and Saratoga Knitting Mill. But ask employees in the mill just *how* they want things to be different, and most of them speak only vaguely about "having more of a voice" and "management should consult with us more." As a survey of employee attitudes by Cornell University researchers shows, "employees are unhappy about the lack of information-sharing between management and the workers," according to Stern. And true to the statistics of the study, workers in the factory are quick to reel off a list of complaints: managers keep information secret, managers ignore worker demands for health and safety improvements—managers ignore workers, period.

Workers say the *spirit* between managers and employees should have changed. "We all thought we'd have a lot closer organization than what we had before," says Vogel. "With Sperry it was hammer and tong, you had to fight for everything. Seeing as how we're stockholders now, we felt we'd be able to sit down [with management] and come up with much better and easier solutions to problems."

Vogel and other employees insist they don't want, or expect, to be involved in making daily management decisions. "You can't afford to have committees meeting all over the place," Vogel argues. Indeed, "our findings show," reports Cornell researcher Stern and Tove Helland Hammer, "that at least initially, there is very little interest in participative management on the part of . . . workers." But in informal interviews, many workers declare that when management is considering major corporate decisions "they should call us in and give us a voice."

For instance, some employees say they want the unions to have voting representatives on the board of directors. "The employees and the management should be *equal* on the board of directors," says Vogel.

When the worker-community corporation first bought the factory, managers did offer two board seats to union officials, which the union—under orders from the International—refused. But since then, both the local and the international have changed their minds—in fact, Vogel now insists "the employees and the management should be *equal* on the board of directors," with each side controlling half the board. But managers in the plant are balking. Today, two union officers may participate at board meetings, without the power to vote. And when the board members consider any matter they consider "privileged information"—in effect any matters they wish to discuss in secret—they ask the union officials to leave.

A growing number of employees are saying, furthermore, that the unions should also take part in making decisions affecting them such as layoffs. "You better believe we want power over that," Vogel says, "we've had two layoffs already."

One of the most bitter worker complaints at Herkimer is that management bought multimillion-dollar subsidiaries—without even consulting the rank and file first. "That's *our* money they're spending," says Joseph LaBate, a 17-year veteran at the mill, who coats wood planks with sap so the stains will hold. "If they wanted to buy that plant they should have gone before the people and said, 'Should we do this?' And then they should have gone along with what we said." Before the workers bought the corporation, LaBate says, "Sperry Rand ran the plant the way they saw fit and they paid our wages and it was none of our business what they were doing. But we own the plant now. If I own my own home or my own business, I want to run it the way I see fit. I ain't going to have anybody tell me how to run it."

Union officers are talking tough. "Management thinks they're so god almighty," Vogal says. We're telling them, 'You're there because *we* put you there, just don't lose track of that. If you don't do a good job for us, we'll vote you out.'" But so far, it is unclear whether the rank and file will ever have the passion, the stock votes, or the unity necessary to shake up the decision-making structure in their plant. Managers don't appear interested in sharing fundamental powers. "It's very important to have input from the employees," vice president D. A. Norton says. "In fact we've started a suggestion box where employees can make themselves heard."

Most workers feel too powerless or resigned to use their minority ownership power to pressure for change. At the first stockholders meeting, only about 100 people showed up. "People complain and bicker in the shop," one worker says, "but they don't come to a stockholders meeting and cast their votes. And what good would it do if they did? Management would just do what it wants anyway."

And although workers will eventually own a majority share of the corporation on paper, through the ESOP, there are no plans yet to pass *voting* control of the ESOP stocks from the management board of trustees which now controls them to the individual employees.

Sources

South Bend Lathe, Inc.

"Unusual Financing Gives 500 Workers Their Own Company," *Wall Street Journal*, July 8, 1975.

"Employees Acquire Factory," by Joel Weisman, *Washington Post*, July 19, 1975.

"Salvaging a Plant the Kelso Way," by Karen Arenson, *Business Week*, August 11, 1975.

"When the Boss, Worker Are One," by Edwin Darby, *Chicago Sun-Times*, July 7, 1976.

"Worker Capitalism a Boon for Cities," by Darby, *Chicago Sun-Times*, July 8, 1976.

"How and Why U.S. Helped 500 Workers Take Over a Machine-Tool Manufacturer," by John Ryan, *Wall Street Journal*, August 16, 1976.

"More Worker-Owners," *Time*, October 4, 1976.

"Employee Ownership: Report to the Economic Development Administration," by the University of Michigan Survey Research Center, Institute for Social Research.

Personal interviews by the editor.

Saratoga Knitting Mill

"Employees Purchase Van Raalte Plant," by Craig Wilson, the *Saratogian*, April 25, 1975.

"Closely Knit Group to Buy Tricot from Cluett Peabody," *Wall Street Journal*, April 26, 1975.

"Workers Buy Textile Mill, Hoping to Revive Its Sales," *New York Times*, April 26, 1975.

Transcripts of proceedings at the Third International Conference on Self-Management.

Personal interviews by the editor with researchers at Cornell University and employees of Saratoga Knitting Mill.

Mohawk Valley Community Corporation

Robert Stern and Robert Cardinaux, "Shutdown at Library Bureau, Case I," New York State School of Industrial and Labor Relations, draft manuscript.

Stern, "Library Case II," draft manuscript.

Robert N. Stern and Tove Helland Hammer, "Employee Ownership: Implications for the Organizational Distribution of Power," manuscript, 1979.

William Foote Whyte, "In Support of the Voluntary Employee Ownership and Community Stabilization Act," March 20, 1978, draft manuscript.

Personal interviews by the editor.

COLLEC-TIVES

It's a winter's Saturday morning at the Bethesda Community Food Store, in a suburb of Washington, D.C. But it could be any one of hundreds of worker self-managed collective food stores sprinkled across the nation. The store, the size of an old-time mom and pop grocery, is squeezed among an auto supply shop, a jeep showroom and a greasy spoon luncheonette in a car-jammed shopping district.

The first aisle of the store isn't reserved for food but for neighborhood communications. There's a large bulletin board, two layers thick with file cards seeking "sensitive woman to join communal house" and yoga students, offering recipes for sesame seed buns and soybean casserole, and condemning ITT interference in the Third World.

I take a worn, wrinkled shopping bag from a recycled bag bin, pass "Breast Milk Is Best" and "Kick the Junk Food Habit" posters, and stop at the pasta stand, nine varieties of whole wheat noodles sold in bulk form from the cardboard cartons they were shipped in. Shoppers clutching empty jars from home crowd the bulk liquids stand, a rack of five-gallon jugs sticky with six different kinds of oil and three varieties of honey.

A member of the board of directors, an economics professor at a local university, is unloading baskets of tomatoes, leeks and yucca root into the well-stocked produce bins. Other volunteers are slicing hunks of cheese from a large wheel and piling them in a cooler stocked with 40 different domestic and imported varieties. I take a carton of milk from the small dairy cooler; "We feel that food is a basic right and that it shouldn't be sold for a profit," a sign proclaims. "Milk, being a staple necessary to most diets, is being sold for only a few pennies above our costs so that those in need can afford it."

The guts of the collective food store, at center aisle, are 60 plastic barrels filled with grains, legumes, beans, seeds and flours which most supermarkets shunt aside—exotic foods such as rye flour and soy flour, bulgur wheat, millet and rye berries, wheat flakes and turtle beans, sunflower seeds and soy grits, macadamia nuts and dried pineapples.

I squeeze past the community craft stand—home made pottery, jewelry and teashirts for sale—and join the long checkout line, waiting for the lone, painfully slow, volunteer cashier. Most of the shoppers clutch a few sacks of flour and beans, a couple vegetables, perhaps a jar of wildflower honey and some dried fruits. Average purchase: about $8 each.

The collective surge

The scene at the Bethesda Community Food Store is being repeated at hundreds of stores across the country, in towns from Philadelphia to San Francisco, Boston to Seattle, Ithaca to Atlanta, Minneapolis to Ann Arbor. For the Bethesda grocery—with its sticky honey tins, whole wheat lasagna, toiling board of directors and all—has joined the most important surge of nonprofit, politically motivated enterprises since the New Deal promoted co-op stores and factories as

a path out of the Great Depression.

Not all the collective stores sell food. Washington, D.C.'s two dozen collectives include record stores and plant shops, a women's radio studio and a law office, a magazine, a graphics firm called Art for People, and a small printing plant. In Boston, there are more than 50 collectives working in architecture, auto and bicycle repair, bookselling, child care counseling, therapy and crafts, waste recycling, health care, law, house moving, woodworking, carpentry and even community organizing, among other fields, according to an educational collective called Vocations for Social Change. In Minneapolis, one of the two dozen collectives is making high quality clothes.

But whatever products or services they sell, collectives usually share three crucial elements in common:

- First, they do not sell their goods for profit; in fact, most collectives call themselves *anti-profit.*

- Second, they are worker self-managed, usually an extraordinary form of decision-making called "consensus." This means that "all workers have equal input in the running of the group" and "everyone in the collective must feel comfortable with a decision before it is finalized," according to Vocations for Social Change.

- Third—and members of collectives say this is most important—collectives do not exist primarily to sell their specific products, or even primarily to provide its members with a livelihood. They exist to promote and serve as a model for radical social and political change. "The creation of a work collective . . . is a political-social statement in itself," declares Vocations for Social Change, which promotes collective enterprises across the U.S. "People in collectives aim to spread these ideals throughout society. We want to show that worker ownership and control [are] not a pipedream, but a real possibility that has been blocked by those who stand to lose their political and economic power in a worker-controlled economy."

"Selling food isn't our goal," as one worker in a

Boston researchers found that shoppers who shun supermarkets for nonprofit food stores could save 33 percent on fresh produce

Washington, D.C. collective food store explains. "It's just a pretext for building living and breathing models of revolutionary change."

Revolutionary islands

In economic terms, the collective movement across the country is miniscule: Washington, D.C.'s entire network of collective food stores grosses about $2 million a year in sales, approximately 1/80 the amount which Safeway Stores, Inc. sells each year in the same city. But collective workers say that achieving economic size is not necessarily an essential goal. "I don't think it's reasonable to assume that some day the nonprofit food movement will suddenly appear on the Fortune 500," says Chris Simpson, who has helped organize collectives in Washington, D.C. "The worker collectives are like revolutionary islands."

"We must view them [collectives] as models and not as the ultimate end," declares the newsletter *Alternative Economics* (November 1973). "We can't out-compete the capitalists, but we can establish a good number of models to influence" others to change.

To understand how a collective works—to understand its achievements and problems—it is important to understand how most collectives are born and how they grow. For the political goals, the work structure and the finances of a collective enterprise shape one another.

Most collectives are born not with capital, but with volunteer labor and sweat. When Safeway opens a new supermarket, for instance—the corporation opens 125 in an average year, according to a recent annual report—it spends more than $1.2 million just building and stocking it. But when organizers decided to launch the Bethesda Community Food Store, they had to knock on hundreds of doors in the community until they sold $8,000 worth of food coupons, redeemable for groceries at a future date. When student organizers of a collective food store in New Haven went

looking for seed money, they struggled to raise $2,000 in donations from friends and neighborhood residents plus $900 from a benefit dance.

Washington, D.C.'s first nonprofit collective food store, Stone Soup, was just barely born with $25,000 from wealthy donors and friends. Organizers could afford to rent only a crummy building in an economically depressed neighborhood, where mostly white radical collectives, public interest firms, and wealthy young professionals in renovated townhouses merge with a low-income population of Mexican-Americans and blacks. "We poured money into renovation, the building was a rat tin, totally burned out," organizer Steven Clark said. "At times we'd run out of money and have to stop work until we could go out and raise some more money." Stone Soup finally opened its doors with 1,600 square feet of groceries, about five

<table>
<tr><td>

A collective definition

"Collectives are a way to work toward social change, to develop personally and politically, to learn and develop skills, to cut down on individualism and promote cooperation and group accountability, to provide financial support, to give emotional support and love while working toward a movement committed to socialism and real democracy."

Vocations for Social Change
Work Collectives

</td></tr>
</table>

percent the size of an average Safeway supermarket.

From the first day, Stone Soup—like most collectives—was wracked by financial problems. Crippling labor costs ate up the biggest single chunk of the budget. Since Stone Soup was so small, there wasn't much shelf space to stock food. Workers had to restock items constantly. As sales volumes increased, the stocking problems got worse. Even with volunteers helping them out, the members of the self-managed collective had to keep hiring more collective workers, driving labor costs so high that the store couldn't accumulate a financial cushion in the bank. When sales suddenly slumped the first summer, as most supermarket sales do, the store plunged into a financial crisis. "We started bouncing checks and suppliers cut us off," one organizer said. "We had to cut salaries and had to go out borrowing money again just to stay alive."

Achieving goals

In spite of their difficult birth in such impoverished financial soil, collectives across the country have achieved some of their goals to a remarkable degree.

One of the most important goals, for instance, is to provide the community with *nonprofit* goods or services—which, collective workers say, should mean charging lower than normal prices. When I stopped

by a Safeway supermarket in Washington, D.C., shoppers were loading their carts with half gallons of milk for 81¢ compared to only 72¢ at the Bethesda Community Food Store collective around the corner; eggplants and cabbage at Safeway cost 2½ times as much, and cheeses sold for at least 10-20 percent more than the collective food store's prices. Such savings are not unique to Washington. When Boston University researchers Ronald Curhan and Edward Wertheim surveyed 24 nonprofit food stores in the Boston area in 1971, they found shoppers could save 33 percent, compared to supermarket prices, on fresh fruits and vegetables.

Consumers can expect to find lower prices at other kinds of collectives, too. In Washington, D.C., where the going rate for most lawyers ranges from $50-$100 per hour, the collectively-managed law firm of Dodson & Luxenberg has been charging most clients from $35-$45. And at the North Country Department Store in Minneapolis, shoppers can buy tools and household items ranging from knives to cast iron skillets at prices at least 25 percent less than conventional stores would charge.

Another important goal of virtually all collectives is to provide special, *community-oriented services.* "Our philosophy is to serve people, not profits," one Washington, D.C. collective worker says. Most food collectives, for instance, attempt to shift consumers away from synthetic and highly processed foods and promote a wholesome and nutritious diet, instead. That's the opposite of conventional supermarket sales techniques, which steer shoppers toward the foods which are most highly processed and richest in fat, sugar and artificial additives—the foods, industry journals indicate, which generate the highest profits. Most food collective stock few if any "junk foods" in the first place; shoppers are hard-pressed to find a food in the store which isn't nutritious. And when collectives do stock items which workers consider unhealthy, they often hang up posters or leaflets encouraging shoppers *not* to buy them. One Washington collective carried bacon, which often contains cancer-causing nitrosamines—but then handed out leaflets explaining why bacon should be avoided.

The food collectives offer other unique services as well. For a while, the Fields of Plenty food collective in a low-income neighborhood in Washington, D.C. was delivering groceries, for free, to senior citizens. The collective provided free breakfasts on the weekends to kids on the block, and always kept a box of "free food" near the store entrance, for any community residents who couldn't afford to buy it.

Or consider the Southside Community Garage, in Minneapolis. The garage was launched by four full-time workers plus four part-time mechanics in the fall of 1971. At first, the collective workers merely repaired cars, for low rates. But then "the mechanics realized that they were feeling drained by doing only repair work," according to a leaflet written by a member of the collective. "They were anxious for contact with people, not just nuts and bolts." So the collective mechanics launched an unusual system in which "car owners fixed their own cars, with the mechanics teaching the owners."

Nourishing the soul

Many collective workers say they have created still another kind of alternative to conventional stores or enterprises—an alternative which is less tangible than the lower price of carrots or legal services, the rich variety of whole grains, or do-it-yourself auto repair. This alternative is a *spirit* which permeates many collectives, a kind of warmth and comraderie among workers and customers which satisfies some of the human needs often forgotten in the cut-and-dried world of profit-making businesses. For instance, some of the people who work and shop at food collectives seem almost starved for a sense of communion with the earth and with food—and in a small way, the collective food stores help provide it. Workers—and shoppers—in the Washington, D.C. collectives talk with pride about how the grains and beans must be scooped by hand and weighed on a scale, not in a plastic bag, as if the act of scooping kernels of rice into a bag with your hands is more nourishing to the human soul.

For many shoppers, doing volunteer work in the store once a month fulfills another need. "I can't tell you how much joy I feel working here," says one volunteer in a Minneapolis food collective. "In a way it's brought back the days when a grocery was a social event—people around the wood stove, drinking coffee, talking. We do the same thing here, slicing up wheels of cheese, drinking herb tea and talking. And maybe it sounds corny, but I feel I'm doing something important for my family and community."

Stroll into the book section of the Minneapolis North Country Department Store, and you can browse over the new books—priced at about 30 percent off the cover price—in an old easy chair. Reading literature on collectives across the country, in fact, one often gets the sense that the quality of the relationships among workers and customers in the stores are far more important than the relationships between sales and profits. The 1976 Safeway Annual Report, for instance, ends with the note that "Capital expenditures for 1977 are expected to approximate $270 million." But a recent report on the Boston Food Co-op, a worker collective, ends with the observations that "Relationships among staff members have always been more intimate than what one would expect to find in a traditional job" and that, "Staffers need to be open, to confront others with minimal emotion, and to make themselves confrontable."

Community control?

One of the major aims of many collective enterprises is to give the *community influence*, and perhaps even formal control, over shaping the kinds of products and services the enterprise sells, and the manner in which it sells them. Just as workers need control over their workplace in order to protect themselves against the abuses of management, many collective workers argue, so consumers in the community need some control over the enterprises which serve them in order to protect themselves from abuses by business.

To achieve this goal, many collective stores have structured the enterprise as a cooperative. The co-op has "members," defined perhaps as shoppers who pay annual dues, or work a certain number of hours each month in the store; the members elect a board of directors, which formulates general store policies, and hires the staff, which runs the store day-to-day as a collective.

At the Bethesda Community Food Store, for instance, anyone can become a member merely by working three hours a month in the store. The members elect eight consumers who, together with the collective staff of four, comprise the board of direc-

---

How to get a consensus

Democratic decision-making in a collective is based on one fundamental concept: *all workers take an equal part in making major decisions.*

Living according to this fundamental rule, virtually all collective workers will tell you, is difficult, frustrating, and above all, time consuming. Most collectives use the principle of *consensus.* "This means," according to Vocations for Social Change, "that no decision is finalized until everyone in the group feels comfortable with the decision and is able to implement it without resentment. The skill of coming to genuine consensus decisions is a real and a hard one."

The experiences of numerous collectives suggest that the vital elements of successful collective decision-making include:

- Every member of the collective must have equal power. This means that no one person can be allowed to accumulate the special knowledge and authority of a traditional "boss."

Collectives use a variety of techniques to achieve this "equality of power." The most common one is *job rotation.* If every worker learns every job, collective workers say, they can contribute knowledgeably to every decision; no one person will accumulate unique expertise which will allow him or her to wield special authority, as others are forced to sit back in ignorance.

At a collective newspaper in California, according to researcher Rothschild-Whitt, each worker spends 20 hours per week editing, 10 hours writing, and 10 hours in production tasks. At the Stone Soup food collective in Washington, D.C., workers rotate jobs as often as every three hours — the same person may work at the cash register in the morning, fish counter at noon and in the stockroom in the evening.

Collectives which have coordinators or managers handling administrative tasks usually rotate that position, too. Stone Soup, for instance, installs a new worker as coordinator every three months.

tors. The board sets general policies for the food store, but when there have been especially controversial issues, the decision has been referred to a vote by all the "members"—that is, all the members who happened to show up at the monthly general meeting. Other food collectives have tried more informal "community control" plans: at one time, Stone Soup defined its voting community as anyone who showed up at the weekly policy-making meetings.

But at most collective food stores, "community control" has remained a more elusive and undefined goal. Most collectives have "community" boards, where shoppers can write comments and suggestions. At Stone Soup, one day, a shopper scrawled a request for a certain brand of peanut butter, and the collective scrawled an answer: "We'll try to get it in the future." If community members wish to attend the regular collective meetings, and voice their opinions—but not cast votes—they're welcome to do it. In effect, the community usually does exert more influence on collective food stores than shoppers do on Safeway—but often only because the stores are so much smaller and the attitude of the collective workers is receptive to community ideas. When it comes to legal community power on paper, shoppers often don't have any more power in their neighborhood collective than in a corporate supermarket.

Decision by consensus

Perhaps the most important goal of most collective enterprises is *to manage the business democrati-*

- Every member of the collective must have an equal opportunity to debate an issue, or voice an opinion before a consensus decision is made.

  Collective workers note that if some members of the collective feel afraid of talking in the groups — or if a few members tend to dominate the groups — part of the collective will in effect be cut out of the decision-making process. This weakens the collective's commitment to a decision, and can create resentment and hostility among members of the collective. Some collectives, as a result, have a rule that *every worker in the collective must voice an opinion* at a meeting, before a decision can be made. Other collectives pass rules which prevent any worker from speaking more than once until every other worker has already spoken.

- Every member of the collective must be honest and open about his or her feelings — or relationships between the workers will deteriorate, and the collective will be unable to make effective group decisions.

"People's fears can lead to subtle agreements not to talk about certain issues or [not] to deal with certain problems," writes Vocations for Social Change. "This can stifle and then kill a collective."

To encourage collective members to share their emotions honestly, many collectives hold "criticism-self-criticism" sessions at the end of every meeting. Members use this time to voice criticisms or complaints about the way they and others have handled the week's work or personal realtionships.

- Finally, a successful collective requires commitment. Without special commitment, collective workers say, they aren't likely to survive all the frustrations and pains of earning low salaries, laboring long hours, and constantly working out emotional conflicts. "Often the only thing that keeps a collective together throughout its conflicts," writes Vocations for Social Change, "is the conviction that the experiment of collective decision-making has a great inherent value, a value that makes the pain and work worthwhile."

cally, collectively—"to show that worker ownership and control (are) not a pipedream but a real possibility," as the Vocations for Social Change says. To a considerable degree, many collectives have succeeded.

At some enterprises, where the staff is small—there are only four full-time workers on the Bethesda Community Food Store collective, and half a dozen on the Boston Food Co-op Collective, for instance—all decisions are made at a weekly, or several times weekly, staff meeting. We try to hash out a consensus," as one worker says, "so at least if everyone isn't thrilled about the decision, no one is actively against it." At People Clothes garment collective in Minneapolis, "we all meet and make decisions while we sew," says a collective member, Susan Shroyer, "we can't afford to take off time to hold meetings."

At these small enterprises, decision-making often becomes an informal process which the staff members handle on an ad hoc basis, whenever an issue comes up. "The way it works in our store," one collective member in Ann Arbor says, "if we're all around when the milk distributor wants to know how many cases to send us, we all stop what we're doing and agree on a number. If only one of us is around, we make the decision on our own and hope the others agree when we tell them later."

Informal decision-making like this can work with a small staff, but as the staff grows larger, collective decision-making becomes more difficult. When I stopped by Stone Soup recently—the structure changes so frequently, as collective members try to find the "perfect" system, that by the time this is published, the information may be obsolete—the collective of 10 workers had worked out a democratic decision making structure which looks like this:

From day-to-day, the store is in effect "managed" by three coordinators, who rotate every three months. That way, everyone gets the opportunity to learn managerial tasks, and no one can absorb too much power, which would destroy the egalitarian spirit of the collective. The coordinators handle decisions such as ordering, stocking, and pricing. Fundamental policies of the collective—for instance, whether to carry

nuts from a "Third World" country, or bacon with sodium nitrite, how much to pay staff members, how to divide working hours—are made at weekly meetings of the entire collective.

The collective members and 15 "support workers," part-time workers who are voting members of the collective, meet weekly on various subcommittees to draft policies on food and nutrition issues, fiscal plans, bookkeeping, and community outreach; the subcommittees then recommend policies to the full collective for a consensus or, when a consensus just can't be reached, for a majority vote. According to one consensus decision by the Stone Soup collective, all the workers in the store rotate jobs several times each *day*; one worker might work at the cash register in the morning, work at the fish counter in the mid-afternoon and in the stockroom in the evening. "All of us learn every job," says one collective member, "which is not only good for us as individuals, but also good for the collective. We learn that no one is indispensable."

The New Haven Food Co-op staff collective has forged a more rigid structure. The day-to-day work of managing this supermarket-sized cooperative, housed in an old A&P, is handled by three autonomous teams. The "meat room team" of workers handles all meat ordering, cutting, pricing and wrapping—collectively; the "floor team" handles the ordering, stocking and pricing of canned goods, produce, dairy and frozen foods; the "front of the store" team manages the cash registers and bookkeeping. The entire collective meets regularly to forge policies which affect the operations of the entire store.

What goes wrong

In spite of their many successes, political collective enterprises across the United States confront serious and painful problems.

The major dilemma which troubles most collectives is lack of adequate cash. From the first day a collective enterprise forms, its fundamental nature guaran-

Democracy at the press . . .

"Collective Impressions is a non-profit, community-controlled, collectively-run, alternative print shop," begins a leaflet which the Washington, D.C. collective hands its customers. "As an alternative business it is an example that business can be responsive to the community, that cooperation makes better 'business sense' than competition, that concern for the community's needs is a better incentive than profit."

The print shop began in 1973 in a spare room in a church; by 1976 the business had expanded so much that the four-person collective moved into its own shop in downtown Washington. The print shop opened after months of difficult renovations — difficult because they were so extensive and because only one of the collective members had ever had construction experience.

By the spring of 1978, the collective had expanded to a full-time staff of six—none of them members of the original collective, however, which disbanded for higher paying jobs after "burning out." Salaries range from $2.88 to $4 per hour; annual gross revenues are $80,000 and "we've just passed the point of breaking even," a collective member says. Following are the collective's original "goals for the shop and for ourselves as workers":

- Good quality printing can be provided at lower prices than profit-motivated shops charge.

- The process of work need not be exploitative if the shop is organized as a workers' collective. A work situation should be responsive to the needs of the workers as well as to those of the community; therefore, good wages and benefits are essential.

- We see our skills as printers and the power that gives us as a community asset. In the interest of sharing that asset, training is an important part of our program. We trained two apprentices . . . last year. One, a young woman of sixteen, stayed with us seven months and became an integral part of both the shop and the collective. We are particularly sensitive to the difficulties women have finding opportunities in the trades and, thus, place a high priority on training women.

- In an effort to "demystify" printing we use a detailed billing system which itemizes and reflects the shop's real costs for each printing job.

- We also began and will continue a series of seminars and workshops to share our printing skills and collective work experiences with the community. Our workshop on layout tips was particularly well received (50 people attended), illustrating that good printing and visually attractive layout techniques are important aspects of effective communication, particularly in a generation raised on Madison Avenue.

- Unlike traditional profit-motivated shops we believe the community is more than a group of potential customers. We encourage members of the community to be participants in the decisions affecting the shop. To this end we will continue to hold open community meetings once a month and keep open financial records for all to scrutinize.

- We see printing as inherently political since it is the process through which ideas are spread. We feel responsible for what we print. We will not print racist, sexist, or classist material. We are particularly interested in serving community groups involved in radical social change.

. . . and at the needle

One of the few collectively managed garment factories in the United States is People Clothes, a small clothing shop in a run-down neighborhood of Minneapolis. People Clothes was launched in 1970 by three workers at one of the local food co-ops; the workers had been sewing sturdy drawstring pants and shirts in their own homes and then selling them in the basement of the co-op. The operation was rapidly expanding, and so the workers applied for (and received) a $10,000 grant from a local Community Development Corporation, moved into a shabby storefront, and expanded to a full-time working collective of eight seamstresses.

Today the eight workers are producing 20 different designs from scratch, including men's cowboy shirts, pants, and a variety of women's clothes. People Clothes sells their goods wholesale to the local collectively-managed department store, a co-op in Seattle, plus a few small stores in the Minneapolis area. The clothes are not cheaper than many factory-made clothes — shirts run at least $20 a piece — but they are well made.

All major decisions are made at a weekly meeting of the collective. "We all sew while we meet," says co-founder and collective member Susan Shroyer, "because we can't afford to pay people just for meeting time." Decisions brought before the collective involve issues such as working hours, what kinds of designs to produce, hiring new collective members, or even asking troublesome workers to leave. The collective workers also decide how to price their garments. "To get the price we add up the cost of the materials, plus the time required to produce the item, rated at $4 an hour, and then we mark all that up 33 1/3 percent," says Shroyer.

The collective selects a manager and assistant manager who handle purely administrative chores, such as filling wholesale orders, buying and stocking materials, organizing the financial records, "and stuff like sweeping the floors and carrying out the garbage," says Shroyer. Working as manager isn't considered a prestigious job, but a sacrifice: "We were the only two people in the collective willing to take the job," Shroyer says. In fact, while the six sewers can earn up to $4 per hour — they get paid by the finished piece — the managers get paid only $3 per hour.

Shroyer says the collective members have never been satisfied with the inequality of the piece method of paying wages, "But we just don't know how to figure out the wages any other way. We'd go broke if we paid a flat rate, because everybody doesn't produce at the same speed." One advantage of the piece rate, some collective workers say, is that workers who don't

tees that financial security may remain painfully beyond its reach.

Members of Washington, D.C.'s legal collective originally set their fees at the low rate of $16 per hour, hoping that lots of low-income citizens who need legal help would be attracted to their firm. With a high volume business, the lawyers figured, even $16 an hour would pay the overhead and provide a decent living. Instead, they could barely cover the losses they suffered when clients with politically "worthy" cases, but little money, didn't pay. As a result, the collective approached the brink of financial collapse several times during its four-year existence Now it has increased its fees more than 100 percent.

The Southside Community Garage in Minneapolis struggled through a "very precarious existence," until finally folding, one collective member writes, mainly because the low rates of $4 an hour, compared to at least triple that rate at commercial garages, had starved the firm's bank account.

Perhaps the collectives most seriously pinched by financial woes are the food collectives. The anemic

Numerous collectives have collapsed because the workers are filled with enthusiasm and commitment—but know little about business

feel energetic occasionally can work more slowly and relax, "without feeling guilty we're dragging the whole group down," as one member says.

In spite of its steadily increasing orders, People Clothes finds itself in a fragile financial state. "We're hovering around the break-even point," Shroyer says, "we're close to going under and close to making it." Moving to the storefront added overhead expenses — rent and utilities, insurance, renovation and repairs — far higher than the collective had expected.

Another problem which has hurt the collective is that workers have been *too* relaxed: most of them had worked at traditional sewing factories before, so when they came to Peoples Clothes, they indulged in the luxury of working slowly without reprisals — and didn't generate enough sales volume to shore up the collective's bank account. "Now we're getting tougher on each other, and everyone's working really well," Shroyer says.

People Clothes can't afford to pay unemployment, and they can't afford to provide health insurance or sick leave. Still, the $3 - $4 per hour that the workers average, says Shroyer, is as good or better than most of the sewing factories in town. "Here we all run the shop," Shroyer says. "In a factory we'd be little different than the machines."

starting budgets and their high labor costs are only the beginning of their problems. Since most collective stores are so small — compare the Bethesda Community Food Store's 2,600 square feet to the 28,000 square-foot Safeway, considered small by industry standards, down the street — they are unable to handle much volume. In the U.S. food business, big sales volume is the key to operating a financially sound business.

"Del Monte wouldn't even look at us twice when we called them," says a former worker at Stone Soup, "because to buy direct from Del Monte you have to buy in semi-trailer lots." That means most food collectives are forced to buy from local wholesalers and distributors by the case, at a premium price. Operating costs in a small collective, therefore, are far higher as a percentage of sales than in a corporate supermarket. Keeping the retail prices low, therefore, means the enterprise cannot possibly accumulate much "surplus" (the collective term for profits) — and that means the store cannot build a financial cushion. Most food collectives are chronically facing a financial crisis, or struggling at a break-even point, at best.

In addition to these economic problems, which are inherent in many small businesses, collectives suffer from less inevitable financial difficulties as well. Numerous collectives have collapsed because the workers, while full of enthusiasm and commitment, know little or nothing about business and mismanage the enterprise to death.

"We took over with absolutely no training," says Stone Soup food collective member Susan Hecht. "Most of our collective had never even worked in a food store. It took us two or three months sort of fumbling around just to understand how to run the business. Our efficiency level was very, very low."

After a jubilant first year in which they earned a $35,000 surplus — almost unheard of in food collectives — staff members of the Bethesda Community Food Store suddenly discovered they were on the verge of a financial pinch. Why? A board of directors committee decided to inspect the chaotic financial books, and found that costs had soared while income had dropped. "I have absolutely no idea what the money situation is right now," the co-op bookkeeper, a member of the collective, said. "We're not into the establishment accountant thing of keeping official records of every little financial detail."

The collective law firm in Washington confronted a similar financial crisis when workers discovered that one of the attorneys had not been keeping accurate and detailed records of his case time or billing clients — meaning the potential loss of hundreds or even thousands of dollars of income.

Painful realities

As financial problems develop, many collective workers say, some of the collective goals may be compromised. Food stores and legal firms can't keep prices as low as they would like. So while the Bethesda Community Food Store offers stunning savings over supermarket prices on many vegetables, cheeses and grains, for instance, it charges more than area super- markets on many items such as oil, butter and eggs, and even some produce. Alternative food stores in Washington no longer carry meat, "partly because so many of us are vegetarians," a worker at Stone Soup says, "but mainly because we can't handle it economically."

In the cold world of shopper comparisons, this means that few shoppers buy more than a handful of groceries at the food collectives. Collective workers get frustrated as they see shoppers hunt and pick up only a few bargain items, and then forsake the collec- tive for a lower price at the Safeway or A&P. "It's really frustrating to see that people who shop here won't support us simply because they believe in us politically," says a worker at the Fields of Plenty collective. Other collective workers assault what they call this "bargain hunter" mentality, or "middle class greed" of shoppers. But the fact is that few people pinched by climbing food prices want to pay higher prices for some items just to support a better political line.

In an effort to keep prices low and attract more customers — and survive — many collectives have felt compelled to compromise other goals. "It's a trade- off," as one Washington collective worker put it, "between political purity and economic survival." For instance, while most collectives view their role as a means of economic self-defense—by protecting workers from inflation, by offering foods at lower prices, and by "not exploiting our workers, like capitalism does"—many collectives must pay their own workers rock bottom wages. Typical wages in the food collectives in the Washington, D.C. area hover at around $2.50 per hour, often without health

insurance, compared to a possible $6.73 per hour plus health benefits at a supermarket down the street. Mechanics at the Minneapolis collective garage were earning "bare subsistence salaries," according to one report, while a collectively run newspaper staff in California worked a 40-60 hour work week for a maximum $300 per month, according to Cornell University researcher Joyce Rothschild-Whitt.

In Boston, salaries at collective enterprises range from $75 per week at a bookstore to a relatively luxurious $150 per week at a collective food store, according to Vocations for Social Change. Some col- lectives make up in part for the low pay: one Boston collective buys lunches for its members every day, and many pay a special allowance to collective members who have children.

"What is the future of this wave of businesses if they can't stand as viable alternatives for everyone?" asks the Washington, D.C.-based newsletter on self- management, *D.C. Economics*. "Since at this time, if salaries were raised across the board, we would all fold."

The subsistence level of salaries in many collectives has far-reaching impact on the kinds of people who work in the enterprises, as well as the kinds of service they give to the community. In one sense, the low pay can be a kind of asset, according to Rothschild- Whitt: "the practice ensures that their staff will continue to be made up of people whose dedication is to movement goals, not to protecting their jobs. Lean salaries assure the organization that its workers are committed, that they are engaging in a labor of love." But the lean salaries also guarantee that the collectives will have a rapid turnover, as workers tired of a subsistence life-style move to higher paying, "straight" jobs. It also means that in spite of their goals of serving the "working class" and minorities, most collectives — even those located in minority neighborhoods — are staffed primarily by young whites from upper-income families. These are people who may not have much money themselves, but have access to money whenever they really need it. At the food stores Rothschild-Whitt studied, the mean parental income of the staff workers and board of directors members was $46,000.

"The low salaries which are inherent in these businesses," remarks *D.C. Economics* in an article about Washington's collectives, "exclude a large segment of the neighborhood [the neighborhood has a large population of low-income blacks and Chicanos] from ever participating in the stores as workers."

Some collective enterprises, however, have made a determined effort to pay themselves adequate wages. Art for People, the Washington, D.C. graphics firm, charges enough for their services to pay collective members from $10,000 (for a single worker) to $18,000 per year (for a worker with three children). "Our goal has been to create a real alternative," says Dick Anderson. "The whole idea has been to allow people with children and normal expenses in our society to work in a democratic setting and still have an adequate life-style and wage. We don't want people to have to feel guilty," Anderson says, "about living comfortably."

Trying to survive

As a result of all these financial pressures, collectives are sometimes forced to spend less and less time pursuing their political goals and more and more time merely trying to survive. Efforts to forge strong ties with the community can fall by the wayside; "after you've spent 60 hours a week practically living in the store," says a member of a Washington, D.C. food collective, "you just don't have much energy left to go out and organize the community." One free health clinic in California, according to Rothschild-Whitt, began to provide certain services it didn't feel deserved top priority, simply because these services would attract funding from some well-heeled sources.

One of the most difficult pressures on workers in most collectives — also one of the collective's most important rewards — is the process of democratic, group decision-making. Workers at the Southside Community Garage in Minneapolis summed up the problem: "Most of us do not know how to make decisions ourselves as well as we need to," the workers wrote. "All of us have to some extent been trained to depend upon others for direction . . . we still need to develop better skills in making policy as a group."

Vocations for Social Change echoes the same sentiments: "We need to be patient in developing democratic decision-making skills," the collective writes. "The supposedly democratic society in which we live has not prepared us for understanding or creating a truly democratic society."

Vocations for Social Change has summed up the most important traits and skills required for effective group decision-making (see Box). When some of them are lacking, the decision-making process breaks down, causing inefficiency, financial problems, and emotional strains within the worker collective. Collective workers often joke about the long, exhausting meetings they must endure just to reach a consensus on minor issues, such as where to put a whole wheat pasta stand. "If we can't agree on how to agree whether we agree," a cartoon in the Vocations for Social Change guide asks, "how do we decide on what to do next?"

"The worst of collectives," the Guide quotes one worker at the Women's Community Health Collective in Cambridge, Massachusetts, "is meetings, meetings, meetings." The collective must "endure a weekly seven-hour meeting at which all issues are talked through and decided," the Vocations for Social Change booklet says — but such a grueling meeting is by no means uncommon in collectives across the country.

Burning out

The net result of all these obstacles and pressures on worker collectives tends to be a peculiar disease, unique to political activists, known as "burn-out." "Burn-out," as one Washington, D.C. food collective worker explains, "means that I'm exhausted and drained after four years of subsistence salaries, 50 hour work weeks, endless meetings which take hours to reach a consensus only to have someone complain the next morning they don't agree with the decision, and always being on the verge of financial crisis." She quit the collective and moved to the country. "The turnover in work collectives is rather high," Vocations for Social Change notes, "many people leave collectives because they are just plain burned out, and thus may not do any political work for several years as a result."

In spite of all the problems, worker collectives keep proliferating across the country, even as old collectives from the first half of the decade are dying. Many collective workers talk about the months or years they spent working collectively as one of the most important periods of their lives. "I grew incredibly," one worker from Ann Arbor, Michigan, says, "I learned more about working with people and taking responsibility for myself than in six years of college. I have an entirely different perspective on what it means to work, I mean, how work doesn't

have to be something you go to, because you *have* to, but how it can be something really important that you *love*."

For the first time in U.S. history, there are promising financial and educational resources taking shape which could give worker collectives an important boost. The most important is the new Consumer Cooperative Bank, created by an act of Congress in 1978. The bank, nourished with a $350 million Treasury loan that will eventually be paid back with interest and sales of bank stocks, is designed exclusively to make loans to nonagricultural co-ops. Most of the loans will go to consumer co-ops, such as grocery stores—and worker self-managed collectives may well be among them. The bank will also provide technical assistance to co-ops, such as help in organizing co-op finances and decision-making structures. Collective workers hope that by tapping some of these new federal resources, they can make the long-term prognosis for cooperative and collective enterprises a brighter one.

Sources

No Bosses Here: A Manual on Working Collectively, by Boston Vocations for Social Change, Strongforce Series, Fall 1977.

Non-Profit Food Stores, A Resource Manual, Strongforce Series on Worker/Community-owned Businesses, 1977.

Joyce Rothschild-Whitt, "Problems of Democracy," *Working Papers for a New Society*, Fall 1976.

"A Look at Stone Soup," by the Bread and Roses Collective, *D.C. Democratic Economics*, Summer 1976.

"The Southside Community Garage: Progress Toward Worker Self-Management," by Ken Meter, mimeograph.

Daniel Zwerdling, "Shopping Around: Nonprofit Food," *Working Papers for a New Society*, Summer 1975.

Interviews by the editor with collective workers in the U.S.

PLY-WOOD CO-OPS

Rudy Anderson, member of the board of directors of the $25 million Puget Sound Plywood, Inc., arrived late for an interview. He had been busy patching up holes in veneer inside the sawmill. When he finally showed up he wasn't wearing a pinstriped suit but sawdust-covered overalls. "I'd shake," he said, showing his dirt-layered hands, "but mine are kind of filthy."

Anderson was a board member of a rare breed of corporation in United States history—one of about 16 currently operating, worker-owned and worker-controlled co-operative plywood factories in the Pacific Northwest. Most other worker self-managed or worker-owned companies are isolated anomalies in their industries—enterprises such as the Vermont Asbestos Group, International Group Plans, or the Cooperativa Central.

But the plywood cooperatives are heirs to a movement. The first cooperative formed in 1921, when a group of 125 lumberworkers,

At a typical board meeting, members voted to sell some company stocks and purchase a $15,700 saw. Next they voted to fire a worker who had been caught smoking marijuana

carpenters and mechanics pooled their savings, chipped in $1,000 each, and built their own plywood mill in Olympia, Washington. The plywood industry was still in its infancy. And as Olympia Veneer prospered, earning a reputation for high quality products and innovative manufacturing techniques, it inspired the formation of perhaps 30 other worker-owned and controlled plywood mills.

The precise decision-making structure changes from co-op to co-op, but the basic principles remain the same: each worker owns one share of the factory and casts one vote in company-wide elections. The workers cast votes on everything from choosing the board of directors—usually around seven or nine workers from inside the mill—to formulating corporate policies such as sick leave, purchasing equipment and making real estate investments.

Every worker earns equal pay, from shopfloor sweeper to the co-op president, and every worker receives an equal share of the annual profits (or, as the co-ops call profits, the "margin"). And when workers have a gripe they take it right to the board of directors, because the board members they elected are working at the machine next to them in the mill.

The plywood cooperatives suggest a proven model which other factories can follow as employees attempt to establish a self-managed and worker-owned enterprise. In a nation where the word "cooperative" usually conjures images of a small grocery store or food buying club, the Northwest plywood mills suggest that the cooperative structure can help bring workplace democracy, profitably, to factories as well.

Building democracy for survival

The workers who built the plywood co-ops were not inspired by socialistic ideals, but merely by the desperate need to find work — to survive. Like the miners at the Vermont Asbestos Group, many of the co-ops sprouted from the ashes of privately owned companies which were shutting down as the owner invested his capital elsewhere or went bankrupt.

Washington state's Hoquiam Plywood Company began as a private corporation in 1946, which went bankrupt only seven years later. Ninety-nine workers scraped together $1,500 each — they cashed in their stocks and savings bonds, emptied their bank accounts and borrowed from their friends — and two years later they had bought the mill.

In Tacoma, Washington, the owner of the 26-year-old Oregon-Washington Plywood Company closed the factory doors in 1949 as he watched plywood prices decline and sources of timber dry up. But buoyed by the success of four other successful co-ops, 188 workers contributed $2,000 each — half cash, half on installment — slashed their normal wages to generate operating capital, bought the mill, and renamed it North Pacific Plywood co-op. In a year plywood was back in a boom market and the co-op has prospered since.

A few co-ops, such as Olympia Veneer and the Linnton Plywood Association near Portland, Oregon, started from scratch. "We started out in order to create job security," one Linnton worker-owner told University of California researcher Paul Bernstein. "It was the Depression. Finding work was real tough. Several of us who'd worked in plywood mills, plus a few loggers and mechanics, decided we might as well try to create our own company."

It's tempting to ask "how well do the plywood co-ops work" — but the spirit and economic success of these industrial democracies vary widely from one company to the next. One of the most successful co-op factories, successful both financially and in its commitment to cooperative self-management, is Puget Sound Plywood. The basic governing unit at Puget Sound is the nine-member board of directors, elected by popular vote among the 270 worker-owners in the mill. The board hires a general manager, an outsider who does not own a co-op share, to manage the day-to-day business. The rest of the administrative staff, including the treasurer, is elected by the entire workforce.

Researcher Paul Bernstein describes some of the plywood cooperatives' most important historical achievements:

- They invented the "working share", which guarantees for each worker-member the rights of ownership, labor and self-government on an equal basis;

- They have worked out a legal identity of workers' control, through existing state laws, either by incorporating as a cooperative or as a jointly held corporation;

- They have created "workers' councils" in the United States without waiting for either a socialist revolution or a change in union ideologies;

- They have worked out a mechanism to equalize income distribution.

In the boardroom

In many cooperatives the workers surrender their potential power to the hired manager, who ends up controlling the co-op as autocratically as any conventional executive would. The worker-elected board rubber stamps the manager's decisions, and the enterprise becomes cooperative in name only. But at Puget Sound Plywood one gets the sense — talking with workers, sifting through minutes of board and membership meetings — that the worker-owners control the most fundamental corporate decisions.

At a typical board meeting — the board usually meets at least twice a month — members voted to sell some company stocks and they hashed out a position on some upcoming negotiations over construction of a log-hauling road. Next the board voted unanimously to fire a worker who was found smoking marijuana; possession of illegal drugs was one of the few offenses for which a shareholder could be dismissed from the co-op. At most co-ops, Paul Bernstein notes, workers who are dismissed or disciplined can appeal to the board. If the board upholds its original decision, the worker can appeal to the entire membership for a vote.

The board ended its meeting with a vote to purchase a new $15,700 rollfeed skinner saw. The board has delegated authority to the manager to spend $500 without consulting members first, but whenever a major expenditure comes up — over $25,000 according to the Puget Sound bylaws — the board must take the decision directly to the entire membership.

The worker-owners at most companies meet at least twice a year, and some meet three. At a typical membership meeting at Puget Sound Plywood, 73 percent of the workers showed up. And the workers say they get together for special meetings whenever a pressing issue demands it. "We had six special meetings (of the members) last year on just one issue, when we wanted to spend half a million dollars on some timber in Alaska," says the elected co-op secretary. "We also had a special election to purchase a $750,000 veneer plant."

One year earlier the members had voted to buy a new $50,000 water pumping system which would recycle water rather than dump it into the bay — but not until members of the machine committee, workers in the shop, had traveled a bit and investigated the pump market and recommended the system they liked best.

Worker power in the plywood co-ops, like in any corporation, is often measured not by formal board meetings nor by votes taken, but by the *informal* power of workers to influence the board of directors' and manager's decisions. In many of the factories, the members exert enormous power over the board of directors, partly because they work side by side on the job. "In a big private outfit, the directors make the decisions and never give the little man a chance to say anything," says Hoquiam Plywood board member Vern Wolfe. "But here, we board members step right out onto the coals. When we go back to the plants from a board meeting, we're just another one of the guys."

Keeping tabs on management

The workers make sure their opinons are heard. "We usually get to work at least half an hour early, get together with the guys and hash things out if some important issue is coming before the board," says Earl Altes, Jr., a young bark stripper at Puget Sound Plywood. "We've been looking at some property lately and I've been doing quite a lot of checking with the board. How much timber is it? What's the quality and the long range prospects? What rights agreement do we have? I'll pass board members in the plant and ask how sales are doing this week, or maybe say, 'Hey, I heard we got stung on a deal.' "

"And if the board members don't listen to us," says Bob Prescott, a crane operator at North Pacific Plywood, "well, they're not on the board of directors next year."

The rapid turnover on some plywood co-op boards suggests the members don't tolerate an unresponsive board director who does not vote in their best interests. In a recent year, four of the nine members of the North Pacific board were defeated, while at both Hoquiam and Puget Sound, two directors were ousted. "Some of the members felt he was getting too snotty," a Hoquiam worker explained when asked why one of the directors had lost reelection. "So we voted him down and clipped his wings a bit."

The worker-owners in many of the plywood co-ops also exert considerable power, if only informally, over the day-to-day actions of the hired manager. Some of the most convincing evidence of the workers' power comes from the managers themselves. "In a private corporation I'd answer to only one or two people," said Hoquiam manager Peter Majar. "But here, I answer to a whole membership. I'm very hesitant as far as making decisions goes. I'm never in a position to take any kind of gamble because they (the co-op members) are always second-guessing me.

"It would be a heck of a lot easier to manage a private corporation. When you're a manager here, you just don't walk up to a guy and tell him what to do. Here they all have a say and tell me, 'No we

won't do it that way.' And I always have to consider," Majar said, "that the guy I'm talking to today may be on the board of directors tomorrow."

The structure of the plywood co-ops — a manager hired to run the business day-to-day, yet accountable to the entire membership — sets the stage for an important conflict which confronts most worker self-managed firms. On the one hand, the members in the mill are supposed to control the long-term policy decisions of the corporation, and they wield the ultimate power to fire the manager if they wish. Yet from day-to-day, the manager runs the corporation and in effect directs the very workers who have hired him. Workers feel a constant tension between delegating enough authority to the manager to allow him to make creative and effective decisions, while not surrendering too much authority to the manager and in effect abdicating their cooperative power. In the same vein, workers face constant tension between challenging the manager's decisions in a constructive and creative way, to protect their best interests, while not challenging the manager so relentlessly that he feels imprisoned and paralyzed to act.

When interests conflict

Typically, the most important conflicts between managers and worker-owners surround financial decisions. Managers feel caught between what the worker-owners demand and what *they* believe would be "best for the business." In many cases, the workers' relentless demands *do* seem to protect their financial interests, by preventing the manager from taking the sort of risky gambles which better befit a Wall Street broker than a worker-owned co-op.

"If this were a privately owned corporation I'd make different economic decisions," said Berchal Monteith, manager at North Pacific Plywood. "I'd take more gambles, make more investments, try different pay scales and that sort of thing. But here, the men have bought a job and they want to take that money home with them. I can't say the hell with it, because it's *their* mill. Most corporate managers don't give a goddamn what the workers take home. They just want to see some big profits."

But sometimes, the workers are short-sighted. In their desire to take home as much money as possible they neglect the need to plow some of the surplus back into the company to buy better technology, to make plant improvements, perhaps to build up a financial cushion for a possible bust in the plywood market — all sound investments which will bring them more money in the long run. "The membership," as Hoquiam's Majar said, "thinks of investing money in capital improvements as taking money out of their pockets."

"Suppose I think we need a new barker, which I do," said Cal Lloyd, manager at Everett Plywood, "and suppose you have 300 people out there in the mill who want a 25¢ raise. Now who wins? Everything in this mill is political — even the monthly statements are political, because there are so many owners looking at it, criticizing it. Earlier this year, the workers voted a pay raise of 25¢ an hour. And the mill was *losing* money," Lloyd said. "But the board had to politically support that raise, in order to keep their jobs. I had to allow a 13-year-old machine to go without being replaced. Now if this were a private firm, the modernization program would be on a continuing basis. But unfortunately most of the work in a co-op is done on the squeaky wheel method — you know, why fix it until it breaks down?

"On the other hand," Lloyd said, "the board voted to put in a new green end when we were almost broke, while the year before, when we *could* have afforded it, the workers voted to take the money home. Now I'm trying to get one piece of machinery replaced, a veneer stacker. Whatever happens I'm going to sell them on that piece of equipment," Lloyd said with determination, "I know I will."

The inevitable question

These chronic financial conflicts raise the crucial question inevitably asked of worker self-managed firms: how can workers who are not specially trained in business make sensible decisions worth millions of dollars? The answer, according to members of the plywood mills, is that workers rely on their common sense: as they participate in making financial decisions, they learn. Members at the co-ops are encouraged to learn about business matters by taking part in board meetings and by browsing through the latest corporate financial statements. At Puget Sound Plywood they're lying around the lunchroom; workers browse through 10 pages of itemized debits and credits from the cost of the glue stock and office phones to the latest veneer sale, while sipping coffee and munching donuts.

Co-op members say one of the best ways to educate themselves about business matters is to serve on the board of directors. At some co-ops, members come and go so frequently on the board that membership practically rotates. But in the end, members say, their biggest incentive to learn about finance comes from their emotional and financial stake in owning the business.

"We don't have any high-priced engineers, no staff of lawyers like the big companies do," said Hoquiam board member Vernon Wolfe. "You take a hundred blue-collars in any business and you'll find enough of them who can run the business. One man will learn from another. The men around here, their book knowledge isn't so great, but they're concerned and they just know what's going on."

"All it takes is common sense to make good decisions," Puget Sound board member John Vaughn said. "When we don't know something we're briefed by somebody who has the information we need, and that gives us the knowledge to make our own decisions — about *our* business."

Outproducing the competition

And even if the financial decisions in a plywood co-op aren't quite as astute as they might be if made by an experienced corporate financial expert, the plywood co-ops are doing something right. As researcher Paul Bernstein says, "the enormous forces of productivity often generated in self-managed and self-owned firms can more than outweigh the inefficiencies of semi-amateur management.''

Periodic surveys have consistently shown that the plywood cooperatives outproduce conventional plywood mills. A study in the 1960s, according to researcher Katrina Berman, showed the worker-owned firms produce 30 percent more per worker-hour than traditional firms. Even the U.S. Internal Revenue Service, in a tax case against the plywood co-ops, essentially confirmed co-op data showing the co-ops are 25 - 60 percent more productive than conventional mills.

Worker-owners attribute their impressive productivity to their emotional and financial involvement in the mills. "It's pretty much like working for yourself," said Rudy Anderson, a 30-year veteran of Puget Sound Plywood. "The more effort you put into it, the more you'll get out of it. I've worked in seven plywood companies since I was 15 years old. At the other companies you're only interested in getting in your eight hours and taking home the check. But here it's altogether different. It's *our* money that's involved. There's always the possibility that we could work harder and make more money. The harder we work, the more money we make. And that's the beauty of a co-op."

Breaking down barriers

Worker ownership and control at the cooperative plywood mills has in many cases broken down the hierarchies and inequalities which separate workers at a conventional company. One of the hallmarks of virtually all the plywood co-ops is equal wages, for every member from the shop sweeper to the worker-elected president. Even the board of directors members don't get paid extra, except perhaps a symbolic dollar per year at Puget Sound. "I get no more compensation than the janitor does," said board member John Vaughn, "plus all the responsibility and all of the abuse." A few years ago the board of directors at Everett Plywood voted to set up a hierarchy of pay scales for different jobs, but the membership overwhelmingly defeated the proposal.

Some workers, Bernstein reports, do resent the equal pay scales, however. Highly skilled workers, for instance, are disgruntled that workers with far less experience and expertise should earn as much as they do. But for the most part, the equal pay scales have helped break down the notion that one job in a mill is more or less prestigious than another — which is not to say that workers don't feel that one job is more desirable than another. Workers in many of the mills move from job to job with ease, unhampered by the competition and jealousy which cloud the process of job transfers at a conventional firm. They rotate jobs not to relieve boredom so much as to help out where extra hands are needed.

"I've worked at least half the jobs here," says Earl Altes, at Puget Sound, "if no one else is available, or someone's sick or takes off. I may not like them, but I'll do the best job I can. That's the attitude of most guys here. If you've got an investment in the company you'd like to do a little bit better."

Members at the plywood co-ops are paid by the hour. The pay is not called "wages," as in a conventional firm, but an "advance on patronage receipts" — that is, an advance on the income the co-op expects to have earned by the end of the year. Workers at the factories often earn considerably more than average workers at conventional unionized plants, perhaps 20 percent more per hour. Plus, at the end of the year they receive a share of what's left over, a "refund" on the co-op "margin" — a share of what conventional firms would call profits.

The different terms represent more than semantics. At a conventional company the profits are considered private wealth to be spent however the private owners wish. But at a co-op, as Paul Bernstein points out, the philosophy holds that "the wealth of the firm resulted from its members' labor, and the amount they did not receive as compensation advances during the year is what has accrued into the margin surplus at year's end. It is thus 'refunded' to them." In a recent year at Hoquiam, for instance, each worker-owner received

At most of the plywood co-ops, layoffs don't exist. When the market goes bad and the mills lose money, the workers cut their pay

an extra $2,800 refund at the end of the year.

In most of the plywood co-ops the board of directors sets the amount of the hourly advance and the annual refund. The system gives co-op workers a degree of job security unparalleled by conventional companies in the United States. At a traditional firm, if the profits aren't as high as the management would like, the management says it is "losing money" — and lays off workers. At most of the plywood co-ops, layoffs don't exist. When the market goes bad and the company loses money, the workers vote to cut their hourly pay, across the board.

"If things get bad we'll all take a pay cut," said Earl Altes. "You don't want to milk the cow, because if you milk the cow, there's nothing left. And *we* lose the company."

"We overpaid ourselves last year," said Lloyd Gausta, the elected secretary at Puget Sound Plywood, "so we cut the hourly advances this year." At Everett Plywood, hourly advances have even fluctuated from one month to the next. In one of the few exceptions to the no-layoff rule, workers at Ft. Vancouver Plywood Company voted to close down the mill temporarily during the housing slump of 1974.

Co-op members also enjoy other benefits, such as insurance plans, discount gasoline, free lunches — all voted by the board and the membership. At mills such as Hoquiam, workers receive a generous, self-voted, paid vacation of four weeks. Some companies, Bernstein reports, allow members to take up to three months unpaid vacation with board approval. And some co-ops even allow members to "quit," and then return to the co-op when they wish, with full voting rights, as long as they hold onto their shares.

"This is my fourth time quitting," one worker said as he prepared to leave the co-op to strike out on his own in the gravel business. "It's not that I dislike it here. But we all have the opportunity to quit and try something better. If you can't better yourself on the outside, you can always come back to work here. As long as you own that share, you own your own job."

Plywood flaws

The plywood cooperatives' version of self-management has achieved important successes, but the co-op factories still have serious flaws. One of the most nagging problems which plagues the co-ops is frustratingly familiar to virtually every self-managed firm: many workers don't care to participate. Even at the most successful and democratically-managed co-ops, there are segments of the membership which other worker-owners scorn, for their "anti-co-op" attitudes. "A minority here never seems to realize they're working for themselves," Hoquiam board member Vernon Wolfe said. "They'd just as soon see a piece of machinery break down so they can go home for half a day. They don't realize it's *their* company."

Ironically, it was the manager at Puget Sound Plywood who complained that many members don't participate enough at membership meetings. "Many take the attitude that they don't know enough about the issues to make a decision on their own," he said. "They're reluctant to participate because they're afraid they'll be wrong; people will say 'that's a stupid idea.' " And some workers, he said, ignore the business at the meeting. "There's always a group just waiting for the tavern around the corner to open."

Although there are no comprehensive studies to confirm it, researchers report that the democratic spirit at the plywood co-ops tends to suffer as the firms get larger. Hoquiam, with only 99 owners, has a strong spirit.

But at Everett Plywood, with more than 320 worker-owners, for instance, there are widespread complaints that too many workers are not interested in the mill. They point especially to younger workers who, unlike the veterans who helped build the mill from the ground up, have no deep emotional commitment to the job. "I'd say 70 percent of the people here just don't give a damn," said one member of Everett Plywood. "We shouldn't have to have any foremen here, people should work on their own. But there's so much crapping around and jealousy and lack of cooperation that we *have* to have foremen,

How to perpetuate the plywood co-ops

One of the major developments which threatens the long-term survival and growth of the worker-owned plywood firms is the fact that the co-ops are not perpetuating their self-management structure. New workers can't afford to buy $25,000 shares and become voting members of the co-ops, and old-time members are voting to sell out the firms to conglomerates.

The problem, proponents of self-management say, is that the cooperatives are legally structured in such a way that workers can become voting members only by investing capital—buying a share. The solution: structure the self-managed firms so new members acquire voting rights *simply because they work there.*

"A self-managed firm should be defined and operated under the humanistic principle of active participation," says Cornell University researcher Jaroslav Vanek, "and not under the principle of capital ownership."

How would it work? Vanek and members of the Ithaca Work Group, which promotes self-management, suggest the self-managed firm would actually be owned by an umbrella, non-salable "supporting corporation." The supporting corporation would be controlled by representatives of the firm, and of any other self-managed firms in the community, and perhaps even by representatives of the outside community. It would lease the plants to the members who worked there, and the workers in each firm would run the firm as they do today, under the cooperative self-management structure. Workers might own symbolic $1 membership shares in the firm, which would be issued when they joined the co-op and which would have to be returned when they left.

just like in a regular mill. A lot of the problem is caused by these younger guys coming in. They just want to put in their time and take home the paycheck."

A recent board meeting told the story: "Absenteeism continues to be a major problem," the board complained in its minutes, which noted that board members discussed why several other co-ops were so much more productive and profitable than Everett was. Members of this co-op were discouraged. "If you can tell us how we make this co-op work again," one veteran said, "you'll make yourself a lot of money."

The breakdown in co-op spirit is one of the most serious problems threatening the survival of some worker-owned plywood mills. The mills may unwittingly be fostering this breakdown by hiring new workers who are not enfranchised shareholders but merely hourly workers, like those in any conventional plant. The hourly workers earn about 50¢ per hour less than the co-op members, receive no share of the profits (or margin), cast no votes — and usually get assigned to the noisiest and dirtiest jobs. At Puget Sound Plywood for instance, about 10 percent of the workforce was comprised of these hourly employees during a recent year, while almost a third of the workers at Hoquiam were nonshareholders. The trend in some co-ops to expand their workforce with hourly workers is creating a hierarchy of employees — "first class" co-op members and "second class" hourlies — which seems inimical to the egalitarian co-op spirit.

Why are co-ops resorting to nonmember labor? Ironically, one of the characteristics which helps preserve worker power at the co-ops is the same characteristic encouraging them to weaken it: worker ownership of *shares* in the firm. Here's why: when the co-ops were first launched 20 to 30 years ago, workers could buy a membership with only $1,000 to $3,000 per share. As the co-ops have grown and prospered, the shares have soared in value; a share at Puget Sound Plywood is worth well over $25,000. To become a member of the co-op, a prospective worker must buy a share, either from a current member who wishes to quit the co-op, or from the board of directors, which controls first option to buy back shares when a co-op member leaves.

Buying one's way into membership of a cooperative mill, then, requires a substantial outlay of cash. Most co-ops do allow payment on credit — perhaps 10 percent down, then a couple hundred dollars per month — but for workers already in debt on their homes and cars and medical payments, buying a share is an enormous burden to bear. As a result, fewer young workers are trying to become members today, and co-ops have often been forced to expand their workforce with nonmembers.

"Collective selfishness"

The co-ops, of course, could create *new* shares which would cost far less money, if the members merely voted to do it. But many co-op members fear that creating new shares would dilute the value of their own shares — and they want to *maximize* the value of their shares to finance their retirements. Self-management researchers often call this syndrome, "collective selfishness."

So, many co-ops are becoming closed shops of sorts, dominated by older men, some in their seventies (the plywood co-ops don't force early retirement), "just biding time until they retire," as one co-op member says. These workers formed the co-ops to buy their own jobs, not to create ongoing social institutions which would propagate the co-op ideal even after they're gone.

Many co-op members say they could care less if their co-op disappeared — and in fact, some co-ops have eagerly been trying to sell out to conglomerates. Two worker-owned mills have sold out, by a vote of the worker shareholders, to ITT and the Times-Mirror Corporation in the last several years. Workers at Everett were disappointed that a tentative offer by the Japanese Mitsui conglomerate had fallen through. No wonder: the workers at one co-op which sold itself, according to Bernstein, each received almost $200,000.

Unless the workers at the 16 surviving plywood co-ops make a determined effort to recruit young members who will carry on the co-op tradition, the cooperative movement in the Pacific Northwest could die during the next decade. It would be ironic, for renewed interest in cooperative enterprises is just beginning to bloom. Despite their problems, the cooperative plywood factories have succeeded in ways which provide an important model to other workers interested in building self-managed firms. It's true, as researcher Bernstein points out, that the plywood co-ops enjoyed some historical good luck: during the early years when the co-ops were founded, for example, the plywood market was booming. The fledgling co-ops of the 1940s and 1950s didn't face the enormous conglomerates—Weyerhaeuser, Georgia-Pacific, Crown Zellerbach—which would make it difficult for new plywood firms to join the market today. The plywood co-ops have also benefitted from some

Where are the unions?

With few exceptions, workers in the plywood co-ops do not belong to unions. It's not because they feel antagonistic toward unions, but because they say they don't need them.

"Why do we need a union when we make all the decisions in this company, like decide wages and benefits and run the whole shebang ourselves?" one Hoquiam worker said. Pay in the worker-owned mills is usually considerably higher than union wages in conventional plants, and the worker-owners award themselves more lucrative benefits.

One of the exceptions is Everett Plywood, where the union has survived since the days when the mill was privately owned. But other than handling grievances, job bidding, and organizing the annual picnic and fishing expedition, workers there say, the union doesn't play a significant role.

unique characteristics of the plywood industry. A trade group called the American Plywood Association, which has representatives from worker co-ops on its board, has sponsored some of the most important research and development in the industry—the kind of research which private corporations usually finance in other industries, and which the individual co-op mills could not likely have afforded.

Researcher Katrina Berman, however, stresses that the worker-owned plywood mills have succeeded *despite* serious *obstacles* in the plywood industry— such as the wildly volatile price and demand for plywood. If worker co-ops could succeed in this unstable market, Berman argues, producer co-ops could succeed in a wide variety of industries, especialy industries which are labor-intensive as the plywood mills are.

But perhaps the most compelling testimony of the co-op achievements comes not from statistics but from the members themselves. They say working in the worker-owned mills has created a new work spirit and a new feeling about their lives. "I used to work for Boeing aircraft," says Earl Altes at Puget Sound. "All I ever got was the runaround. I was always nervous and tense. But here I feel more at ease. I have peace of mind, and this is important to me. When I know I have a job to do, and it depends on me, I like that. I can take pride in my job, even mine, and it's not the most important one out there. Because when you put them all together, they're important. I can take pride because I'm working for myself."

"It's like my garden at home," said Hoquiam member Al Filyaw. "I sure get a kick out of planting it, and taking care of it—and watching it grow."

Sources

Katrina Berman, *Worker-Owned Plywood Companies, An Economic Analysis*, Washington State University Press, 1967.

Paul Bernstein, "Worker-Owned Plywood Co-ops in the Northwest," *Working Papers for a New Society*, Summer 1974.

Bernstein, "Worker-Owned Plywood Firms Steadily Outperform Industry," *World of Work Report*, May 1977.

"Where the Workers Run the Show," by Daniel Zwerdling, *The Washington Post*, September 2, 1973.

Interviews by the editor with employees of the plywood co-ops.

COOPER- ATIVA CEN- TRAL

While most of the nation's five million migrant and seasonal farmworkers drift through their annual work cycle — another farm and another crop, another boss and another uncertain low wage — 75 Mexican-American farmworkers and their families in California's Salinas Valley are proving that a farmworker's life can be dramatically different.

Until 1973, many of these farmworkers were typical subsistence migrants and share-croppers who followed the cotton, lettuce, peach and plum crops from Texas on up north. Most of them worked each season for a wealthy Salinas rancher who drove through the fields in his gun-gray Jaguar. But the migrant's life is behind them. For in 1973, community organizers funded by the U.S. Office of Economic Opportunity bought the ranch—and today, the farmworkers collectively own and control their own $2 million, 900 acre strawberry and vegetable co-op.

All the fundamental decisions on the ranch, from what types of berries to plant to how to distribute the profits, are made by a nine-person board of directors elected from among the workers in the field, and by monthly votes of the entire co-op membership. In an industry where exploitation and poverty are considered the norm, many farmworkers and families on the Cooperativa Central are earning up to $25,000 each year.

While many co-ops traditionally deteriorate as the members relinquish their power and defer to a powerful manager, the members of this co-op are continually increasing their collective power and making sure that the manager operates strictly on their behalf.

There have been few cooperative farms in American history: utopian ventures such as the Brook Farm in Massachusetts sprouted briefly in the 1800's and then died out within a few years. During the New Deal a handful of agricultural cooperatives struggled off the ground in the southwest, but they faded quickly too. The Cooperativa Central is the largest and most successful living model which shows that the historic vision of farmworkers working the land democratically can come true in the 20th Century United States.

Democracy by dictate

The Cooperativa Central did not have a democratic birth. The co-op, like the Consumers United Group insurance company in Washington, D.C., was essentially a democracy imposed by beneficent dictate. A California community action agency, called Trabajadores Adelante (which means "workers forward") had received $1 million from the Office of Economic Opportunity to launch local economic programs, and staff organizers were eager to form some co-ops. With no firm plan to guide them, the organizers recruited 15 migrants for a board of directors and—with no membership to join them—began shopping for a large patch of land.

"We were looking for anything—lettuce, tomatoes, anything—that would go," recalls Armando Piña, a former TA organizer. "We didn't have in mind to be a strawberry co-op." The organizers wanted to take over an existing ranch so they could absorb the farmworkers already in the fields as co-op members, and hook into the existing marketing networks. A few co-ops which TA had tried to build from the ground up had gone bankrupt. But most of the private farmers whom the organizers approached refused to sell. "A lot of them told us they were against people getting all that money from the federal government, out of their taxes," Piña says.

But finally the co-op organizers found a ranch for sale. It was a successful strawberry ranch, with good land, a reputation for good berries, and a private owner who was in poor health. He agreed to sell to the farmworker co-op, rather than sell to private corporations which had submitted offers, he said, because "I don't like the way the corporations would treat these people in the fields." Trabajadores Adelante was also willing to pay what some observers say was an inflated price, $350,000 for a package deal including rotten machinery and broken-down sheds that a large corporation with bargaining power would likely have refused to buy.

Next the organizers went shopping for financing. They approached at least half a dozen banks, which scoffed at the notion of a farmworker-controlled co-op, before the Bank of America finally agreed to make a $270,000 loan; $110,000 of the bank loan was guaranteed by the Opportunity Funding Corporation of Washington. With the Bank of America loan plus another $175,000 in OEO funds, the TA organizers closed the deal.

The entire co-op deal—the loans, the purchase agreement, the insurance, the marketing and contract arrangements, even the articles and bylaws—had been forged before any other farmworkers on the ranch had even heard about it. "All the negotiations were done in secret because we were afraid other farmers might find out and put pressure on the owner and the bank not to sell," Piña says. "When we finally called the big meeting for all the farmworkers and their families and told them we had bought out the ranch and they could join as members of the co-op, a lot of them were angry. They said they should have heard about it first."

But 300 people from more than 60 families on the ranch attended the first meeting, and most of them decided to join the co-op. Farmworkers from 25 families at nearby ranches also signed up. Each member, usually the father or mother from each family, chipped in $50 in membership fees, to be deducted from future paychecks. Each member and his or her family got their own plot of land, apportioned according to how many family members they expected to work on it. Since the co-op had not been the farmworkers' idea to begin with, few of them cared about the social ideals which motivated the organizers to create it. "The idea of a co-op as a democracy was secondary to them," Piña says. "The first thing they asked was 'How much money is this going to put in my pocket?'" Seventy-nine members and their families became charter owners of the Cooperativa Central.

Co-op organizing handbooks usually stress that a co-op is likely to survive only if the grassroots members create it. Co-ops organized by dictate, as the Cooperativa was formed, usually lack cohesion and eventually fail. But the Cooperativa Central has been a remarkable exception. From the beginning, organizers say, they asked themselves the crucial question: would the farmworkers use their cooperative ranch as a democratic tool for changing their economic and political lives? Or would they merely keep picking berries as they had before, following orders from a boss, and perhaps earning some more money in the process?

Strings attached

The financial institutions pressured the farmworkers to follow in the second direction. When the Bank of America approved the co-op loan it demanded, as part of the contract, that the co-op retain the same general manager, salesman and office staff which had run the ranch under private ownership. The bank required the co-op to maintain an advisory board, which included outside businessmen and the former ranch owner, at a salary of $800 a month.

Keeping the competent general manager, Tony

Rodrigues, and salesman Alex Bordges made good financial sense; many co-ops have failed because they lacked competent management, and strawberries are a notoriously high risk, perishable fruit which demand even better management skills than most crops. But the arrangement also guaranteed that the fledgling co-op members, most of them with less than an elementary school education, would be unlikely to assert themselves as a collective. Rodrigues was a stubborn and abrasive sort who openly battled to retain absolute control over the ranch despite its new cooperative ownership and structures. "I've been managing strawberry farms for over 20 years," he said angrily. "Who the hell are these farmworkers trying to tell me what to do?"

During the first year, members say, they seldom challenged Rodrigues' judgments; the ranch operated as a cooperative in name only. "Many members got discouraged and we lost 20 members in the first year of operation," one co-op member told participants at the Third International Conference on Self-Management. But during the second season in 1974, the mood of the farmworkers changed. For the first time since the co-op had been formed, members say, they

For the first time since the co-op was formed, the farmworkers began to understand that the ranch truly belonged to them—and they could exert potentially enormous power

began to understand that the ranch truly belonged to them and that they had potentially enormous power. Although the members still did not initiate many changes in their worklives, they began to challenge Rodrigues and salesman Bordges, demanding them to justify every major decision and explain how it would benefit the ranch.

"The members are always asking Tony (Rodrigues), 'Why did you do this?' or 'How come you want to do that?'" Piña said at the time. One could see the members asserting their powers at the weekly board of directors meetings. The nine board members took a few hours off from picking berries under the relentless 90° sun to meet with the manager and salesman. The board room was in the corner of a dilapidated old barn, with cold cement floors, a sagging, ragged couch, and a "conference table" slapped together with a dozen nails and a few gray boards.

At a typical board meeting, the members told manager Rodrigues—as a young farmworker translated to English, for the manager spoke little Spanish—that they wanted him to clean up the field toilets. Next they voted to grant one of the co-op members two weeks leave in Mexico. It was a controversial decision since the member would be leaving his plot of land, called his "company," at peak harvest, and other workers would have to pick his berries instead. If the member stayed away longer than two weeks, the board warned, they would parcel off his company to the other members.

After considerable debate the board members voted to order the manager to delay spraying the fields with a certain pesticide until he had investigated its potential effects on both the plants and the workers' health ("I'll spray anyway," Rodrigues boasted later, "they won't know the difference"). The workers argued with salesman Bordges, whom they discovered had been giving away free crates of strawberries to buyers. Bordges—who kept referring condescendingly to the co-op members as "sharecroppers," which the translator tactfully converted in Spanish to "companies"—insisted the handouts were valuable sales gimmicks, while the farmworkers argued they were a

drain on the workers' income. They compromised: Bordges could continue giving out free crates, but only if he cleared each gift with the board in advance.

And finally, just before adjourning to the fields, the board of directors voted to forbid the salesman to market any strawberries through a distributor who had also been handling produce from a nearby ranch, where the United Farm Workers were on strike. Although the Cooperativa has no union—members say they don't need one since they own and control the ranch—most of the pickers support the United Farm Workers' struggles.

Bit by bit, the farmworkers in the co-op began to chip away at the general manager's powers and to assert more and more control over the ranch. While the manager had previously enjoyed the authority to spend $1500 in a single transaction without getting permission, the board voted to slash his discretionary spending to only $500. "I guess they don't trust me," Rodrigues complained. While Rodrigues had previously hired and fired the handful of truck drivers, crate loaders and tractor drivers who worked for the co-op by the hour, the co-op membership elected its own committee to take control over hiring and firing instead. While Rodrigues had bitterly opposed the idea that the co-op should lend money to its members—many of them families with eight to 12 children and hard-pressed for grocery money until the peak harvest rolls in—the co-op members voted to grant loans at less interest than they could ever negotiate at a bank.

One of the most symbolic confrontations flared over the members' proposal to plant 14 acres, not with strawberries but with pinto beans—a Mexican-American staple whose price had recently quadrupled in the grocery stores. Rodrigues argued they would make more money with strawberries. "What he really meant was he'd be making more money if we raised strawberries since he gets a commission, three cents a crate," one young co-op member said. "We said, 'Tony, *we* want pinto beans.'" Later that year, the co-op harvested and sold its members about 20,000 pounds of pinto beans, at the low price of 25 ¢ per pound.

Seizing control

Today, the worker members have taken complete control of the Cooperative. In 1975 they fired the manager and salesman, and elected one of their fellow farmworkers as manager instead. Since then, the farmworkers have elected a new manager from among their own ranks at least once a year, sometimes even more frequently. While most co-ops would consider the frequent change of managers a sign of membership weakness and indecision, co-op members see it as a plus. "The revolving door is a good sign," says Steve Huffstutlar, until recently an adviser to the co-op, "a good sign that members are constantly involved and looking for change and improvement."

The Cooperativa pays an independent broker a 7 percent commission to market their fruit, but they keep close watch over his marketing methods. Members of the co-op have also ousted most of the old board of directors, whom they felt were too closely identified to the conservative Rodrigues and Bank of America management; the farmworkers keep electing new members to the board each year, "kind of like a rotation," one member said, "so that everyone will have a chance to serve on the board and make decisions."

How does a farmworker like Felipé Ramos, with virtually no formal education, take on the position as manager of a $2 million strawberry ranch without any special training or managerial experience? Ramos, the first in the line of farmworker-elected managers, had previously worked as the co-op's elected quality control inspector, while his family worked on their plot of land harvesting berries. "We're helping each other," one member explained, translating for Ramos, who doesn't speak English. "If Felipé doesn't know something then we ask somebody who does, and that way we're all learning as we go along." Under the new democratic spirit in the co-op, the members don't consider their elected managers to be Rodrigues-style tyrants, who bark orders; the manager serves simply as an administrator who carries out the board of directors' will. 'I'm just called the production

manager, I can't do what I want," Ramos said. "I have to do what the board wants." The Cooperativa Central, as a board of directors resolution made clear, is now run strictly by committee. "From this date," the Board declared, "The Executive Committee is to be considered itself exclusively the General Manager."

The board of directors members have been so anxious to avoid the managerial tyranny under the former Rodrigues regime, that they have gone almost to the opposite extreme: they refuse to delegate any significant authority to the production manager. "Even though I can spend $500 on my own, I ask the Board everything," one production manager said. "If I have to take a truck to the garage to fix the brakes I ask permission from the Board. I had to buy a new water pump for $250, so I decided I had better ask to play it safe. This morning we needed to put some fertilizer over there," the production manager said, pointing to a section of the field where members were picking strawberries, "and we needed to hire four workers to put it on. I had to keep going back to the board members in the field, again and again, to ask each one who he wanted me to hire. It's sometimes hard to bring the board members together to make those decisions because they don't want to stop working in the fields. They have berries popping out of their ears."

Democracy in a barn

While the production manager feels pressured to refer almost every decision to the Board, the Board of Directors members in turn feel a responsibility to share virtually every major business or policy decision with the entire membership, even if a vote isn't required under the bylaws. "We are completely democratic," says member Javier Ruiz, a panel member at the Third International Conference on Self-Management. "Everything is done by majority vote. The workers meet at least once a month in the conference room we fixed up in the barn—I'd say at least 50 or 55 of the 75 members usually attend—and they hire and fire, they decide how much acreage we should plant, who to sell our berries to, and they make a lot of financial decisions.

"For example," Javier Ruiz says, "members vote on buying new equipment, like a tractor or expensive office equipment. Members voted on which freezer company to sell to, and which one of the trademarks we wanted to use. Recently the Board voted to accept a new member into the co-op, but the members overturned the decision at their monthly meeting because they felt he wasn't qualified. We had some old houses on our property which we were just using as storage sheds, and some members thought we should rent them out to families. The Board voted not to lease them, because the houses are not up to code, but the members overruled the Board because some of the members need housing very badly. We're going to try to bring the houses up to code soon."

At one meeting the co-op members voted to have an independent audit of the office books, in addition to the standard audit the co-op has each year—not so much because the members mistrust any of the elected officers, one member explained, as because after working so long as sharecroppers, the farmworkers have a healthy skepticism toward managers in general. And recently, the general membership voted to make loans to needy members, even if those members are already in debt—breaking a previous co-op rule. "Everyone voted to waive the rule, because last year there was a terrible rain at peak harvest, and a lot of members need the money badly," Ruiz says. "For years no one cared about the farmworker," one member explains. "Now that we own our own ranch, we like to take care of each other."

When observers ask Ruiz how the co-op can expect to function efficiently and profitably when the board and general membership insist on taking part in so many decisions, he laughs. "If they have any doubts send them over here and we'll show them," Ruiz says. "We've been in this system five years, and it's always worked this way."

"Member participation here is as strong as ever," says Steve Huffstutlar, until recently a full-time paid adviser to the co-op. "Sure, it gives anybody working

for the co-op headaches, nightmares and hives to always have someone looking over your shoulder. And that's the way it should be."

While the democratic spirit at the Cooperativa Central has grown strong, the major development which has impressed the banks and other observers in the local financial community has been the co-op's financial success. In 1974 the co-op borrowed more than $100,000 from the Bank of America to pull it through the season; in 1975 the co-op drew on its own burgeoning financial reserves and didn't borrow one cent. Sales have topped $2 million, twice the income in 1973, and the Cooperativa has maintained if not improved the quality of its strawberries. "We won two firsts and two seconds this year at the Salinas Valley County Fair," said one co-op member, pointing proudly to the ribbons hanging on the Cooperativa's office wall.

Up from poverty

The Cooperativa has also been an important financial success for the individual members who work there. When the ranch was privately owned, the farmworkers got paid a fixed rate per crate, period. Under the co-op formula, the members get 50 percent of

Cooperativa members say their incomes have quadrupled since joining the co-op ranch. In 1976 the average farmworker earned $25,000

the going price for every crate of strawberries they produce on their plots of land, or "companies" as members call them; the co-op coffers get the other half to pay for the communal supplies and services, such as fertilizer and pesticides, seeds and planting, irrigation, marketing and other services.

If members wish to hire pickers by the hour to help them out during the peak harvest, when berries are exploding on the fields, it's their business—and they must pay the pickers out of their own pockets. "Most of the members usually hire relatives or friends, to help them out when they need work," one member says.

At the end of the year, after all the costs have been paid, the co-op distributes the surplus—what the private owner would have kept as profits—among the members.

For the first several years, the co-op apportioned the surplus based on a complicated formula which combined each member's total production plus his or her yield per acre. By taking yield per acre into account, the co-op was attempting to reward members for hard work and efficiency. But the formula was hotly contested by some co-op members, partly because it was too complicated for them to understand, and partly because members felt it penalized those who happened to get a poor piece of land. Now the co-op simply distributes the surplus in proportion to each member's gross sales. "People are still complaining," one co-op worker says, "but at least everyone understands how it's being done."

Whatever the inequalities in the system, Cooperativa members say their incomes have tripled and even quadrupled since becoming members of the co-op. A look at a recent annual payroll shows the Cooperativa Central members are doing well: the farmworker with Company No. 34, for instance, who farms 3.23 acres, earned $20,956 plus a share of the profits, while one with Company No. 74, farming 3.57 acres, earned $17,522 plus profits. In 1976, the best year ever, co-op members earned an average of $25,000, including profit sharing and deferred payments. Under a financial plan adopted by the farmworkers, members re-

ceive only 20 percent of their share of the profits in cash; the rest is funneled into a certificate of deposit account, which the co-op uses for working capital. The members get paid back in a few years, with eight percent interest. In a typical year, the co-op can generate about $200,000 in working capital that way. And meanwhile, members are saving money at a high rate of interest.

As members of their own cooperative ranch, the farmworkers at the Cooperativa are achieving economic security which most farmworkers never dream possible. "Some sharecroppers working on private ranches are making good money," says Ruiz, "but the important thing is they don't have any future. If the employer doesn't want you, you're fired, that's it. Here, at the Cooperativa, the only way you can get fired is if you don't produce anything. And you always have a share. A member leaving now takes $7,200 to $10,000 for his share."

The members' economic situation has improved so much, Ruiz says, that "for the first time many members have houses now. They've been making more money now that they're in the co-op, and they've been buying property."

Nagging problems

The Cooperativa Central is succeeding better than any other agricultural co-op, but it still confronts some nagging problems. The co-op could do even better financially, members say, if more of the farmworkers and their elected leaders were better educated and possessed keener managerial and business skills. The current production manager, during the harvest of 1978, "is completely illiterate," one co-op worker says—adding, however, that the manager "is one of the most knowledgeable members about the business."

"We still have a lot of members, including the board and manager, who don't know too much about the [financial aspects of] business," says Ruiz. "We have a problem with lack of education. Most of the people

Another co-op blooms

The success rate of farmworker co-ops had not been encouraging—until recently. A handful of co-ops sprouted near the Cooperativa Central, also with the help of Trabajadores Adelante, around the same time the Cooperativa formed. But they were small, with only a handful of families, and after only one or two seasons they died. "They can't make it because they have no money," said farmer organizer Armando Piña, "and can't find good management." It's the familiar co-op lament.

But now six successful co-ops have sprouted near the Cooperativa Central. One of the success stories is the Cooperativa Campesina ("farmworker's co-op") near Watsonville, California. This co-op, which also grows strawberries, is especially significant—because unlike the Cooperativa Central, which took over a successful ranch—the Cooperativa Campesina started literally from the ground up. "It began when some farmworkers in a TA-sponsored adult education class asked me how they could go about starting a co-op," says Tereso Moralez, a TA organizer and co-op member, as he picks berries in the blazing sun.

Eight of the farmworkers approached the local Central Coast Counties Development Corporation for some technical assistance, found seven acres of land up for lease, and started searching for seed funds. The farmworkers were "flatly refused" by the Farmers' Home Administration, according to a CCDC pamphlet, "which voiced skepticism for economic success by a group of inexperienced low-income persons."

"We couldn't get any loans at banks," Moralez said, "and farmers wouldn't lend us any equipment." What the farmworkers did have was $2,300, the fruit of $5 contributions which each of the eight organizers deposited in a savings account every week. Four of the organizers dropped out of the project because they thought the co-op would flop, but the other four bought some seeds and some equipment and planted six acres of squash and zucchini.

Now that they had some experience—and produce—to show to the money lenders, the co-op organizers were able to scrape up funding. They got $100,000, repayable over five years at one percent interest, from the Office of Economic Opportunity and another $150,000 in loans from the Wells Fargo Bank (five other banks had turned the farmworkers down). Moralez and the three others fanned out into the community to recruit members for their co-op: they knocked on doors, put some ads on local radio, tacked announcements to community bulletin boards, and received 150 applications.

With the help of the CCDC, the organizers leased 80 acres of good land and planted some strawberries, cabbage and zucchini. By 1974, the Cooperativa Campesina was flourishing with 30 members and their families and 160 acres of fruit. Sales that year topped $1 million. "This valley looks beautiful," Moralez said, pausing in mid-row and looking over the land, "with all the families out there, everybody working hard."

While farmworkers at the Cooperativa Campesina have achieved unqualified financial success, they have never exerted democratic control to the degree that the farmworkers have at the Cooperativa Central. One reason is that the Wells Fargo Bank granted its loan with strong strings attached: the co-op board must be controlled not by the members but by representatives of the CCDC, three votes to two. The co-op has also kept the number of members to a minimum, preferring to hire large numbers of hourly pickers to help out instead; hourly workers, in fact, outweigh the co-op members and their families by a large margin. The arrangement has tended to dilute the collective spirit. And since the co-op's land is split into several different parcels each about a mile apart, the members don't have much daily contact which might foster a sense of unity.

"They're individual businessmen," the co-op manager said. "It's not a communal operation, not a bunch of families working together. What we're here for," he said, pointing to the small administrative staff, "is merely to perform services for these small, individual growers."

Still, the co-op has brought the farmworkers dramatic financial success. The $300,000 in loans was paid ahead of schedule, according to the CCDC, and the average family income has zoomed from $3,500 a season to more than $12,000. Some families, like the Moralez family—he has 11 family members working two acres—earn $20,000 a year. The families have proved that farmworkers with little but vision and hard work can build their own cooperative ranch from the ground up.

"Farmworkers have been transformed into farmers and managers," the CCDC declares. "Even more importantly, with a relatively stable economic base established, they can now control their destiny and that of their families to a degree never before possible."

"We proved something that wasn't proved before," Moralez said, munching on a strawberry. "Like they said, we didn't have any education to run a co-op. We didn't have experience, we didn't have credit, we didn't have nothing. Well, now we have all this," he said, sweeping his hand over the families and the pickers and the ranch.

here have never gone to school or gone beyond the second grade." When the co-op was first formed, some of the younger and better educated members organized some classes to teach members rudimentary business and management skills, and to teach them the principles of agricultural marketing. "But no one came," one of the member-instructors said.

And although an increasing number of members have been plunging into the monthly meetings, and taking an active role in co-op debates and votes, many of the farmworkers at the Cooperativa still sit back in silence—only to complain after the vote that things aren't going the way they'd like.

Some co-op members also complain that colleagues are not doing their jobs. For example, co-op members elected a committee which was supposed to inspect the quality of the berries around the ranch, and help members who were facing special production problems, but members said the committee never did its job. The farmworkers elected one of their fellow members to attend special educational seminars held periodically by the California Strawberry Advisory Board, so he could bring back the latest information on strawberry techniques, "but he never goes to them," the production manager said with a shrug.

And like members at other self-managed firms, both the board members and the general membership need special training in how to conduct democratic, efficient and productive meetings. "Sometimes we sit there for four to six hours and do everything but get down to business," one member said. "Every little thing becomes such a big issue."

Despite the problems, the Cooperativa has been flourishing, and growing, too. Even most members' lack of a formal education, while perhaps slowing the co-op from reaching its full potential, is not holding it back. "That's why they have me here," says Ruiz—a member of the co-op who used to work in the fields, but is now paid full-time to advise the board and members on business and financial matters they don't understand. "I don't tell them what to do, I just explain to them all the business factors so they can make their own decisions," Ruiz says. "They've been around—they've been working at this business for years. The people here don't have no white collar guys managing them, *they* are the manager. They just have a guy like me who makes recommendations. But they make up their own minds.

"Sure, we still have members who don't speak up or say anything, and we still have members who don't agree about anything," Ruiz said. "But the important thing is, they have a chance to decide. They're part of the decision-making body. They're managing a $2 million business. There's members who don't ever vote or show up at the meetings, but the business is moving ahead, it's not holding back for them. But when they want to participate more, they'll have the chance."

Visions come true

When the Cooperativa Central was founded, the Trabajadores Adelante organizers had fiery visions of raising the farmworkers' consciousness and fomenting social change. Somewhere in the co-op office files, organizer Pina dredged up an old proposal for forming a co-op, filled with stirring-sounding plans to make the farmworker "totally self-sufficient in his role as farmer, businessman, co-op member and member of the Mexican-American community." There was more of the lingo of government-funded social idealism—talk about educating members through "teacher and resource mobilization," forming day care centers "to provide children with meaningful, integrated experiences," and there were lots of democratic organizational flow charts.

In the world of co-ops, visions such as these seldom become reality; they usually remain an activist's dream. But at the Cooperativa Central, many of the visions are now coming true. Ever since the co-op began, members have dreamed of making themselves "totally self-sufficient," as the proposals said, by expanding beyond their 200 rented acres, dependent on a land-owner's lease, and diversifying beyond fragile and risky strawberries. If they could only diversify into other crops, members dreamed, they could finally

work at their Cooperativa on a year-round basis, instead of from only spring though fall, as the strawberry business provides.

So, last year, the Cooperativa used $200,000 in revolving funds, plus a $1.9 million bank loan, and bought 700 acres of good land. As this booklet goes to press, the farmworkers are planting 200 acres of cauliflower and broccoli; 100 acres of mixed vegetables such as romaine, butter lettuce, leeks and red cabbage; another 150 acres of strawberries; 160 acres of beans, carrots or potatoes; plus 100 acres of pasture for raising 20 beef cattle, which the farmworkers will slaughter and sell at a low price to co-op members and their families.

"We're still experimenting with the vegetables," says one co-op worker. Unlike the strawberries system, there will be no individual "companies" in the vegetable fields. The entire acreage will be farmed collectively, with co-op members working a certain number of hours prescribed by the board, with members' approval. Income from the vegetable fields will be shared equally. Since none of the farmworkers have much experience with vegetables, they have hired a private vegetable grower as a consultant.

In another dream come true, farmworkers with the Cooperativa Central are finally going to get some decent housing. With a state-approved grant, the co-op will build 50 low-cost homes on its new land, and rent them to the co-op families who are neediest.

One of the most important questions which confronts most co-ops is this: How will the co-op regenerate and keep bringing in new members, to make sure that as old members leave, the enterprise will survive? Some of the plywood cooperatives in the northwest are dying out precisely because the workers have made it difficult for new members to join. Several years ago, it looked as if the Cooperativa might be moving in the same self-destructive direction, when members voted to freeze membership. "If new people come in, it just creates more problems; personalities conflict and people disagree, and things like that," one member said.

But since then, the co-op membership has changed

its mind. In the past two years, as veteran members left, the co-op has accepted a substantial number of new members, swelling the membership ranks from 52 to 75. To become a member, the farmworker must buy membership rights for $8,000-$10,000, plus another $6,000-$8,000 in future revolving fund certificates (that is, in the member's future share of the profits). "It sounds like a lot of money," one co-op worker says, "but it isn't really so bad because a member can join for as little as $500 down." The Board of Directors selects the new members, usually friends or relatives of current members, but must submit the applicants to the rest of the co-op membership for approval.

Sowing democracy

Expanding the number of members within the co-op is only one part of the Cooperativa's effort to keep the co-op ideal alive. The farmworkers in the Cooperativa Central have also launched an extraordinary effort to nourish the growth of more farmworker co-ops. The Cooperative Central has launched its own co-op training center, a wholly controlled subsidiary funded by the state government, called Technica, Inc. At the training center, housed on the grounds of the Cooperativa Central in a mobile trailer, veteran Cooperativa members have been teaching members of six other fledgling co-ops, from Salinas to Santa Maria, how to set up and run a farm co-op.

"Thirty-nine members of the Cooperativa are the 'peer' trainers," says Javier Ruiz. "They will teach everything from their own experience." There will be 100 students there this summer (1978), all from other, operating co-ops, taking four hours of training in the classroom, and then four hours on the job at their own co-op. Already, 28 members of one new co-op, called Agricola—all of them trained last year by Technica—are farming 100 acres of strawberries; another co-op, called Unida National, whose members are also being trained at Technica, are starting to farm 150 acres with 57 members.

Ask Ruiz how farmworkers with no education can conduct the co-op training, and he laughs. "Our co-op members have been in this business five years," he says. "We have been a successful co-op. If we can show other people our way of management, maybe they can be successful like us. I don't have anything against college people with a degree," Ruiz says, "but we've been through it. We've experienced it, in the fields."

The 75 farmworkers in the fields of the Cooperativa Central may accomplish what workers at the nation's other self-managed firms have so far failed to do: they are transforming their lonely and isolated success into a growing movement.

Sources

Interviews by the editor with members of the Cooperativa Central.
Transcripts of the Third International Conference on Self-Management.

The first democratic business school in the nation

One of the most critical needs in enterprises which are attempting to democratize the workplace, as virtually every case study in this book makes clear, is basic training in the art of running a democratic business. There has never been a business school in the nation which prepares people for the task. That is, until now. The New School for Democratic Management, based in San Francisco, California, has taken an important step toward filling the need.

The New School bills itself as "the only business school to address directly the particular and unique problems of worker and community-owned factories" and other enterprises and institutions; the goal, the school founders say, "is to help community-oriented and democratically-organized enterprises become self-sustaining and able to expand."

There is no lack of business schools in the U.S. But, as the New School points out, "Traditional business courses don't address the problem of under-capitalized businesses trying to exist in limited markets alongside powerful competitors. Traditional texts don't include case studies of the successes and failures of such businesses. And perhaps most important, existing business schools don't consider the problems and possibilities of democratizing the structure of management, the organization of work, or the patterns of ownership; rather, they discourage such ideas and plans."

Since 1977, the New School has launched a series of workshops, each three to five days long, in cities such as Seattle, Minneapolis, San Francisco and Austin. The Seattle session drew more than 100 students from businesses, government and social service agencies in six states plus Canada. The 15 faculty, who work only part-time for the school, included business consultants, university professors, community organizers and a congressional aide. Courses ranged from Starting a Business and Marketing to Bookkeeping and Accounting, from Legal Structures for Self-Management and Women in Business to Democratic Management and Criticism-Self Criticism techniques. Back home in San Francisco, the New School conducts a 10-week night school program for workers in the Bay area.

The New School for Democratic Management has been negotiating with a city government in Ohio to launch workplace democracy training programs for city employees; the school also is trying to organize special sessions across the country for labor leaders and union members. Unfortunately, the school is suffering from one of the same problems it was designed to help correct: lack of funding for democratic enterprises. Its foundation money is stretching thin, and the school reports it is having a difficult time raising more cash. A bill now before Congress, the Voluntary Job Preservation and Community Stabilization Act (see back of the book) would provide federal funding to keep organizations such as the New School alive. It is a crucial goal, since right now, the New School for Democratic Management is the only one of its kind in the nation.

IGP For sheer political drama, the board of directors elections in February 1977 at the Consumers United Group, Inc., beat the Carter-Ford election cold.

Consumers United — usually called International Group Plans, or IGP — is the $60 million, worker-managed insurance corporation just ten blocks from the White House in the financial heart of Washington D.C. The 340 secretaries, accountants, file clerks, salespeople, and other employees own half the corporation and elect by popular vote half the board of directors.

The results of the national presidential campaign meant no more than political variations; the structure of the nation would remain basically the same. But the outcome of the IGP elections promised a dramatic difference. For the incumbent board was staging a coup of sorts, trying to impose more traditional corporate work styles. Board members were proposing widespread layoffs in a company that forbids laying off workers. The board wanted to bring back worker attendance records in a company where keeping track of attendance is forbidden. And the board wanted to give the power to fire workers to management in a company where firings are controlled by a worker court.

But the entire board was ousted, and the workers elected a new board with "democratic" views. "It was a major showdown, a turning point," one insurance clerk said. "The people — and democracy — won."

The board of directors elections at IGP went unnoticed in the press. But in just five years this insurance corporation has developed perhaps the most extensive experiment in worker self-management in North America. It's an ongoing experiment, not a finished model; the democratic decision-making structure changes so often as workers grapple for the "best" system, that a description of the corporation one year may well be obsolete the next.

But more than any other enterprise represented at the Third International Conference on Self-Management, IGP offered a model suggesting that worker self-management — not just worker ownership or worker participation — can work in a contemporary, sophisticated U.S. corporation. IGP is a modern white-collar company in a competitive market using advanced computer technologies. It's a successful corporation that earns close to $1 million profit a year. Workers at IGP aren't left-leaning college graduates like workers are in so many collectives, but are instead a typical assortment of middle and lower income office workers — 46 percent white, 43 percent black, two-thirds female, and only a third with college degrees.

Most important, IGP is a firm where rank and file employees really do exert fundamental powers. For example, 85 percent of the workers turned out for the board of directors election, an enviable turnout in any political campaign. "Look, just say we are completely in charge of our own jobs from day to day," a claims clerk told me. "I mean that individuals like

myself, making close to [IGP's] minimum wage, make decisions on our own that could affect a whole insurance plan, such as whether certain people are eligible to receive claims or not — decisions which only a manager could make at any traditional insurance company."

And the workers at IGP have used their powers to fashion benefits which most U.S. workers can only dream about. In a city where many white-collar clerks start at $6,000 per year, IGP employees have voted a minimum wage over $10,000, plus a share of the corporate profits. In a nation where most workers get a few days paid sick leave, the IGP rank and file have voted paid sick leave for three months.

The lessons IGP offers are not all about success, however. The company faces some serious problems and has made some serious tactical mistakes from which workers and students of workplace democracy can also learn.

The self-management system at IGP remains wobbly and sometimes embattled, plagued by managers who resist giving up their traditional powers and by production clerks who don't know how to assert their newly obtained powers. Some employees at IGP say they could care less about making important decisions which shape their work lives.

"I would love to go back to a traditional company, punching time clocks and being told exactly what to do, when and how to do it," one clerical worker said. "I just can't stand the confusion anymore."

The experience at IGP suggests that the journey to self-management in a company is difficult and painful —but rewarding. But then, so is any social change. "If I were at a traditional company I'd still be just a clerk," says a college dropout who started as a clerk at IGP. "But here I've been elected to committees where I've learned skills I never could have learned in school—how to work with people and how to run a multimillion dollar business."

From insurance to revolution

James P. Gibbons, the current president, founded

James P. Gibbons

IGP in 1964 with three partners and an IBM 1401 computer. Gibbons had earned a reputation in New York as a spectacular insurance salesman, and now he wanted to try a new marketing concept. Instead of using a sales network to sell insurance door to door, IGP would sell group health insurance by computer-ized mass mailings to members of large groups—from the Air Force Sergeants Association to the staff of *Family Health* magazine. The idea took off, and in five years Gibbons had 100 employees handling $10 million in premiums.

Gibbons says he considered business just a way to

"What I've done is to create the first corporate power structure in this country which the employees have the power to change as they want . . . a total revolution"

make a living while he pursued his visions of social and political change. He marched — and was twice arrested — in antiwar, antipoverty, and civil rights protests; he says, "I was marching for the power of the people to control their own lives.

"I had always thought I'd sell the business and use the money to set up some sort of foundation, like the Stern Fund or something, and give money to political causes," Gibbons says. He sits at his desk in an open office pool of rank and file clerks; there are no "elitist" executive offices at IGP. "But then I started thinking, "What's the point? Set up another foundation that is trying to change the very people and system that gives us all our money? It occurred to me what we really had to do was create an economic institution that was self-sufficient.

"And that," Gibbons says, "is when I became consciously committed to making this company a self-sustaining, living model of social change.

"What I've done," he says, "is to create the first corporate power structure in this country which the employees have the power to change as they want. I'm not talking about anything short of a total revolution."

The birth of democracy at IGP was a paradox. Gibbons imposed self-management on the workers as the enlightened monarch of a tiny nation might liberate the masses by beneficent dictate. One day in spring 1972 he announced he was transferring half the company ownership to the employees in a non-salable, profit sharing trust. Six months later he announced that employees would begin electing half the board of directors (Gibbons appoints the other half). And then he began creating a network of employee committeess which, he decreed, would gradually make the corporate decisions traditionally reserved for the executives.

To understand the evolution of self-management at IGP, workers there say, it is important to underscore one point: Gibbons never pursued self-management for self-management's sake. "Hell no, self-management isn't the end objective, the end objective is

maximizing humanness," Gibbons says, " creating an environment of justice, equity, equality, beauty, truth — an environment where each member of the community has the opportunity to grow and develop in his or her own unique way, to self-actualize."

The main reason for self-management, Gibbons says, "is to give workers the power to protect themselves against arbitrary uses of power by management. But if we achieve self-management without achieving these other goals, I'll consider the experiment a failure."

Many companies around the country that have instituted some form of worker participation have used it as a tool for making the business more successful. But in Gibbons' revolution, the business itself has become the tool — the tool for creating a radical society, "a utopian community," as Gibbons puts it. He has proclaimed his goals in a credo, emblazoned on a silver poster and taught to new employees their first day on the job:

- Goal I: To build a lasting economic institution which helps satisfy the real needs of our client organizations .. and to provide quality service .. [while] making enough profit to keep the corporation in existence . . . .

- Goal II: To build this institution on a foundation which maximizes the humanness of everyone involved, and which creates a new ethic for economic institutions — an alternative model for business.

"The very idea of creating a humane society within a business institution," Gibbons acknowledges, "is an enormous paradox."

IGP government

Gibbons and IGP employees have spent five years groping for a sensible decision-making structure. There have been so many committees created, modified, abolished, then resurrected again that even veteran employees can't remember them all. In early

Benefits of self-management

Worker-owners at IGP enjoy the kinds of benefits that most of America's 86 million workers only dream about. Formulated and passed by the employee-elected congress, the CRA, and then approved by the board, benefits include:

- minimum annual wage: $10,600 plus profits.

- flexible hours: set your own hours between 7 a.m. and 7 p.m. Some employees work four days a week.

- no attendance records: everyone leaves a few hours early or takes a whole day off from time to time. As long as you get your work done, no one minds.

- vacations: no less than two weeks a year, and "no more than the job responsibilities, team, and team leader will agree to." Some clerical workers take a month off.

- unlimited sick leave: the company pays your full salary for 90 continuous days, then you go on disability. You're guaranteed a job with the same salary whenever you come back.

- maternity leave: three months at full pay.

- tuition paid: take a course at a local university that relates somehow to your work, and the company will pay you back. "I'm taking psychology and philosophy," a files team-leader says, "so I can better understand the 'girls.'"

- first crack at job openings: all vacancies are offered to IGP employees first.

If your team votes to fire you, you're not yet out in the cold. You can appeal to the employee court while receiving full pay. If you do leave, you can start over at a new company with good will and a clean slate. IGP won't put any negative information in your personnel file.

1978 the basic structure at IGP looks like this:

- The *worker teams* are autonomous work groups throughout the company, each with about six to a dozen employees who perform the same job. Clerks who pay claims to military clients, for instance, work on the military claims team. Although team power has never been defined on paper, in practice the teams are virtually responsible for organizing and managing the company's day-to-day work, and handling staff hiring and firing.

- Each *department* is composed of several teams. Department-level decisions, such as staffing levels and budgets, long-range objectives, and coordinating the work of the teams, are made democratically by a *department operating committee*. The committee includes the *team leaders* (a worker representative elected from each team) and a *department coordinator* whom the team leaders help select. A department coordinator doesn't have the powers of a traditional corporate department head, but is supposed to guide the staff and carry out the decisions of the operating committee.

- Each *division* includes several departments. Division-level policies are made by the *division operating committee*, which includes the department coordinators, a representative elected by the workers, and a division coordinator elected by the department coordinators. The division coordinator — called a "center forward" in IGP's lingo — is supposed to carry out the decisions of the committee, not give orders like a boss.

- The *corporate operating committee* is made up of the handful of top managers who run the corporate business from week to week. It's the least representative committee of all. Except for one member directly elected by the workers, the members are hired by the board. The corporate operating committee reviews all major policies and corporate operating strategies devised by the lower committees before sending them for approval to the board.

- The *board of directors* is half chosen by Gibbons and half elected. The board is supposed to be the ultimate decision-making body, the final vote on major policies from investments to sick leave to wage scales.

- Two of the most important committees operate somewhat outside this chain of responsibility. The first is the seven member *personal justice committee*, the worker-elected court. Official IGP policy guarantees its workers "full protection of your individual rights as a citizen of these United States, in particular freedoms articulated in the Constitution and known as the Bill of Rights." In practical terms, this means that "All decisions of the Personal Justice Committee shall be final," as the policy says, on disputes over pay, promotions, leave policy, job transfers, almost anything. The only exception is firings, which employees can appeal beyond the elected court to a special committee of three worker representatives and three managers. "It's sort of like the Supreme Court reviewing death penalties," Gibbons says.

- The committee that created the worker court is the *community relations assembly*, or CRA, the worker congress. Its 20 representatives are elected by popular vote, each by "constituencies" of about 15 employees. At least one CRA representative sits and votes on virtually every major committee in IGP, which ensures that at least one direct representative of "the people" votes on every decision.

  But the heart of the CRA's job is to formulate all the workplace policies that directly affect employees, from vacation rights to production standards, from hiring guidelines to wages. The CRA doesn't have final say, according to corporate policy; it sends its recommendations for "review" by the corporate operating committee and "approval" by the board.

Does it work?

When visitors observe IGP, they begin to ask the employees, "But does it *really* work?" It's a simplistic question that reduces the complex power relationships to an absurd yes or no. The more revealing questions include: how much power can employees exert over their day-to-day work life? How much power over the corporate finances and business? How much power can employees exert over financial questions that directly affect them, such as wages and benefits? And just as important: no matter how much or little power the employees have available through formal voting, how much power do they actually assert?

When it comes to the day-to-day life in this "economic community," as Gibbons calls it, the rank and file employees have enormous power available—and they use it. File clerks making under $11,000 a year hold an impromptu meeting one morning and vote to revamp the entire central files system, the guts of the corporation. Clerks churning out new insurance policies take a break to decide who should answer the telephone; they vote to rotate the hated task. A team of researchers, who answer clients' questions about their insurance policies, votes to hire a job applicant they interviewed the day before. The department coordinator hasn't even met her. "A department head," one researcher says, "shouldn't stick his nose into team business."

The worker teams also wield effective control over firing fellow employees, although the power is slightly ambiguous since team leaders and department coordinators also have the power to fire; the company has never firmly resolved just whose power should take precedent. In practice though, the rank and file employees have made firing a rare event in this company. A small drama flared one day in the life insurance department, when the team leader tried to fire a worker he said "wasn't producing." He quickly backed down when the worker's teammates marched angrily to his desk and declared he had no right to dismiss a teammate without consulting the team first.

Some employees at IGP complain that it's becoming *too* hard to get rid of troublesome and unproductive employees—"it's kind of scary to stand up to someone you've been friends with and say, 'sorry, you're not working out, you've got to go'," one claims clerk says. But workers do it. "We fired a dude last week," a mailroom clerk says. "When he didn't carry his load we had to do the extra work. We warned him, had meetings with him, put him on probation—he wouldn't listen." The worker appealed to the personal justice committee, but the court upheld the team's decision.

How the employee trust works

When IGP's founder and owner, James P. Gibbons, decided to give away half the corporate stock to the employees, he discovered it wasn't all that easy. Worker ownership and control are so rare in this country that there aren't many legal structures set up to achieve them. Gibbons couldn't just give away his stock, it turned out, without paying astronomical gift taxes.

"It took us almost two damn years just to work out the arrangement," recalls George Allen, a long-time member of the board of directors. "There just weren't any models to follow." What finally emerged: Gibbons doubled the shares of IGP stock in 1972 from 250 to 500. Then Gibbons—technically, the company—"sold" half the stock, or 250 shares, to a special employee trust. Any employee who works at IGP more than six months automatically becomes a member of the trust until he or she leaves.

The trust didn't give the company any cash for the stock; instead it gave the company an IOU to pay back the value of the stock, plus 6 percent interest, over approximately a decade. The value of the stock was fixed at around $1.7 million, based on an independent appraisal of the company's book value.

Now, each year, the board of directors votes to distribute a certain amount of the corporate profits to the workers, by transferring it to the trust. Under IRS regulations, the company can give the trust a maximum amount of profits each year equal to 15 percent of the corporate payroll. In a recent year, for instance, the company made $1 million profit and the board voted to transfer $.5 million to the employee trust, which was somewhat less that 15 percent of the payroll.

But since the employee trust is still paying off its IOU for the stock, it immediately pays back 50 cents of every dollar of profits that the board transfers to it. The company doesn't pay taxes on the profits that it gives to the trust, nor on the money it gets paid back. This means that the company can generate large chunks of capital, tax-free.

Each employee gets credited with an equal share of the profits each year; a manager earning $30,000 a year gets the same dollar amount as a mail clerk earning a third as much. Employees don't actually get to take their profits home, although they may borrow up to 25 percent of the profits they've accumulated at low interest rates—8 percent compared to more than 11 percent they'd pay at a private bank. When employees leave IGP, they will get their share of the profits in one of three ways: all at once, spread over five to ten years, or in the form of an annuity purchased from a life insurance company. They'll also get a portion of the current book value of IGP's stock, based on how long they've worked there.

The clerks paying insurance claims and peering in the microfilm machines don't exert direct power over department and division-level policies, since they don't have a direct vote on the operating committees. But most employees say they aren't interested in worrying about long term planning and budgeting.

They can, however, exert considerable informal power over department and division decisions when they feel the issues touch them directly. For one thing, there's a company commandment called the "IGP Decision-Making Model": it declares that no decisions may be made until all the workers directly affected have been consulted first. But more important, the workers exert power because there is an assumption that leaders are supposed to act on behalf of the employees and are to watch out for the employees' interests.

"We don't assert ourselves very often by taking initiative," says one claims examiner, "but people resist because they know they have the right to resist." When one department announced it was installing a new computer system to keep track of claims, for instance, the claims team announced they didn't like the system and would refuse to use it. "The computer people were forced to sit down with us and design it the way we liked," one team member said.

Managers who don't respond to the rank and file don't survive in their positions very long. "We called our department head before a meeting of the entire department to air a lot of grievances," one researcher says, "and one of the big issues was, do the people have confidence in the top man? We were terribly, painfully honest with him. We gave him a vote of confidence only to give him another chance."

No paper tiger

IGP employees also wield considerable power over the broad policies that govern their work life, through their Community Relations Assembly. On paper, the CRA seems like a glorified employee sounding board, one that has the empty "power" to *recommend* poli-

cies, which managers then can toss in the waste basket—since all CRA policies must be submitted for "review" and "approval" to the corporate operating committee and the board.

Many employees at IGP have never taken the CRA seriously for precisely that reason. Since Gibbons created the committee in 1973, CRA representatives have limped through occasional periods of inertia, paralyzed in self doubt as they ponder whether they really have any power.

"We've had a problem trying to figure out what our role is and what our limits are," one representative said. "Look, none of us have really believed we could ever have the power to do anything important," another said. "I mean, how many of us have ever been on a company committee like this before and been asked to make corporate policies?"

But however powerless these representatives may feel, recent members on the CRA have revised all the major workplace policies and started the disciplinary system working. As IGP employees later told participants at the Third International Conference on Self-Management, it was largely the CRA which drafted the company production standards, after "meeting with the different folks to find out what they thought a realistic standard of performance was," as one worker said. (Ironically, workers told the conference, the production employees and they CRA may have established standards too low, far lower than many workers had achieved before the standards were drafted. Workers who were paying 300 claims a week now pay only 175 under the standard; "and the quality of that 175 is not nearly as high as when they were doing 300," the employee told the conference).

Gibbons and several board members have consistently prodded the CRA to assert itself more. "The CRA acts like it's asking permission from the operating committee," said one board member, a professor in the school of business at the American University. "But I'd like to see the CRA become equal in power to the operating committee."

Describing IGP through the CRA, the teams, and other committees miss the spirit of employee

There's a sharp dichotomy at IGP between the daily world of work and the world of business. When it comes to making decisions on major financial issues, workers have little voice

power and freedom there, especially compared to employee feelings at traditional white-collar firms. A woman who works as a claims examiner at Geico, a major insurance company with headquarters in Washington, tells what it's like at her office. "A bell rings at 8:30 and if you're five minutes late they reprimand you," she says. She is speaking at home because "I'd get fired if I talked to you at the office. Clerks aren't supposed to drink coffee at their desks and they're not supposed to talk, unless it's about business. Supervisors assign us our work each day, and if we ask questions they tell us 'It's not yours to wonder why, just do as you're told.' I ask questions anyway, and they've classified me in my personnel file as 'insubordinate'."

At IGP, clumps of workers sit on their desks, drinking coffee and chatting about a recent CRA vote to reimburse workers for meals, transportation, and even babysitting fees if they work after hours or on the weekends. Work in one department comes to a noisy halt when the research team throws a baby shower for one of their teammates; the department coordinator doesn't scowl, he takes some wine and a piece of cake. There's no morning bell at IGP. "I've been coming to work at noon lately because I'm training some horses every morning at a stable," a researcher in the life insurance department says. "I stay and work until 8 o'clock."

The Geico employee has "never even met the company president"—but Gibbons and three top managers take 45 minutes one morning simply to meet with an angry IGP employee who has questions about disciplinary procedures "which just can't wait." And workers at Geico are afraid to speak out. At the IGP board of directors campaign assembly during a recent year, one candidate, a 24-year-old claims clerk, declared that "Gibbons has been feeding us a lot of bullshit and it's about time the people bring it to a halt." He received some healthy applause; then everyone adjourned to a conference room for a wine and cheese party and to vote.

When voices subside

There's a sharp dichotomy at IGP between the daily world of work and the world of business. When it comes to making decisions about what insurance packages to market, what strategies to use and what investments to make, the rank and file employees have little voice.

The theory behind the structure at IGP has been that "employees don't have any business making decisions about finances if they don't have financial expertise," one researcher explains. Instead, representatives accountable to the rank and file are supposed to make such decisions. Until a couple of years ago, financial decisions were handled by a finance committee, most of whose members were elected from each department. But it didn't work. For one thing, in the effort to be as democratic as possible, membership was rotated so often that individual representatives couldn't build up enough knowledge about the company's financial structure or about the workings of the committee to play a meaningful part. To make matters worse, former committee members say, many of the representatives had little financial background, and the company made no effort to provide training.

"Frankly, the meetings were terribly frustrating," one elected representative said. "Half the time I didn't know what they're talking about." Both these factors increased the tendency of the chief financial officer, the chairman of the committee, to "play the cards close to his chest," as one finance committee member recalls. "He controls the books, he controls the figures—so he'd make a recommendation and we had little choice but to nod our heads. We should have been more forceful, I know," the representative says, "but we were intimidated."

Since then the finance committee has faded away. Now most of the power to make financial and marketing decisions rests with the corporate operating committee, far from the rank and file, although there are a few possibilities for direct worker involvement. The chairperson of the CRA votes on the committee, but so far none of the chairpersons has learned enough

about the details of the insurance business to take an active part. And the Board of Directors, which is half elected by the employees, does have the power to reject operating committee decisions. A few years ago, the directors acted like the operating committee's rubber stamp—"one year the board hardly even met," recalls former board member George Allen. But the board has been asserting itself more and more as the voice of "the people." When managers on the operating committee insisted that they should control wage scales, for example, the board insisted that *it* would make the final decisions. "The operating committee is mostly managers," one board member explained, "when the people should have a large say in deciding wages."

Workers at IGP do exert substantial power over financial issues that touch them directly. The CRA largely drafted the last major wage scale revision, after consulting with rank and file employees; it was changed little by the board. CRA representatives also selected the company-paid health insurance plan, one of the most generous packages at any company in Washington.

And when really crucial financial policies come up, the board turns over the decision to the entire work force for a vote. It was the rank and file who voted to establish the remarkable, constantly rising minimum wage—now $10,600 per year—and it was the workers who decided how to divvy the profits. Most managers, not surprisingly, wanted to apportion profits as a percentage of salaries. But the rank and file, the two-thirds earning under $14,000 a year, voted to split the profits equally, to president and mail room clerk alike.

Now the caveat

Despite the many successes at IGP, the self-management system does not work as well as it might. For every team that asserts its autonomy and power, employees point to a team that shrinks from responsibility. For every decision that a committee reaches by democratic vote, workers point to a committee that waffles and submits to the decision of a self-styled boss. "There isn't one department in this community where the philosophy is even half working," Gibbons says with frustration. "This place," says a former member of the top operating committee, "is a mass of contradictions."

And the contradictions are nourishing worker discontent. The corporation preaches trust, maximization of humanness, and quality work, yet the absentee rate is increasing, turnover is high (up to 20% during the last few years), and some departments are mired in chronic backlogs and sloppy work. You can read the discontent in managerial memos that float around, warning of "tremendous tensions, anxieties, character assassination and balkanization." And you can read the mood in the only graffiti scrawled on the otherwise spotless men's room stalls. "IGP employees need to organize a union to protect and increase their working conditions," a dissident wrote in bold blue. "Self-management is a clever farce to keep wages low." About 25 percent of the workforce apparently agrees—and told a company-wide survey in 1975 they would support forming a union.

Workers at many companies, according to social surveys, are discontent with the status quo—their lack of power, their isolation, their alienating role as a cog in a vast corporate machine. But at IGP the workers' discontent stems from change: normal corporate power relationships have been turned upside down. Self-management at IGP, far from being a

"clever farce," has put power and responsibility up for grabs, and neither the managers nor the rank and file have ever been trained to handle it.

Advocates who have worked with democratic decision-making institutions emphasize some characteristics that make a self-managed enterprise strong. To begin with, workers need a sense of personal confidence, responsibility, and autonomy to manage their work and to make decisions on their own. An IGP employee, formerly a telephone operator, explains her plight: "At Bell Telephone we had to raise our hands just to ask permission to go to the bathroom. But at IGP we're supposed to do everything on our own. No one tells us anything." "The fact is," says a file clerk who used to work at the post office, "a lot of people need a boss standing over them, telling them exactly what to do."

While workers in a self-managed firm need independence, they also need to feel responsible to the collective. "I thought self-management meant you can get your work done whenever you want," one policy issue clerk complained. She was angry that her team reprimanded her for taking three days off during a hectic week. "That's not self-management," Gibbons writes in one of the two-page philosophical treatises he occasionally passes among the employees, "that's anarchy!"

The committee curse

And if committees are the cornerstone of decision-making—there are so many committees at IGP that one can scarcely count them—employees must master the art of listening to others, sharing opinions openly and hammering out a consensus acceptable to the whole group. Yet too many committees flounder at IGP because workers lack successful committee experience.

Committee members talk at once and can't hear what the others are saying, or they shrink from saying anything at all and let one or two members dominate. Many CRA meetings have accomplished nothing be-

128 IGP

"Lots of us come from such uptight work or school environments that it's hard to eye a less structured situation without suspicion"

cause representatives straggled in 45 minutes late, and team meetings have wasted time because workers felt too nervous to say what they really felt. No wonder two-thirds of the workers told the 1975 survey they think most committees are a waste of time. "God so loved the world," reads the sign on one worker's desk, "that he didn't send a committee."

Yet "The problem is not in having committees," as then board member George Allen wrote in the company newspaper, *Another Voice*, "but in how they operate." Committees of top managers aren't much better off. Managers on the corporate operating committee spent an hour trying to figure out why they tended to ramble instead of focusing on specific topics. They finally realized they had never prepared an agenda.

Many employees do plunge into the democratic decision-making process—over 40 percent of the workers at IGP have served on at least one decision-making committee. But as in any organization, from the PTA to the SDS, when a minority of the participants take on most of the burden they get exhausted before long. "After six months here, you just burn yourself out," says Jane Suppan, a researcher who has belonged to the CRA and innumerable other committees. "And you still have your normal work to put out."

While many employees feel overwhelmed and confused at their sudden rise to power, managers at IGP feel uncertain with their lack of it. "Damn it, don't think of yourselves as mangers, think of yourselves as leaders," Gibbons fumes at an operating committee meeting. "*Manager* implies control; *leader* implies government with equal rights." As self-management advocates emphasize, a good leader shares information with the rank and file employees, delegates power as much as possible, inspires and motivates workers rather than gives orders, and, most important, sees his or her role as working on behalf of the workers, not over them.

"Now you tell me," Gibbons says with a sigh one day, "where you can find leaders who have administrative and insurance experience who also believe in these democratic values? Right—nowhere."

"Managers are afraid and confused here because they lose the power of being the boss," says Del Clark, a former member of the corporate operating committee. More than 18 top managers—*leaders* as Gibbons says—have come and gone since 1974, partly because they couldn't handle democratic-style leadership. "At my last job if a secretary so much as talked back to me I could have said, 'Shazaam, you're fired, finished',," one department coordinator says. "But now at IGP if I try to boss someone around *I* could be fired, or at least deposed. After 20 years in the cutthroat business world, it's hard suddenly having to accept a secretary or mailroom clerk as equals."

Perils of democracy

Most leaders at IGP complain that group decision-making takes too much time in a business that demands quick action; and unless all the members of a committee are doing their required part, workers with committee experience agree, they're right. Some leaders have become so afraid of crossing the line between providing leadership and imposing dictatorship that they shrink from exercising any initiative at all. "And then," one division center forward says, "inertia sets in."

"I'm telling you, it's absolutely impossible to make every decision democratically," says Del Clark, who used to be center forward of the largest division in the corporation, with 200 employees. "Our committee would take three weeks trying to solve a problem I could have solved like that"—he snaps his fingers—"in a couple of days, and we'd get 99 problems a week. The department heads on the committee would all agree to do certain jobs during the week, and then at the next meeting they'd say they didn't have time. So if I took action on my own I'd be accused of being a boss. If I didn't, the work wouldn't get done and as division head I'd be blamed for it. I got so frustrated and confused," Clark says, "I just had to resign."

Continuing education in democracy

Some employees at IGP have suggested ongoing training programs which could better equip them to work together under self-management. They envision:

- Regular seminars for all employees on the history, philosophy and experiences of self-management. If workers at IGP learned there were historical roots to Gibbons' visions—if they knew that workers in Yugoslavia as well as plywood cooperatives in the Northwest were grappling with the same sorts of problems—they might feel more grounded in a movement, rather than alone and adrift.

- Regular seminars on how the business operates, from marketing insurance packages to investment finance.

- Regular forums, perhaps once a month, where top leaders could discuss the current financial status of the business, key issues up for debate in the corporate operating committee or the board, and could answer questions from the employees.

- Weekly meetings between CRA representatives and their "constituents," to share more immediate information about possible grievances or problems, policies pending in the CRA, and new policies that employees would like to propose.

- Methodical training in the art of group discussions and group decision-making, for every committee from the work teams to the board. The training should be handled by full-time employees skilled in group dynamics.

- Special training for every leader—teaching techniques from the art of chairing a meeting to demystifying technical information so the rank and file can understand it.

Now Clark works in a nonleadership position, where he has no direct accountability to other employees.

Combining employees together with managers who are equally unprepared for self-management creates a vicious circle. Teams, the CRA, and other committees don't meet their responsibilities and the work falls behind. Tensions rise as people sense the system isn't working; instead of asking themselves how to solve it they blame their leaders for failing them. The leaders blame the rank and file for dragging their feet and withdraw in defensiveness and secrecy. The workers become more hostile. "And then we all ramble along in no real direction," one researcher says.

The stalemate inevitably ends when a strong leader, usually Gibbons—impatient and furious at the breakdown, frantic for the system to work—plunges into the power vacuum and imposes his own solutions. Workers have watched Gibbons undercut his own carefully nurtured democratic structure many times, pleading "This is a business, we've got to go on." He solves the immediate crisis, employees argue, but contributes to a more profound crisis in the long run: cynicism.

"We have no power to do anything, really," a team leader scoffs after Gibbons has intervened in her department to unjam a work backlog. "Uncle Jimmy tells us we have the freedom to do what we want, but then he just goes ahead and does what he wants anyway."

"Lots of us come from such uptight work or school environments that it's hard to eye a less structured situation without suspicion," one employee wrote in the IGP newspaper. "Knowing only gross manipulation by employers or instructors, we expect it ... At least the old system clearly defines the enemy. Are we strong enough to risk a system where there may not be an enemy, other than our own cynicism?"

But many employees do acknowledge that when the system doesn't work as it should, they are at least partly to blame. "The mechanisms are all here, the freedom and power are all here for us to really take control and run this company the way we want," a

Selecting managers

For two years, starting July 1974, the 340 employee-owners of IGP conducted an astonishing experiment: they elected most of the top managers, by popular vote. From the time Gibbons transfered half ownership of the company to the workers, the community had been debating how to make its leaders more accountable to the rank and file. The board of directors had suggested forming an employee-elected committee to nominate a slate of candidates for each management spot, leaving the final choice to the corporate operating committee. The worker congress (the CRA) had suggested forming a committee composed of management to recommend a slate, leaving the final choice to employee elections. But the policy that became company law was Gibbons' idea, and it gave workers the most power. The workers would nominate the candidates, a joint worker and management committee would certify which ones were professionally qualified, and then the rank and file would elect the final choice.

In one department, the 30 production clerks who process insurance policies for clients like the National Council of Senior Citizens, a $2 million account, elected an affable former supermarket cashier as department head. He trounced a candidate who knew far more about the insurance business but who, one clerk explained, "was always stepping on the people's toes."

In the military department, which handles insurance for members of the Air Force Sergeants Association, the former department head, a retired military officer with a reputation for barking commands, wasn't even nominated. "Sure I would have liked to continue as department head," he said. "But if the people here don't like you, you don't have a chance in hell to succeed."

Over the next two years, employees at IGP elected and deposed numerous team leaders, department heads, and even division coordinators. The elections were embroiled in controversy from the start—partly because some workers were opposed to the principle, partly because the elections were not always handled well.

"The elections have become personality contests," a proofreader in the advertising department said. "We've elected some very nice idiots to run some of the departments." She was exaggerating: most employees said they did not elect any "idiots," but they did elect some leaders more for their personalities than for their administrative ability. Some of these leaders floundered badly, contributing to low morale and "chaos," as many workers put it.

In some departments, competent, experienced leaders became scapegoats for deep-rooted problems that weren't their fault. And the election process suffered from inconsistency: in some departments a leader was elected as soon as the spot became vacant, while in others the top operating committee installed a leader with little explanation and without an employee vote. Some teams and departments were leaderless for months if the employees couldn't find a candidate whom they were willing to elect.

"The elections came too much, too fast, " says a former board member who helped set up the process. "It was an awful lot of political activity all at once for a place that's never had it."

"I just don't think most people here are qualified—I don't think *I'm* qualified—to decide which people are qualified to serve in top leadership positions," a researcher added.

So in mid-1976, the worker congress, the top

operating committee, and the board all voted to revamp the leadership selection process. Here's how it now works:

The rank and file workers still elect their team leaders by popular vote. But their direct participation in the leadership selection process ends there. To select a department coordinator, a joint worker-management "search committee" certifies a slate of candidates who are professionally qualified, and qualified by virtue of their democratic "spirit," for the post; then the team leaders in that department and the other department coordinators elect one from the slate to become department coordinator. Division center forwards are chosen by the same kind of process: after a search committee picks a slate, the department coordinators in the division and the other division center forwards make the final selection.

If president Jim Gibbons leaves the company, the board of directors, the corporate operating committee, and the CRA will elect a new president.

"It's a good system," one claims examiner said. As the community policy says, the people doing the electing now are "completely informed about the expected duties and performance of the leader." Every six months, each leader will be "evaluated"—and ratified or deposed—by essentially the same process. If the workers in any department or division think their leader is doing a bad job, a majority can petition for a special evaluation any time they want.

"I think the people should elect all the leaders some day in the future," a team leader said, "but not until they're all really educated and informed. And that kind of education hasn't been dealt with. You can't allow people to vote who don't understand what the effect of their decision will be."

young claims examiner named Kurt Carr said, before he became elected department coordinator. "Why don't we? I don't want to call it ignorance. Let's call it lack of education—lack of education in democracy."

Education in democracy, many employees argue, is one area where IGP stumbles. The transition to self-management should be expected to be difficult, they say, but Gibbons neglected to make the transition smoother by creating long-term training programs to teach employees self-management values and skills. IGP has made some attempts at education: new employees take orientation courses in the philosophy and finances of the business, and at one time the board of directors held seminars with workers to teach them how the employee trust works. Over the years the company has hired various consultants to help committees work more effectively.

But these sporadic attempts to spread a little democratic or financial knowledge among the work force don't work. Gibbons acknowledges it: "I'm tired of these ad hoc, hit or miss part time efforts to solve problems. We need a long-term training program, and I want someone to get to work on it fulltime." But he adds in the same conversation: "People don't understand that we don't have the luxury of time for all this training. We're not an educational institution, we're a business, and we have economic problems that have to be solved."

What are the long-term prospects for self-management at IGP? Although the tensions are healthy—they indicate that the corporation doesn't squelch people but nourishes intellectual and emotional ferment—they are reaching a stage where they will move people in one of two directions: toward a more stable and smoothly working self-management structure, or toward a more traditional corporate hierarchy.

"We're at a critical turning point in this community," Gibbons acknowledges, "where the experiment is up for grabs. The people here have the power to throw me out, throw out all the values I stand for, even piss on me if they want."

For a time in 1976 it seemed as if Gibbons' values would be thrown out. The company, like the nation, is constantly swinging through varying political moods and 1976 was the year of the conservatives. To begin with, IGP faced considerable financial pressures: after 10 years of spectacular growth the company's income began leveling off, partly because of the nation's economy and partly because, after years of dominating the mail order health insurance market, IGP began to face some stiff competition.

Although the corporation was making a profit, some employees felt it wasn't making enough, especially at a time when some long-term debts were coming due. And employees were tiring of the constant changes in Gibbons' experiment. "People tend to be a lot more conservative when things keep changing," one researcher says. "They need something secure and stable to hold on to. And here," he laughs, "what you write about us today will be totally different six months from now."

The rank and file employees voted their mood in that year's board elections: they defeated the "liberal" candidates and elected a Washington bank president and an IGP manager known for his traditional, straight-line approach to business. Gibbons, who in the past appointed such people as a Marxist economics professor and a civil liberties lawyer to the board, picked three top managers with conservative fiscal reputations. "I figured it was time to put some financial knowledge on the board," he recalls.

To a point, most employees seemed to approve of the new climate. The CRA and the board revamped the election process so rank and file employees had far less power in selecting top leaders, and workers started putting more pressure on fellow employees who took too much advantage of liberal leave. "The place has the feel of a Republican administration," said Kurt Carr at the time. "The company is really cracking down now and becoming more conservative, and putting emphasis on the bottom line. But I think it's a healthy thing for democracy here in the long run. Things were getting too chaotic. We just have to

be careful that it doesn't swing too far in a conservative direction."

The pendulum swings back

But the climate did swing too far as top managers on the board and the operating committee began to argue that IGP's preoccupation with democratic values and workplace freedoms was damaging corporate profits. When a board resolution called for the end of some of IGP's basic workplace freedoms, however, the political mood swung back. The managers were ousted from the board, and a new group of directors known for their "liberal" and democratic outlook were elected to control the corporation. Gibbons' new appointees included Michael Maccoby, a self-management specialist who helped design the United Auto Workers-management Work Improvement Program at Harman Industries, and a production employee. "I'm saying, 'let's put people on the board again who will implement people policies, and not just think about profits," Gibbons said.

The recent events at IGP—the widespread conservatism, culminating in the unsuccessful effort by top managers to toss out fundamental worker powers and freedoms—suggest that IGP confronts a difficult paradox. As the workplace democracy grows stronger and employees feel more assertive, the workplace democracy itself may come under increasing attack. For until recently, most employees, including top managers, went along with Gibbons' visions even if they grumbled under their breath. "Nobody in this company comes right out and says to Jim's face, 'democracy sucks,'" a former board member said. But as more and more employees feel assertive, those who oppose Gibbons' goals are boldly speaking out. And the strongest opposition is among some of the leaders, who feel they have the most to lose.

"I came to IGP hoping to make vast sums of money," a former member of the corporate operating committee said, "but I've finally accepted the truth. This is not a company where any of us will get rich. Do you know that Jim could make $1 million a year if he wanted, yet when the board tried to raise his salary from $50,000 to $150,000, he threatened to quit? There are no stock options for us; a guy making $25,000 a year will leave with the same money after 20 years as a mailroom clerk making less than half as much. We don't get power, or prestige—most of us don't even have a private office. Democracy is nice," he said, "but I'm not sure I want it at my business." A few months later, he quit.

Ironically, one of the major obstacles to full self-management at IGP, employees say, will continue to be its most dynamic force—Jim Gibbons himself. The employees at IGP never asked for self-management. Gibbons alone dreamed the self-management vision, imposed it on the employees, and with his charisma made it work. But now employees say Gibbons' role is starting to stunt self-management's growth, for the employees can't quite shake the notion of Gibbons as the beneficent monarch and themselves as grateful subjects.

"I know I've got to go," Gibbons says, "because this experiment won't really have worked until it can function without me." He talks about giving his half of the stock and his board of director seats to a trust which would be controlled by IGP's clients. That would make IGP a worker and *community* controlled firm, the community being the company's clientele. So far, the plan is still a dream, primarily because the clients have expressed little interest in becoming part-owners of the corporation.

Questions for the future

IGP employees are asking difficult questions that every self-managed enterprise must ask and answer. Can a workplace democracy survive if some of the employees don't care to participate? According to the extensive but unscientific 1975 survey, less than half the employees who responded wanted "a lot of say" over selecting management, and not even one-third said they wanted "a lot of say" over hiring and firing fellow workers and deciding how corporate funds should be spent. The statistics coincide with workers' own perceptions; as one employee told the participants at the Third International Conference on Self-Management, "I would estimate 35-40 percent (of the employees) carry around in their gut the concern for the survival and the perpetuation of the enterprise, and are the ones who are most frustrated when contradictions erupt" and the self-management system doesn't work like it should.

The company confronts serious problems because not enough workers take an active part in company affairs, yet some employees argue that demanding worker participation is itself an "antidemocratic" rule. As one employee told the Third International Conference: "We might have done participative overkill to the extent that people really feel under pressure to participate and be involved. Somehow they perceive—and maybe it's real—that the amount they participate is tied to their rewards, to their status, to opportunities to really move through the organization. Our assumption had been up to rather recently that people who do not participate in the community's activities were not committed to the goals, principles and ideals of the company—which we're getting to discover is a wrong assumption. We have begun to emphasize, if people choose not to participate, 'you can be involved if you like, but if you don't that's OK.'" "Participation does not mean that everyone *must* participate," former board member George Allen wrote. "It only means that each person is given the *opportunity* to do so."

And IGP employees are asking other questions. Can a workplace democracy survive if some employees, including some key leaders, oppose it? Should the company hire only job applicants who swear they're committed to Gibbons' goals? Must every employee share the same values for the humanitarian structure to survive? Some employees suggest careful screening of job applicants: "We certainly don't want to hire people here who are opposed to the whole idea," says one veteran IGP employee. But others argue that rejecting workers who don't embrace the democratic and humanitarian goals is to *sabotage* those very goals.

"What some people are demanding is that we all have to share the same goals," says Fran Heaps, an administrator, "and I say wrong. As a citizen of this country I don't have to have the same values as my next door neighbor, do I? We have systems and safeguards in this country which give me the right to be who I am. Yes, some managers tried to toss out the system, but the people stopped them—which shows that the system works."

Despite its flaws, the system at IGP does work. Along with their griping, most employees acknowledge the company is the best place they have ever worked. "I've been offered far more money at other jobs, and sometimes I've been tempted enough to go for an interview," one employee says. "But the moment I walked in and saw all those rows of robots I knew a conventional job wasn't for me."

"We do bitch and complain an awful lot," says Jane Suppan, a researcher. "But it's like complaining about your own family. Deep down you really care what happens to them and love them. The truth is, IGP is the best thing that ever happened to me, so amazing that I feel trapped here. I'm trapped," Suppan says, "because I couldn't ever go back to a normal job again."

The 340 rank and file workers and managers are operating this $60 million corporation, and making a profit, with a degree of freedom, democracy and equality never before achieved by a major U.S. corporation. If they're facing problems, every corporation faces problems. The difference is that workers at IGP can shout their complaints and problems if they want, without fear of getting fired. More important, they've got the power to change their corporation.

Sources

Daniel Zwerdling, "At IGP, It's Not Business as Usual," *Working Papers for a New Society*, Spring 1977.

Zwerdling, "The Day the Workers Took Over," *New Times*, December 10, 1976.

Interviews by the editor with employees of International Group Plans.

Transcripts of the Third International Conference on Self-Management.

AU When people advocate bringing worker participation or self-management to an autocratic workplace, they usually envision machine operators in a smoke-belching factory or rows of robot-like typists in an office. But there is another workplace which traditionally has functioned as an autocracy, yet which students of self-management have usually ignored: the university.

In a typical university, top administrators hand out budgets and directives which the middle managers (the department chairpersons) must obey; the middle managers exert almost total control over hiring and even firing the supervisors (faculty). And in turn, the supervisors decide whether the production workers (or students) get promoted or flunked. The analogy is not exact, of course, since in this workplace the production workers, or students, are paying for the privilege of attending the institution. But the analogy is close enough — for in American higher education, the autocratic powers of university deans, department chairpersons, and faculty are legend.

The economics department at the American University, in Washington, D.C., operates under a dramatically different system. As the department brochure boasts, life in the department is "democratically structured." The chairperson, traditionally like a despot at many universities, has been stripped of most power and transformed into an administrator. Today all fundamental decisions are made democratically by a faculty-student council. The council, which is controlled to a considerable degree by the students, makes all basic decisions from admitting students to hiring professors, from deciding the curriculum to granting tenure.

The self-management system in the economics department suggests that universities, like any other workplace, can benefit from a self-management structure. But the experience there also points out the tensions, frustrations and problems which confront any workers who move from an autocratic system toward a democratic one. Bringing self-management to the university is, perhaps, a vivid way to begin teaching students what it takes to live and work in a democracy.

A rebellious birth

The faculty-student democracy at the American University economics department was born during the student rebellions of the late 1960's. The economics department already had reformed the process for selecting the department chairperson; instead of being appointed the chairperson was elected by the faculty, by majority vote. Several years before, the faculty had added nonvoting student representatives to the department faculty council.

But then came the student rebellions of 1968, and students at AU seized several campus buildings. Rather than send in the police, as many universities did, the administration negotiated a settlement with the students which paved the way for a more democratic student government. Under the new system,

university policies were formulated by a campus senate, one third administrators, one third faculty and the rest students. The university administration urged individual departments to adopt the same system, and most did. But most departments sharply limited the power of these councils by defining their decisions as merely "recommendations."

Several professors in the economics department envisioned a more powerful role for the faculty-student council. They hammered out a set of bylaws, then lobbied for support among their colleagues, and faculty-student self-management was born.

The way things work

As the bylaws spell it out, the department is managed by a council composed of all the faculty plus half as many student representatives; therefore, the students cast one third of the council's total votes. During the 1976-77 academic year, there were 18 faculty and nine students on the council; three student representatives were elected by undergraduates, three by graduates and three by PhD students.

The council, according to the bylaws, has "exclusive exercise of authority" over academic policies, including "developing academic programs, admitting students, granting fellowships, hiring faculty, and making decisions on faculty promotions and tenure." The faculty-student council elects the chairperson of the department, but under the self-management system the chairperson is little more than an administrator. In fact, the bylaws practically apologize for having one ("the faculty has a chairman who executes the policies collectively established," the bylaws explain, "for reasons of expediency").

Although the council is designed to exercise final control over all fundamental decisions, several committees chosen by the council screen various proposals and formulate recommendations for council approval:

- The *faculty affairs committee* — three faculty and one student — exerts considerable power over hiring new faculty and promoting current faculty,

because it screens applicants. "The committee doesn't make decisions but it filters recommendations to the council," says former department chairperson Howard Wachtel. "The committee recommends what type of economist to hire — political, Marxist, or traditional — and then it pares down the number of applicants from around 300 to 20."

- The *educational programs committee* — three faculty and three students — screens proposals for new courses or any changes in the curriculum, recommends candidates for fellowships, and formulates guidelines for all the important comprehensive exams.The committee also makes final decisions on admitting new students to the department. "This is an especially powerful role, admitting the PhD's, Wachtel says, "because the committee can admit only 15 or 20 applicants out of 80 or 90 applicants each year."

- Departmental grievances and disputes are referred to a *grievance committee*, comprised of equal numbers of faculty and students, which meets only a few times each year.

- And finally there is the *executive committee* — the department chairperson, the chairpersons of the faculty affairs and educational programs committees, plus one graduate and one undergraduate student. The executive committee is charged with managing the department affairs week to week — setting up council agendas, scheduling courses, resolving small disputes and handling other administrative details.

Dramatic changes

Since the faculty-student democracy was born, department faculty and students agree, it has dramatically changed the character of the entire economics department. "When I came to this department from the University of Oklahoma, it was run completely hierarchically," says professor James Weaver, co-co-editor of the book, *University and Revolution.* "The chairman was appointed top-down by the administration with no role for the faculty in that choice, and the chairman really was an autocrat. We, the faculty, had no power in hiring, firing, promotion or tenure. And the administration's control over the teaching was incredible. We all had to use the same textbook, had to give the same final. It was a highly regimented way of life.

"Now," Weaver says, "the faculty and the students have an awful lot of power, you wouldn't get any dissent on that. And the chairman really is powerless." At a typical meeting of the department council, an observer discovers, the chairperson plays a far less visible role than many of the faculty and students. He often asks the council, "So what should I do, what do you want me to tell the dean?"

Under the original bylaws, the faculty in the economics department was to reign supreme, even though students would have considerable voice. Giving the faculty two-thirds of the council votes, for example, was designed to make sure the faculty could ultimately control the department.

"A fundamental principle underlying the function and governance of the department is that its faculty possesses, and is in the process of enhancing, the knowledge, the skills, and the experience in the discipline for which it is established to instruct, investigate and help coordinate the total resources available to it," the bylaws declare. "As a matter of principle, then, the policies of the department should be determined by its faculty . . ." The bylaws add that "voting student representation is deemed desireable" in order "to institutionalize the contribution of student insight and understanding" and "to insure a regularized way of remaining sensitive to student need and interest." But in practice, the students in the economics department have been far more powerful than their one-third minority would suggest. For one thing, there has been a spirit in the department receptive to student proposals. When the students take a unified position on a matter which directly affects them, such as curriculum, the faculty has usually gone along. The students have also become the most important swing bloc when the council casts a vote. The faculty in the economics department have been fractured just about equally among conservatives, liberals and radicals, while most of the student representatives have tended to be radical. When the radical faculty and the student representatives vote as a bloc, which they often do, they can control the council.

Today, students in the economics department at AU are able to *vote* for innovations and changes in their education which students at other universities have had to plead for. "There's no problem getting any courses taught that students want," says PhD candidate Chuck Sherer, a former representative on the council. For instance, students have proposed, and the council has voted to create, special courses on women and economics, economic history of the labor movement, and black political economy.

The students have pushed for, and won, major changes in the department course requirements. "We've eliminated almost completely the course requirements for doctoral programs which the students didn't like," Wachtel says. "Most departments in the university require students to take required courses for about half their course load. But because of students on the council, we now require only about four prescribed courses, or one eighth of the total course load."

At most universities, comprehensive exams for graduate students have always been scheduled at the convenience of the faculty; at AU, the student votes on the departmental council have swayed the system so that exams are scheduled at the convenience of the students. "And as a result of student pressure on the

Today, students in the economics department at AU can vote for changes and innovations in their education. Students at other colleges can only demonstrate—or plead

council," says Wachtel, "we've introduced a special comprehensive exams preparation course, to help students prepare for the exams. In another department that wouldn't ever have happened."

Voting for help

During the 1977 academic year, the council called a special session to discuss widespread student complaints that some of the courses taught by graduate fellows were boring and a waste of time. "If the chairman had his way," said professor Larry Sawyers, "the senior faculty would simply take over and the grads would be relegated to discussion leaders. But the students and the junior faculty were opposed to letting the faculty take over, which would deny graduates that teaching experience. The graduates wanted more teaching *help*, and said the experienced staff had been ignoring them."

The council voted to allow graduates to continue to control their courses, but also voted to form a special seminar in which the graduates could get badly needed guidance. "Instead of dumping on us, the department supported us," one graduate said with relief.

The democratic council has also shaped the character of the faculty in the economics department. In most universities, new faculty are hired by the chairperson, perhaps with some recommendations from the current teaching staff. But the system here has given students considerable control over the *kinds* of economists the department has hired, as well as control over which individuals have joined the staff.

"We've hired six or seven new faculty in the last couple years," Wachtel says, "and since hiring new faculty requires a two-thirds vote of the council, the student vote is crucial. It takes a tremendous amount of time building consensus toward a decision. First we have to build a consensus about what kind of economist to hire — do we hire a Marxian or a traditional economist? — and then we have to build a consensus on which individuals we want."

Largely because the self-management system has

given power to students and young faculty who tend to have radical politics, the economics department has hired an unusually large number of progressive and radical faculty. At least a third of the faculty call themselves Marxists: this has earned the department a reputation as one of the few university economics departments in the nation which gives Marxist-oriented research courses equal weight with traditional economic points of view.

The self-management system has also turned the task of granting or denying tenure — legendary in American universities for its secrecy and political intrigue — into an open and democratic process.

Traditionally, the chairperson and the already tenured faculty would give an applicant their stamp of approval — or their kiss of academic death — with little or no explanation. Applicants who failed to get tenure would never know who squashed their future plans, or why. But in the AU economics department, professors who are applying for tenure have total access to their personnel file. They can read everything that has been written about them, and know exactly who said it, too. Professors can even encourage students to write letters of support. "No other department in this university, and as far as I know, no other university in the country, would allow the professors to open up their personnel files this way," Wachtel says.

When the department was building its student-faculty democracy council, it was clear the chairperson and tenured faculty could no longer control the tenure process. But the tenured faculty, still a powerful force, opposed the notion that the student-faculty council should assume complete control. They compromised: first, a committee comprised of all the tenured faculty, plus one nontenured professor, plus a student, screens candidates and sends its recommendations to the council. Then the department council votes on a final choice.

How does the department resolve a disagreement? Until several years ago, faculty say, the committee and the department council always agreed on the same choice — so democracy triumphed while the tenured faculty felt satisfied they still influenced the process. But recently there was a major clash. The committee voted 8-3 against a young professor, a Marxist; the council voted overwhelmingly *for* him.

The professor says he never felt the decision was politically motivated, although students who launched a campus-wide protest believed it was. The department chairperson attempted to resolve the dispute by voting to grant the professor tenure, only to be overturned by the dean—who has always had, but rarely exercised, the technical right to overturn department policies—who in turn was overruled by the university vice-president. So the professor received tenure, but the dispute has left some lingering political tensions.

The dispute points out one of the contradictions in the department's democratic system. Although the university administrators have seldom exercised it, they have the ultimate power to reject any of the department's decisions — which means that, should an autocratic administrator take power, the department's decision-making process could potentially become a sham.

Democracy to excess?

Many self-management systems suffer because the employees don't participate enough and shrink from exercising their power. But there's no lack of participation in the self-management system in the AU economics department. Most of the faculty and students are highly articulate and self-confident; "our problem is never that people don't participate," one faculty members says, "it's the reverse—everyone wants to talk everything into the ground two or three times over." Some professors charge that the students and faculty, especially the students, wield *too much* power: they say self-management is going too far. "I support the self-management system strongly," says Wachtel, "I was on the committee that drafted the rules. I was a strong advocate of 'all power to the council.' But my experience has been sobering. I agree that excessive democracy has led to an erosion of self-management."

What does Wachtel consider excessive democracy? Wachtel and other faculty, as well as students, say that "self-management" has come too often to mean that the entire council should decide every issue, no matter how routine or trivial.

"The original idea was that the council would make broad decisions on curriculum and vote on promotions and hiring," says Wachtel, "and the executive committee, on advice of the other committees, would decide the one million smaller issues. For example, maybe there's a small conflict between the chairman and a faculty member, or someone doesn't want to teach a course at a particular time, or they've got to come up with some budget information — the executive committee would handle those. But that hasn't happened. A major problem now is that people come to the council as a final place of appeal for every issue. They don't like to go to the committees. They want to force the whole department to make a decisive vote. So now we have the entire council deciding who should teach what course, who should get what office space — resolving every dispute which comes up when a faculty member doesn't like something the chairman or some committee did — I mean, we were meeting every week for at least two or three hours, and it's utterly draining and exhausting."

Delegating authority to the chairperson or the committees — a normal process in many self-managed systems — has become practically taboo in the economics department. "The chairman is really powerless," professor James Weaver says. "The point has come where the chair can't make day-to-day decisions. If he decides something that people don't like they bring it up to the council and reverse him. Well, that's fine for really important issues but not every picky detail. The problem is, we haven't ever defined well what should be an *administrative* decision, and what decisions need a democratic *consensus*."

The council representatives have been talking about changing the bylaws to define more rigorously just what issues should be delegated and what issues require a department-wide vote. "There's a tendency in both business enterprises and in self-governing institutions," Howard Wachtel told the Third International Conference on Self-Management, "to think that self-management or work decision-making means that everybody decides everything. My own feeling is that if you try to set up a situation where everybody's supposed to decide on everything, in the end nothing will get decided. It will degenerate into administrative chaos, which will lead to the destruction of the very system of self-government."

Another mixed blessing in the self-management system, faculty and students seem to agree, is that the atmosphere of open debate and challenge has tended to sharpen political and ideological differences — so much that virtually every issue becomes a political issue, forcing students and faculty into opposing political camps.

"It seems as if there are no longer votes simply for the sake of having the best quality department," one professor says, echoing a widespread complaint. "All the votes are aimed toward preserving the proper ideological line." The political climate usually pits the conservative faculty against the radical faculty and students, with the "liberal Democrat" faculty caught somewhere in the middle. "It's produced a sort of 'up against the wall' spirit in the department at times," says Weaver, "and trust and respect essential to make the self-management system work have broken down. There's a faction of radicals who, any time a decision goes against them, mount a political campaign."

Weaver cites an incident in which a PhD candidate failed his comprehensive exams in Marxian economics, because two of the three professors on the jury failed to give a passing grade.

Instead of taking his comprehensives over again, Weaver says, "he insisted the failure was politically motivated, and took the issue to the department council, organizing meetings, petitions, putting tremendous pressure on the professors to change their grade." One professor changed his mind under political pressure, and the student passed the exams.

Even the three department secretaries, treated like machines in most offices, elect one voting representative to the council and plunge into department politics. One of the most bitter fights inside the department erupted when a secretary refused to type letters or reports to which she objected on political grounds. The council split down the middle when the chairperson attempted to fire her, although he eventually won and the worker was dismissed. In another incident the secretaries refused to organize the comprehensive exams and set up the schedules, because students were displeased with the scheduling. "I had to do it myself," the former chairperson says, "and a segment of the faculty complained I was undermining the solidarity of the secretaries."

But some of the radical faculty and students charge, as one professor says, that "most of the divisiveness in the department comes from tenured professors who have never really been reconciled to a democratic way of making decisions or to a Marxian economics program."

"Self-management requires enormous good will — there has to be a lot of reconciling," Weaver says. "Self-management requires you to be able to compromise and negotiate. But that's what has too often been in short supply."

Pains of responsibility

Self-management also confronts members of the economics department, students and faculty alike, with some painful responsibilities, such as critically evaluating their peers. "A system of self-management has an ideological premise of solidarity," Wachtel told the Third International Conference on Self-Management, "you know, 'everybody's in this democratic decision-making process together.' But that premise clashes with the educational function of critical evaluation."

For instance, faculty say they find it difficult to vote against a colleague who is up for tenure, in a department council meeting — even if they feel the colleague is not qualified. "Voting against someone is almost like voting against themselves. It's the kiss of death, especially when the job market is so lousy," as Wachtel told the conference.

Students find it hard in council meetings to judge fellow students—yet when student-faculty committees and the council take over the job of dispensing and denying fellowships, they *must*. According to department rules, graduate students cannot renew their fellowships if more than 30 percent of their courses are incomplete (the department council voted a much more lenient standard than the rest of the university, which sets the limit at 20 percent). But now that students help control the fellowships, according to former chairperson Wachtel, students who have not completed as much as half their courses are getting their grants renewed.

The self-management system has made the economics department a kind of island in the university, with its own rules and its own unique ways of making decisions. This unique work style creates occasional conflicts between the department and the university administration. The university administration, for instance, requires department chairpersons to take responsibility — under a written contract — for a host of specific decisions and tasks. Yet as former economics department chairperson Thomas Dernburg says, "as far as the department is concerned the chairman is not much more than an administrative secretary."

"I'd get a phone call from the administration telling me 'it's your responsibility, do it,' " Wachtel told the Third International Conference on Self-Management. "But I couldn't do it without subjecting myself to the censure of the department.

"On January 20 I'd get an administration memo saying I *must* send decisions on new faculty salaries by February 4," Wachtel said. "Hell, salaries are an incredibly complicated issue in the department, and we debate for weeks and weeks every year. But the council won't, can't meet for another week. What do we do? The administration is tired of hearing us say the decision will take longer, because we have to make the decision democratically. They'll say, 'We'll make the decision instead.' "

Now the backlash

The administration is distraught by what it considers to be overly permissive standards passed by the department council. For example, graduate fellows persuaded the council to reduce their workload from teaching two courses a week to teaching only one. The administration was displeased; while it didn't veto the decision, it struck back by allocating a third less fellowships to the economics department the following year.

"The administration thinks we're crazy," chairperson Dernburg says, "they're always threatening to step in and make sure it's run the way the university expects it to be run. People around here (on campus) talk of putting the department into receivership."

There's even a faction in the economics department which advocates cutting back sharply on self-management, and pulling in the reins on student power. "It might mean giving students less participation and giving the chairman more authority," says Dernburg. "I just don't think it's really been all that healthy an influence.

"I don't think we get good decisions; what we get is extra hassle. Not that I don't like students and don't respect them," Dernburg says, "but it's silly, this idea that students should be involved in everything. Take this business of hiring new faculty for example. Students are of no use because they don't know what the hell some fellow is talking about [when he is describing his research]—not that all the faculty do either," he laughs. "But I mean, experience does count for something, doesn't it? But this system denies it. Do you know that we have a department that has never had a faculty meeting? That's incredible. Students come to *all* the meetings. I think we should sharply restrict the role of the students."

The economics department at American University is a case study of a self-managed workplace plagued by problems and frustrations and constant ferment — yet, students and faculty alike say, they wouldn't trade the problems for the stultifying autocracy of a traditional department. The department may be

"Self-management has made the students much more exciting to have in the classroom. There's no other place I would want to teach."

plagued with problems and conflicts, most students and faculty say, but the problems and conflicts are handled in the open.

"This system is still infinitely better than the traditional way," says professor James Weaver, "it's infinitely better to have a voice than be powerless in an autocracy. It's reinforced my conviction that self-management is a *good* idea. If things are bad, we can do something about it. Before, if I didn't like what was going on I couldn't do anything but kick my dog. Now I can take the problem to the council, or to committee. We can even recall the chairman if we think he's not doing a good job."

The self-management system has also torn down the traditional hierarchy which separate professors and students into rigid classes. "When I went to school, an assistant professor didn't ever go to the same parties as an associate professor, let alone a full professor," says professor Larry Sawyers, "and let alone students, who didn't associate with any faculty. But here there's a free mixing; you'll often find students mixing with professors at a party." Sawyers attributes the change partly to the era, but also to the sense of equality self-management has brought to the department.

Despite the problems and squabbles, many students and faculty agree self-management has made the economics department a more exciting and higher quality place to study and teach. "One of the paramount results of self-management," Wachtel says, "is that now we put enormous emphasis on the quality of teaching — because student members on the council keep pushing teaching quality. Without the students there putting on the pressure, we wouldn't give a thought to teaching quality. We'd worry only about research.

"So although I talk a lot about my gripes," Wachtel says, "still I think it's a very exciting place. There's no other place I would want to teach. Self-management contributes to my sense of excitement, and it does force us into an atmosphere with good discussions about curriculum, about grades, about what the students and faculty see as priorities. Other departments can get stagnant doing the same old stuff over and over. And self-management has made the students, because they do feel so much a part of the department, much more exciting to have in the classroom. They come to class from committee meetings where they've been talking with the faculty as equals, and they're far more willing now to ask challenging and stimulating questions. I wouldn't trade it," Wachtel says, "for any other system of education."

Sources

"Statute of Academic Governance," Department of Economics, The American University.
Interviews by the editor with members of the economics department at American University.
Transcripts of the Third International Conference on Self-Management.

BRITAIN

**British Business is Enraged
By Promise of Worker Power**

*LONDON, JAN. 26, 1977 — Despite out-
raged cries from Britain's business, the Labor
government today promised "radical" legislation this year to put workers on the boards
of all large corporations.*

*The plan for worker directors . . . would
enable unions to pick a number of directors
equal to those chosen by stockholders in all
firms with 2,000 or more employees. More
sweeping than any existing European version
of industrial democracy, it would give
worker representatives a powerful voice in
every major corporate decision.*

The Washington Post

With the Bullock Report, as Britain's
controversial worker power proposal has
come to be called, workplace democracy
has officially arrived as a major public
issue in Great Britain.

Observers in Britain say the public awakening to the workplace democracy issue has been a slow, but gradual process. Unlike other European nations such as France and Sweden, where workers' control has long been considered a highly visible, if widely debated, political issue, worker self-management has never been widely discussed in Britain — at least, not before the past decade. There *were* flurries of worker self-managed enterprises established during the 1800's; by the year 1900, there were about 2,000 worker producer cooperatives in England, according to the *Economist* magazine.

But, like the worker cooperatives which sprouted in the U.S. during the 1800's, most of the British self-managed firms died from lack of capital. "Today only about 20 of these earlier worker co-ops survive," Richard Fletcher told participants at the Third International Conference on Self-Management, "and the majority are in financial difficulties."

The British trade union movement, like its counterpart in the U.S., grew strong on a philosophy opposing the notion of workers' control, embracing instead a strong collective bargaining relationship with management.

But during the past decade, British delegates told participants at the Third International Conference on Self-Management, union and public opinion on the self-management issue have changed rapidly. "The movement for workers' participation in management and control," says Walter Kendall, a leading British advocate of workers control, "has now begun to flourish and show life anew."

Signposts toward democracy

Observers point to the following signposts which, they say, suggest Britain is heading toward more workplace democracy:

- Since 1964, a labor organization called "Voice of the Unions" has held nine national conferences, each attended by a thousand trade union delegates, to "carry the message of workers' control to the broadest layers of the trade union and socialist movement," according to Kendall. The large attendance at the conferences, plus the large circulation of a rank and file newspaper, *The Voice of the Unions*, which advocates workers control, suggest that acceptance of the idea is spreading in the trade unions, according to some observers.

- In 1968, there were "two significant strides" toward workplace democracy, according to G. David Garson, professor of political science at Tufts University. First, the British Labor Party called for corporations to "open the books" — to open their financial records to union representatives. Second, union and government officials launched a campaign to "establish workers' councils with powers of oversight in nationalized steel" companies, Garson reports. A compromise plan provided instead for placing worker representatives on the boards of directors of the steel firms.

- Starting in 1970, there has been a rash of worker "takeovers," or "work-ins," as they are called, at companies which management planned to shut down. Best known was the massive work-in by 700 workers at the Upper Clyde Shipbuilders in 1971. When management announced it was closing the shipyards and laying off the workers, the employees seized the yards and kept the business operating on their own until the conflict was settled.

Another widely publicized work-in occurred in the Plessey Ltd. torpedo factory, also in 1971. The management announced plans to close its plant due to "falling international demand," as Garson reports. "Rather than leave, the fired workers voted to take over the works, which they did. After a 20-week occupation, an agreement was reached whereby a new joint company was formed to develop the ... works as an industrial site." Garson stresses that "Neither Clyde nor Plessey led to workers' control, but both raised control issues and intensified labor militancy on such issues as assertion of the right to veto plant closings." Kendall reports

"The aim is to give workpeople collective participation and control over decisions which the collective bargaining and consultative process have not given them"—Bullock Report

there were at least 50 such "work-ins" in 1972 alone.

- In 1974 and 1975, workers at several companies which were closing down negotiated to take over the firms and operate them permanently under worker self-management systems. The government was instrumental in getting financial assistance for the new worker-owned firms, which include a motorcycle factory and a Scottish newspaper (see case studies below).

- In 1974, the British Trade Union Congress — the TUC, a loose federation of unions roughly counterpart to the U.S. AFL-CIO — officially proposed for the first time that workers be placed on corporate boards of directors. Under the TUC proposal, worker representatives, elected through the unions, would take half the board seats on all major companies; the boards would be "the supreme authorities of the companies," according to the Report by the TUC General Council to the 1974 Trades Union Congress. "The aim must be to give legal rights to workpeople of collective participation and control over decisions which the collective bargaining and consultative process have not given them."

The Bullock debate

The most recent and most dramatic development in the trend toward workplace democracy in Great Britain was publication of the report of the government-appointed Bullock Commission, formed in 1974 to explore the future of worker participation in industry. The Commission was set up, according to a government document, "accepting the need for a radical extension of industrial democracy in the control of companies."

The report, chaired by Oxford historian Alan Bullock, largely followed the recommendations of the TUC, as well as one of the nation's most powerful unions, the Transport Workers Union. The plan would affect more than 700 major corporations, employing more than a third of Britain's 18 million workers.

Under the plan worker representatives elected through the unions would take one third of the seats on each corporate board, the shareholders would elect another third, and then the worker and shareholder representatives together would elect the final third of the board (if they couldn't agree, a special government commission would select the remaining directors).

The new plan, said the Bullock Report, would "tap the energies and skill" of the nation's workers by "putting the relationship of capital and labor on a new basis which will involve not just management but the whole workforce in sharing responsibility for the success and profitability of the enterprise."

The proposal is still being debated — heatedly — in the government and in industry. The Institute of Directors, an association of corporate board members, said the plan has "about as much justification as the Emperor Caligula's idea of making his horse a consul," according to *The Washington Post*.

In spite of the protests, a report by the National Quality of Work Center concludes that most managers "seem resigned that board representation (of workers) is inevitable; question in British management no longer seems to be whether Britain will have co-determination, but how much, and in what forms." British public opinion polls and "intense public discussion of industrial democracy," the report concludes, show the public now "generally favors worker board representation."

As social and political pressures nudge Britain toward giving workers power on the boards of directors, some experiences at isolated enterprises suggest that even more extensive systems of worker self-management can work. Three case studies follow: the first focuses on a worker controlled motorcycle factory still going strong; the second looks at a short-lived experiment in worker self-management on a daily newspaper; the third details an entrenched and thriving worker control system in a major chemical products firm.

The Meriden experiment

One of the most important experiments in worker democracy is still going strong, in the British Triumph Bonneville motorcycle factory, in Meriden. Only three years ago, in early 1975, the Triumph plant was a subsidiary of a large privately owned corporation. Today, "All workers, including managers and engineers, are paid equally," write researchers Martin Carnoy and Henry Levin in *Working Papers*. "Managers and supervisors are elected. Workers participate in financial and shop-floor decisions. Jobs are rotated." While the Meriden experience is not the first instance of a worker takeover or worker self-management system in Britain, Carnoy and Levin write, "it is the first in which the workers struggled so long, won so much, and succeeded in getting the government to support their objectives."

The Meriden worker control experiment dates back to September, 1973, when the corporate owner of the plant—Norton Villiers Triumph—announced the factory would be closed in an effort to cut financial losses in the company's Triumph Division, which manufactured the popular Triumph Bonneville motorcycle. [The summary which follows is based partly on Carnoy and Levin's excellent reports in *Working Papers*]. The workers read about their own fate in the evening newspapers sold outside the factory's gates: all 1,750 workers would be laid off, over a gradual five month period.

Instead of going along with the layoffs, Carnoy and Levin report, "800 of the 1,750 workers occupied the plant and refused to leave." As far as the workers were concerned, the plant's financial woes were caused by sloppy management—parts weren't ordered efficiently, workers said, and overhead had ballooned with an unnecessarily large sales force. The corporate owner was planning to call in the police to oust the workers from the plant, but changed his mind when local politicians warned a police action might spark a mass sympathy strike by other workers in the area.

This gave the demonstrating workers precious time, according to the *Financial Times* newspaper—time to start negotiating with the management about buying back the plant and running it as a workers' cooperative.

Negotiations dragged on for more than a year; the number of workers occupying the plant dwindled as financially-pressed workers were forced to find jobs in other factories.

Numerous obstacles and breakdowns in negotiations threatened to scuttle the whole plan: in one instance, for example, the government gave the workers a tentative agreement to lend them enough money to purchase the plant, only to have the corporate owner cancel the agreement by declaring that the purchase price was too low. In another instance, *workers* lobbied against the plan. As the *Financial Times* reported, 1,250 workers at another NVT plant which had been scheduled to take over Bonneville production after Meriden shut down "strongly opposed the [worker cooperative] scheme since they felt it put their own jobs in jeopardy."

But finally, the Labor government's minister for industry, Anthony Benn, helped clinch a deal: the government would lend the workers 4.2 million pounds for 15 years, at 10 percent interest, to purchase the plant, plus another 750,000 pounds as starting capital. In March 1975, the Meriden workers became owners of their own enterprise.

How it works

Here's how the worker cooperative evolved, as reported by Carnoy and Levin:

The workers don't actually own shares in the plant; instead, three shares are held in trust by three trustees, acting on behalf of the worker "beneficiaries."

"Everyone gets the same pay—50 pounds per week—including managers, engineers and office workers. Policy decisions are made by eleven directors, including eight elected supervisors (who come from the eight unions in the plant), an outside representative from the external management (Norton Villiers Triumph), a representative from government, and a representative from the Transport and General Workers Union confederation. In addition, a plant manager sits with the directors to ensure harmony between everyday managerial decisions and board decisions.

"This eleven person committee is responsible for all major decisions in the plant, though financial decisions are customarily referred to a workers assembly. Each of the 280 workers who remained in the plant to the end of the negotiations currently receive five votes in this assembly. New workers (the original 800 who conducted the September 1973 occupation will get first priority in hiring) will get one vote after one year in the plant and an additional vote for every year they put in up to five years. The present plan is to bring the plant up to 'capacity' with 700 workers.

"The management of the firm, though appointed by the directors, is directly responsible to the workers for its policies . . . The demarcation between jobs has disappeared; workers clean up after themselves; jobs are rotated; some teach their jobs to others . . . We observed workers doing several different jobs as they became needed to carry out various tasks . . . This simple change has startling implications for the or-

ganization of work: in place of specialists committed only to the completion of a single operation and having no responsibility for other operations, the Meriden plant's structure encourages each worker to assume a variety of responsibilities. The division of labor between skilled and unskilled workers is thereby reduced, and the division of authority between workers and management overlaps substantially."

The writers report that the mood in the plant has changed dramatically since the takeover. "The most important single change in Meriden, according to the workers we interviewed, occurred in the relationships among the people themselves . . . The machines in the plant are now theirs, and whatever they produced was their responsibility. They now had to deal with each other as equals in a common cause." During the first year under workers' control output per worker soared 50 percent.

An uncertain future

After Carnoy and Levin filed this report, the Meriden plant was hit by a series of crises that threatened to destroy the living experiment in worker self-management. When the workers bought the factory, they had agreed—as part of the takeover deal—to surrender to NTV complete control over marketing of the motorcycles. But NTV's financial empire started crumbling, and its marketing operations crumbled with it—and the Meriden workers began losing enormous sums of money as sales of their bikes lagged far behind production. A coalition of government and industry officials crafted a financing and marketing scheme to save the Meriden plant, but in return they forced the workers to adopt a new management structure. Today, the 720 workers now in the factory have yielded day-to-day control of the operation to five fulltime managers, who are paid professional salaries and are not members of the co-op.

Despite the new management scheme, Carnoy reports, the Meriden workers "have compromised only a little with the strong sense of egalitarianism that developed during the occupation." Co-op members rejected the managers' proposal to impose a hierarchical pay scale; workers are still paid equally, now £68 per week plus another £17 in overtime and bonuses. "The atmosphere of the plant is still relaxed and friendly," Carnoy writes, "job rotation goes on as before . . . Directors are still very much accountable to the membership."

And the workers have used their self-management power to vote themselves benefits "not available in any other plants"—including free life insurance, time off for medical and dental visits, and a remarkable 26 weeks of sick leave with pay. The future of the Meriden plant is still fragile, but the workers are optimistic. The plant is now the only motorcycle factory left in Britain, and by the end of 1979, the co-op workers expect to be operating in the black.

The Scottish Daily News

In March 1974, the corporation which owned the Scottish Daily Express newspaper in Glasgow, Scotland, announced it was going to shut down the Glasgow paper and move operations to another city. The newspaper's employees, however, occupied the workplace—and almost immediately, began negotiations to take over the business.

The events, as reported by researcher J. David Edelstein in *Working Papers*, developed much as they did at the Meriden Bonneville plant. By early 1975, the workers had obtained government loans for half the 2.4 million pounds purchase price—thanks to minister Anthony Benn, who also put together the Meriden deal. Workers helped provide 120,000 pounds by buying stock; the corporation which owned the paper even helped out by buying 750,000 pounds worth of stocks, to be used toward purchase of the plant and equipment. On May 5, 1975, a cooperative of 500 workers began publishing their own newspaper, renamed the *Scottish Daily News*.

"Internally, the co-op maintained the usual chain of command," Edelstein reports. A general manager hired from the outside and a veteran editor wielded day-to-day control, and had the power to hire lower-level supervisors. "But the two officials reported not to a conventional board but to an executive council dominated by elected workers' representatives." The workers' council, according to the *Sunday Times* of London, consisted of 10 members—six shopfloor representatives including a journalist, assistant editor, and four craftsmen, plus the editor, general manager and two outside directors. "This council, together with an 'investors' council, representing outside shareholders and possessing quite limited power, governed the firm. The unions remained independent of these structures and were to retain most of their traditional functions." The Council had the power to appoint or fire department heads, who were charged with carrying out policies of the council on a day-to-day basis.

Under the worker-controlled system, Edelstein reports, labor relations inside the newspaper changed markedly. Workers broke through their traditional "caste" system, which had separated workers with different jobs, and worked together on a more equal basis. For instance, Edelstein reports, one day a worker in the composing room showed up in the editorial offices with some suggestions about how an article could be improved—something a reporter told Edelstein "had never happened to me before in all my many years in journalism."

The workers on the newspaper drafted an informal constitution pledging to deliver a "radical point of view, providing a real challenge to the Right-wing monopoly of the Press." But the experiment was short-lived. While the paper under workers' control started with a circulation of 300,000, higher than ever before, subscriptions started to fall. Financial problems, which had plagued the paper before the takeover, continued to get worse; in desperation, the executive council voted "to hand over executive authority for the paper's circulation and advertising" to a wealthy investor, Robert Maxwell, the outside shareholder's representative on the workers' council. As the paper continued to lose money, the investor started dismantling the worker control structure; workers began to resign in protest; the *Sunday Times* ran a large expose called "How Maxwell Sabotaged the Workers' Dream." Only six months after the experiment had begun, the newspaper closed its doors once and for all. Workers say the newspaper could have continued operations with additional government funding, according to Edelstein—funding which the government had refused to provide.

Scott Bader Commonwealth

About the same time that James P. Gibbons was transforming his International Group Plans insurance company, in Washington, D.C., into a self-managed enterprise, remarkably similar events were taking place inside a chemical products manufacturing company in the Northhamptonshire countryside of Britain. The result is one of the best-known models of worker self-management in Europe, the Scott Bader Commonwealth Ltd.

Scott Bader is owned entirely by a trust representing its workers, a total of more than 400 rank and file employees and managers. Corporate policies are made by a network of worker-elected councils and their elected representatives. The experiment is still changing and evolving—observers in England report that the rank and file employees are taking on increasingly more power. And its profits are steadily rising, reaching 14 million pounds in 1976, more than double its profits only five years earlier.

The Scott Bader experiment was born in the 1930's, when Ernest Bader—a mixture of autocrat, Quaker pacifist, businessman, technician, and Christian socialist—started a chemical manufacturing firm in east London (this description, like much of the information in this portrait, is based on an article by Anthony Moreton in the February, 1973 issue of *The Director* magazine). At first, "Scott Bader was run on quite conventional lines," Moreton reports, "indeed, 'quite ruthlessly,' according to his son . . . All the time, however, he was searching for an ethic, not just an outlet for his pacifism but a way to break new ground industrially."

In 1951, the Bader family gave 90 percent of its stock to the employees of the firm; the family retained 10 percent "to retain ultimate voting power,"

according to Moreton. But in 1963 the Bader family relinquished their 10 percent, and transferred 100 percent ownership of the corporation to a commonwealth of the employees. The commonwealth is in effect a trust of all employees who have worked in the firm for a two-year "probation" period. Once employees become commonwealth members, they have full voting rights. So far, according to researcher Alan Merton, more than 210 of the firm's 315 rank-and-file employees are members.

Bader's blueprint

The Scott Bader Commonwealth self-management system works like this:

• The most important bodies which shape corporate policy are the **Board of Directors** and the worker-elected **Community Council**. The Board of Directors is comprised of six company executives, two representatives elected by the workers, via their community council, and two representatives of the outside community. The Board formulates general corporate policies, hires the company management, ranging from the top executives to the foremen.

The rank and file employees—and owners—exert their power primarily through the Community Council, comprising 16 workers, each elected by a constituency of about 25 workers. Half the council representatives are elected from the factory, a third from the research lab, and the rest are elected by the clerical staff and management. The Council drafts policies and recommends them to the Board of Directors—it doesn't have final decision-making power—and it elects worker representatives to various company committees. But Merton reports that the Council in effect exerts considerable power. "Most of the changes in Scott Bader's internal government were first formulated" in the Community Council, he reports. In addition, the Community Council must approve all executive salaries, according to a rule which restricts the ratio of the company's highest to lowest salary to only seven to one.

Bader's progressive goals

The Scott Bader corporation has committed itself to pursuing unusually progressive social, political and economic goals. Reading some of the corporate documents, such as the following "Code of Practice for Members," from the 1972 Constitution, it is sometimes difficult to remember that Scott Bader is not a small collective of young political activists but rather a multimillion dollar chemicals manufacturing firm.

"We recognize that we are first a working community and that it is our basic attitude to our work and to our fellow workers that gives life and meaning to the Commonwealth.

"We have agreed that as a community our work involves four tasks, economic, technical, social and political, neglect of any one of which will in the long term diminish the Commonwealth. We feel that the practical working out of a balance between the four tasks is a continuing study for the membership as a whole.

"We are conscious of a common responsibility to share our work among ourselves in such a way that it becomes a meaningful and creative part of our lives rather than merely as a means to an end.

"We recognize that there are some members in a position of authority. Such members have a greater opportunity and hence a special responsibility to facilitate the building of jobs which are capable of fulfilling us as people; to act as 'catalysts of common effort' and not as authoritarian 'bosses'.

"We recognize that since management by con-

sent rather than coercion is an appropriate style for the Company, a corresponding effort to accept responsibility is required from us all. This will show in a desire to attend meetings and to participate in the affairs of our community; it will show in increased communication between person and person and between groups and departments . . . above all it will be seen as a genuine willingness to learn, to develop and grow.

"We try to be open and frank in our relationships with our fellow workers, to face difficulties rather than avoid them and to solve problems by discussion and agreement rather than through reference to a third party.

"We are agreed that in event of a downturn in trade we will share all remaining work rather than expect any of our fellow members to be deprived of employment, even if this requires a reduction in earnings by all.

. . .

"We recognize that we have a responsibility to the society in which we live . . . We are agreed that . . . our social responsibility extends to:

- Limiting the products of our labour to those beneficial to the community, in particular excluding any products for the specific purpose of manufacturing weapons of war.

- Reducing any harmful effect of our work on the natural environment by rigorously avoiding the negligent discharge of pollutants.

- Questioning constantly whether any of our activities are unnecessarily wasteful of the earth's natural resources . . . "

Each year there's a "time of reckoning," when a 12-person jury scrutinizes the Board of Directors' performance over the past year

- The rank and file employees exert influence on the company at the grassroots level. All employees, whether they are voting members of the Commonwealth or not, participate in **Departmental Assemblies**, according to Merton. The assemblies are open forums where workers can propose new policies or changes in the decision-making structure, suggest workplace improvements, and air grievances.

- The rank and file workers, meeting in the departmental assemblies, also elect eight representatives to the company grievance board, called the **Reference Council**. An equal number of representatives on the Reference Board are selected by the Board of Directors and Management. The Board, according to Merton, exercises "final authority to settle any complaint or dispute."

- At least once a year, all members of the Commonwealth—meaning all employees who have worked in the firm at least two years—hold a general meeting, at which workers vote on major corporate decisions. For instance, the **General Assembly** must approve any proposed investments over 24,000 pounds; it votes how to distribute the annual profits and how to set salaries (while 60 shopfloor workers belong to a union, the union has agreed it will not bargain for wages as long as the company pays more than the typical union minimum wage. Currently, Anthony Moreton reports, the company pays about 10 percent above union rates. There hasn't been a strike since 1948). The general assembly of workers also votes on new by-laws to the company's constitution. At their general assembly meetings, for example, rank and file workers have voted for a policy which pledges that the company will not lay off workers in times of economic trouble; instead, the company will cut wages across the board, from the shopsweeper to the president. The workers have also voted that their "responsibility to the society" means they will refuse to produce "any products for the specific purpose of manufacturing weapons of war."

Taking management to task

The Scott Bader Commonwealth has developed a unique sysem which gives workers the power to hold management accountable for its performance. Every year, according to Merton, there is a "time of reckoning" at the annual shareholders meeting. Commonwealth members select, by random lot, a kind of 12-person jury to scrutinize and evaluate the Board of Directors' performance during the previous year. If the panel issues a negative report on any of the Board's actions, the Board must take "appropriate remedial action" within three months and then report back to the general assembly. At this meeting, a new panel of 12 workers is selected, again by lot, to evaluate whether the Board's corrective measures were adequate. If the panel still is not satisfied, the Commonwealth Trustees—two appointed by the Board, two elected by the Community Council, two appointed jointly by the Board and Council—must decide whether the Board member or members should be replaced. Merton reports that "This unique method, rather than direct election of all directors . . . has been found by the commonwealth to provide the best check on management's performance while leaving them free of the pressure of a personality contest, which direct election of leaders can too often become."

According to company regulations, at least 60 percent of the common earnings—what a traditional corporation would call its profits—must be reinvested in the enterprise. Workers may distribute up to 20 percent of the earnings, but no more, among themselves as profit sharing payments; the workers must grant an equal percentage of the earnings to a social cause or community organization. For instance, the commonwealth commonly gives money to peace organizations, and it sends weekly parcels of free food to needy elders in the village. So far, according to Merton, the employees have tended to distribute only 10 percent of the earnings as profit sharing, while plowing more than 60 percent back into the corporation.

Sources

Scott Bader Commonwealth Limited Constitution, published by Scott Bader Commonwealth Limited, Wollaston, Wellingborough, Northamptonshire NN9 7RL, England.

"Workers' Triumph—The Meriden experiment," by Martin Carnoy and Henry Levin, *Working Papers for a New Society*, Winter 1976.

"Scott Bader's Bold Experiment in Industrial Democracy," by Anthony Moreton, *The Director* (London), February 1973.

Walter Kendall, "Workers' Participation and Workers' Control: Aspects of British Experience," National Conference on Self-Management, January 1974, manuscript.

"The World of Co-operation," *The Economist*, May 3, 1975.

Richard Fletcher, "Workers' Cooperation in Britain," draft paper at the Third International Conference on Self-Management.

G. David Garson, "Recent Developments in Workers' Participation in Europe," paper at the National Conference on Self-Management, January 1974.

Industrial Democracy in Europe: A 1976 Survey, by The National Quality of Work Center, 1976.

MON-DRAGON

When the London *Observer* published a portrait of Spain's sole but significant model of worker democracy, the Mondragon system of more than 60 cooperative firms, it headlined the article, "Mondragon: Spain's Oasis of Democracy." It was an apt description—for in Spain, just beginning to stretch out of the social, economic and political straitjacket of the almost 40-year Franco regime, the Mondragon cooperative network in the Basque country has long represented a world apart from the economic system in the rest of the nation. But the Mondragon cooperatives are not just a valuable model of economic democracy for Spain; the Mondragon system, as the London *Observer* declared, offers "important lessons for advanced industrial countries" all over the world.

The Mondragon cooperative system is based in the town of Mondragon, in the Basque mountain country 50 miles inland from San Sebastion and Bilbao; the town has a population of about 30,000. In a nation where there are more than 1,300 producer cooperatives, the Mondragon system is by far the largest. The first firm in the network was founded only 22 years ago by a small group of community organizers and workers who had been trained at a technical school run by an activist Catholic priest. The first producer co-op produced small stoves and cooking equipment; by the mid-1970s, the co-op had mushroomed into a network of 65 separate cooperative enterprises, with about 14,700 worker-members, producing a total of $200 million in sales. The cooperative firms include the nation's largest refrigerator manufacturer, and one of Spain's leading manufacturers of machine tools. The Mondragon network also includes an agricultural co-op, a fishing cooperative (which is "not very successful," according to the *Observer*), several cooperative retail stores and a cooperative bank, which supplies investment capital for the industrial co-ops and finances new members of the co-op firms. Mondragon, as Cornell University researchers William F. Whyte and Ana Gutierrez Johnson write, is "a success story in a field where failure has been the general rule"—producer cooperatives. For the number of successful producer cooperatives in the United States and western Europe is small; the plywood cooperatives in the U.S. Northwest are the only successful large-scale co-op factories in North America. These co-ops are low-technology, labor-intensive operations, leading many observers in the U.S. to conclude that producer co-ops can survive only if they are labor, not capital, intensive. Mondragon proves that producer co-ops have other possibilities — for 80 percent of the Mondragon co-op network's sales come from capital-intensive, heavy manufacturing.

Nuts and bolts

Here's how the Mondragon system works:

According to an economic plan established when the first firms were created, the annual profits from each firm are divided into three parts. "Ten to 15 percent goes for social purposes to benefit the community (including support of the educational system)," Whyte and Johnson write. "Fifteen to 20 percent is set aside as a reserve fund to be maintained by the cooperative firm. The remaining 70 percent is distributed to the members in proportion to hours worked during the year and rate of pay received." These "profit-sharing" funds targeted for the workers are not paid in cash, according to Whyte and Johnson, but are put into a co-op operating fund and then considered worker loans, which are eventually paid back to the members at a minimum six percent interest. Increases in the cost of living, Whyte and Johnson report, mean that currently, "members have been receiving about 13 percent on their accounts."

When workers leave the co-op, they can take out 80 percent of the money they've accumulated in their profit-sharing accounts, in cash. When the workers reach retirement age—few workers have, the researchers say, since the average age of workers in the cooperatives is only 32—they may withdraw the rest of the accumulating profits.

This system, researchers report, has allowed the Mondragon cooperatives to become remarkably self-sufficient. One of the traditional failings of most cooperatives is that they are unable to generate or obtain investment capital. But in the Mondragon system, the profit reserves in each firm furnish about half its investment capital. Most of the remaining capital investment capital comes from the Mondragon system's own cooperative bank, the Caja Laboral Popular (which means, roughly, bank of the people's labor).

The Caja, with more than 50 branch offices and about 170,000 members, plays a crucial role in the cooperative's success. The bank finances feasibility studies for new co-op enterprises, and it fronts 60 percent of the starting capital for each new firm (the firm must provide 20 percent of its own startup capital, and the federal government provides the rest). The Caja also covers the operating deficits for each new firm during the first two years of its operation. All of the Caja's investments, including the feasibility study, are considered long-term debts which the cooperatives eventually pay back.

The Mondragon co-ops have become remarkably self-sufficient. Profit reserves in each firm furnish about half the investment capital, and the rest comes from the co-ops' own bank

The people's bank also serves as a personal lending institution, lending money to workers who need to pay the $1,800 membership fee—only five percent down, the rest payable over years—when they join a co-op enterprise. Compare the membership fee to the plywood cooperatives in the U.S. Northwest, where a membership today may cost more than $25,000.

Mixed success

The Mondragon system, observers say, is thriving financially. During the recession year of 1974, Whyte and Johnson report, the system's profits surged 26 percent, and exports increased 56 percent over the previous year. When it comes to worker decision-making, Whyte and Johnson say, the cooperatives are a more mixed success. As in most cooperatives, the general membership of each of the co-op firms meets once a year to elect a board of directors—the Management Board—which then hires the rest of the management. Workers used to get votes based on their level of pay, but in 1972 the cooperative system went to a more egalitarian system of one worker, one vote.

Because the workers have ultimate control over management, researchers say, the co-op managers pay deference to worker interests. "You can't give orders in the tone of a general around here," one senior executive told the *Observer*. "And you can't walk around as if you own the place—anyway, not if you are hoping for reelection. According to the *Observer*, workers say there is a far more egalitarian spirit on the co-op's production floor than in conventional firms. "You aren't pushed around here," one worker told the newspaper, "in the way that happens elsewhere."

In spite of the overall democratic structure, however, the day-to-day operations of the Mondragon cooperatives are not much different than any traditional firm. "While top management is selected by the members," Whyte and Johnson report, "subordinate members of management are appointed from the top down, and the immediate supervisor of the worker members may direct his work force just as autocrati-

cally and inflexibly as his counterpart in the private firm." With few exceptions, the Cornell researchers write, the production process in the co-op firms is structured in the traditional way—the tasks are Taylorized, routinized, often arranged in an assembly line.

Each co-op firm in the Mondragon network has a congress of worker representatives, called the Social Council. In smaller firms, Johnson and Whyte report, representatives are elected by "constituencies" of about 10 workers each. In the larger enterprises—the refrigerator factory has more than 3,000 workers—each representative is elected by a group of up to 50 workers. "The Social Council has no direct power," Whyte and Johnson write, "it functions only in an advisory capacity to management." The Social Council's power as an independent voice of the workers tends to be reduced even further by the fact that the chairman of the management board also serves as chairman of the Council. In some firms, Whyte and Johnson say, it has been "increasingly difficult" to recruit "candidates" to run for the Social Council. Those workers who are most active politically tend to run for the top Management Board instead.

Power battles

Still, worker democracy in the Mondragon system lives; observers report that the rank and file members of the co-ops and the managements have been clashing over some fundamental issues, and the workers have been winning some of their battles. For instance, "when the evening shift workers demanded a wage rise," in one firm, according to the London *Observer*, "They took their case to the general assembly" of all the employees. "The management opposed the demand. But a majority of the votes in the assembly awarded the evening shift an increase of five percent compared with the day workers."

One of the most heated worker-management con-

Self-management advocates in the United States often fantasize about creating schools and training centers which could prepare people in the art of working together, cooperatively. In the Mondragon network of cooperatives, the fantasy has come true. The members of the very first co-op were graduates of a technical school founded in the 1940s; and since then, the school's student population has grown to 2,000. "While the school curriculum concentrates on technical subjects," Whyte and Johnson report, "the school itself is operated in the form of a cooperative, and cooperative ideas and ideals pervade the program." The school has provided the co-op firms with a rich source of skilled workers, skilled in their trade and in cooperative techniques.

troversies has focused on the pay scales. Under a co-op rule, the top salaries in the firms cannot exceed the lowest salaries by a ratio of more than 3:1—compared with conventional firms, where the pay ratios commonly exceed 10 or 20 to one. Professional-level workers and managers want the ratio increased to about five to one: they argue that highly skilled employees are leaving the co-ops to take higher paying jobs in private industry. Rank and file workers, on the other hand, argue that increasing the gap between highest and lowest pay would sabotage the cooperatives' egalitarian spirit. So, Johnson and Whyte report, management proposed a compromise: it would reclassify some of the pay rates at the lower end of the pay scale so that new workers entering certain job classifications would be paid still less, and it would revise the pay rates at the upper end of the scale so that middle managers would be paid more—all the while maintaining the sacred 3:1 ratio.

"(T)his upward and downward shifting," Whyte and Johnson write, "provoked a storm of protest . . . This controversy also brought to the fore other dissatisfactions regarding the pay system." But the con-

troversy exploded not so much because of the debate over pay, as because of the *way* in which the debate was handled. Workers who opposed the management plan "sought to place their grievances before the Management Board," Whyte and Johnson report, "but management replied that, according to the constitution, such matters must be taken up first with the Social Council. While some of the member protesters were in fact members of the Social Council, they had come to the conclusion that this organ was useless as a channel for redress, and they sought to insist upon a meeting with the Management Board. When the Management Board stood firm in its refusal to meet with them, protesters turned to direct action and sought to organize a strike."

The strike involved less than 400 workers, the researchers say, and lasted less than two weeks, but it had serious repercussions. For under a Constitutional regulation of the Mondragon system, the Management Boards have the power to expel workers who strike against the co-op (on the other hand, workers who strike in sympathy with striking workers at other, *non*co-op enterprises receive mild, if any, penalties). Seventeen of the strike leaders were expelled from the co-op, according to Johnson and Whyte—and although the workers got the required one third of the general membership to sign a petition forcing the general assembly to consider overturning the management decision, a majority of the general assembly eventually voted to uphold the Management Board's edict anyway.

Although the striking workers lost their battle, Johnson and Whyte observe, the controversy "precipitated a period of re-examination of the structures and processes of governance of the cooperative." Workers are examining ways to strengthen the social councils, and in one of the co-op firms, one with more than 800 workers, the workers and management have been experimenting with the kinds of job redesign which have taken root in some major U.S. corporations—for instance, semi-autonomous work teams operating under little supervision, team methods of assembling products instead of a dreary assembly line, and similar innovations.

One of the major tasks which lies ahead for the Mondragon system will be one which confronts all self-managed firms, or firms where a self-management system is evolving: educating the workers and managers alike about the nuts and bolts of the business, as well as about the techniques of democratic decision-making. Many workers, according to the London *Observer*, don't know much about their business. "One man," the reporter wrote, "said that 90 percent of what went on in the general assembly meeting was quite incomprehensible to him."

But Johnson and Whyte are optimistic about Mondragon's future. "While the leaders of the Mondragon system naturally take pride in what they have built, they do not take dogmatic positions against change," Whyte and Johnson note. "They are open to new ideas and are seeking to learn from their experience and from the experience of others. Mondragon seems to be an organization that is a learning system."

Sources

Ana Gutierrez Johnson and William Foote Whyte, "The Mondragon System of Worker Production Cooperatives," *Social Experience*, September 1976.
"Mondragon, Spain's Oasis of Democracy," by Robert Oakeshotte, *The Observer* (London), January 21, 1973.

YUGO-SLAVIA

Students and advocates of workplace democracy in the United States eventually must study the evolving system of self-management in Yugoslavia. For Yugoslavia, unlike a nation such as Sweden, is promoting worker self-management not only in industry: the nation has committed itself by law to bring worker control to every office, institution, school and community — to the entire society. "Never before (has) any form of workers' management been completely national in scope nor such an integral part of a national economy," sociologist Paul Blumberg writes.

"The development of self-management in Yugoslavia," as an official government publication puts it, "has initiated . . . the process of transformation of workers into managers of their enterprises and at all levels of social organization. For the first time in the history of human society, workers organized on a self-management basis directly decide on the conditions, means and results of their work."

On paper, the blueprint of worker self-management in Yugoslav factories looks impressive (and surprisingly like the evolving system at International Group Plans in Washington, D.C.). The "supreme authority" in each enterprise is the entire workforce, which votes by referendum on crucial issues such as merging with other firms, relocating plants, and distributing the income. From month to month, according to the self-management laws, the workers formulate policies including the prices of products, production and financial plans, and workplace policies, through their elected workers' councils. The workers' council in each firm is generally dominated by the blue-collar production workers.

The workers also exert indirect control over the day-to-day management of the enterprise, since the management board and plant director are elected by the workers' council, and subject to recall at any time, according to writer Gerry Hunnius.

Participants at the Third International Conference on Self-Management agreed that Yugoslavia has developed worker self-management to a far greater degree than any nation in Europe or the United States — helping transform the nation, researcher Stephen Sachs writes, from a sluggish underdeveloped economy only 25 years ago to one of the fastest-growing, and most decentralized economies in the world. But the panelists also stressed that serious obstacles to full worker self-management still plague the system. "The Yugoslav system is not a complete self-management model," as Tufts University professor G. David Garson writes. The problem, as panelists at the Third International Conference defined it, is this: when it comes to making fundamental decisions about the enterprise, the rank and file workers often don't participate as much as they should, and could — and so the elected managers, who theoretically serve only at the will of the workers, often end up making the major decisions instead.

When reading about how self-management works in the Yugoslav workplace, it is important to remember this: self-management is not an isolated phenomenon within individual enterprises, as it is in the United States. It is an official government policy, which links factories to other factories, to local communities, and to the rest of the nation.

Launching the experiment

Yugoslavia began setting up workers' councils in enterprises as early as 1949. In 1950, the Federal Parliament passed a national policy, called "The Basic Law," popularly referred to as "the law which gave the factories to the workers," according to researcher Rudi Supek. Under the new law, as Blumberg writes, all industry would be operated "in the name of the social community, administered by their working staffs . . . " in other words, operated in the name of the society by the workers.

The nationwide transformation to worker self-management, Supek writes, began slowly. Worker councils were established only in certain enterprises, and even then their powers were sharply limited. For about a decade after "The Basic Law" was implemented, the decision-making in most enterprises was really controlled by the directors of the enterprises, who were then chosen not by the workers but by the government. Furthermore, individual enterprises did not control their own investment capital, the state did.

But as researcher David Tornquist told participants at the Third International Conference on Self-Management, "far-reaching structural changes" in 1965 "expanded considerably the power of the worker councils vis-a-vis the managers" — and gave to each enterprise crucial control over its own investment policies.

Under the 1965 constitution, full power was theoretically placed in the votes of the workers. Here's how it works:

"In all but the smallest enterprises," Gerry Hunnius writes, "the workers elect a workers' council which meets approximately once a month and is charged with making decisions on all major functions

Each company is divided into working units, each with its own miniature workers' council and its own worker-elected management

of the enterprise (prices on its products, whenever these are not controlled, production and financial plans, governing of the enterprise, allocation of net income, budget, etc.). The workers' council elects a management board, in practice largely from its own ranks, which acts as executive agent. At least three quarters of the members of the management board must be production workers," Hunnius explains.

"The Board meets more frequently than the workers' council and works in close cooperation with the director, who is an *ex officio* member. The workers' council is elected for a period of two years, half of its members elected every year. Its composition is supposed to approximate the ratio between production workers and employees. Meetings of the workers' council are usually open and every member of the working collective (meaning the entire work force) is entitled to attend. Decisions are made by a majority vote and members of the council, individually or as a group, can be recalled by the electorate. No one can be elected twice in succession to the workers' council, and more than twice in succession to the management board.

"The management board is elected for a period of one year," Hunnius writes, "and is answerable for its work to the workers' council, which may recall individual members or the whole board at any time . . . The director is the actual administrative manager of the enterprise. He is responsible for the day-to-day operations and he represents the enterprise in any external negotiations . . . He can be removed by the workers' council, which also determines his term of office."

Decentralizing power

In 1971, Yugoslavia enacted still another major change in its evolving self-management structure: since self-management "had generally been found to work better in smaller firms than in large ones," according to researcher Stephen Sachs, the government passed a series of laws which aim to decentralize power and decision-making within every single enter-

prise. The strategy: workers exert their most direct control not at the plant level, but at the departmental level, or, as it's called, the level of the "working unit."

Under the new system, single companies are divided into numerous working units, each with its own miniature workers' council and its own management, a foreman elected by a two-thirds vote of the workers in the unit. Each unit functions practically like a small, autonomous company — the units even buy from, and sell to, other units within the same enterprise, as if they were subsidiaries within a conglomerate. The foreman has no policy-making authority but merely carries out decisions made by the mini-workers' council; the foreman can't discipline the workers, either, but must refer disputes to the working unit's discipline committee. The main workers' council of the entire enterprise intervenes whenever two working units become embroiled in a dispute.

Example: under the plan, Sachs writes, "a furniture company employing 5,000 workers went from four units, each having limited authority under the central workers' council, to 16 autonomous units (of about 300 workers each). Each unit acted almost as an independent business, managing its own affairs and calculating most of its finances on the basis of the activity of the unit itself. The units producing furniture, for example, actually negotiated price in selling it to the retail sales unit since each unit's costs and income are calculated individually, as if that unit [were] a separate firm."

The new system of semi-autonomous working units, observers say, has nurtured signficant advances in democratic decision-making. In small units, as Hunnius reports, the entire working force often assembles to vote on critical issues in "the conference of the working unit," or what in the U.S. might be called a "committee of the whole." Therefore, all the workers tend to play a direct role in decision-making at the working unit level, while they make direct decisions only infrequently at the plant level, in special referenda.

How well does the self-management system really work? The self-management system in Yugoslavia sounds impressive on paper — and to a large extent, the system *has* given fundamental powers to the rank and file workers. According to Garson, rank and file workers have achieved "substantial, if not majority, low-level initiative and influence on policy questions, more egalitarian pay structure, greater job security during economic downturns, greater influence over the immediate work environment . . . and the ability in some . . . percentage of cases of labor-management conflicts to overturn management policy without resort to strikes."

But asking the question, "Does it work?" simplifies a complex system which is evolving across an entire nation. In some factories, observers write, the self-management structure functions smoothly while in other enterprises it breaks down; workers exert enormous influence on some kinds of decisions within a single enterprise, while they exert little influence on other decisions.

Measuring success

One measure of success in the self-management experience is that studies suggest the system has increased worker satisfaction. Hunnius quotes studies showing that "participation in workers' councils and/ or management boards results in significantly greater general job satisfaction," except among workers in highly automated jobs. Furthermore, other studies show, workers seem to perceive that the self-management system has improved their work life. When workers were asked "whether the introduction of self-management had improved their personal position," Garson reports, only two percent of the workers said it had not — and "although a great many were uncertain as to the effect, a majority expressed the belief that self-management had improved their position."

One important aspect of the worker self-management structure is job security: unlike most employees in the United States, workers in the self-managed factories of Yugoslavia control decisions about shutdowns and layoffs. Hunnius describes the case of a

pharmaceutical company, which merged with two other drug companies, and then discovered that the factory could eliminate 10 percent of the employees and save substantial amounts of money. The workers in each working unit selected members of their own ranks who could afford to be "laid off" — workers who had other means of support — and made sure not to lay off workers who had financial burdens and most needed the income. In addition, the workers' council voted to give the 97 laid off workers enough money to sustain them while they looked for new jobs, so that virtually no one ended up jobless.

Rank and file workers in the self-managed firms also have considerable influence on determining wages. Income is handled much as it is at the U.S. plywood cooperatives. Workers are paid a minimum wage; then, once the company has paid its debts, and set aside funds to cover depreciation and pay taxes, the workers' council has the power to invest the surplus or distribute it to the workers, as it sees fit. "The subject of the distribution of income," Hunnius writes, "remains one of the most hotly debated issues in Yugoslavia" — as workers and managers debate whether to put the money in workers' pockets or to invest it. The power to control the surplus gives the workers' councils considerable economic clout, for it means that the rank and file workers of Yugoslavia, through their directly elected councils, control about one third of the investment capital in the entire nation, according to Hunnius.

The most nagging problem which thwarts development of full self-management, observers say, is that too many workers just don't have the education and cultural background necessary to make sound decisions, in a democratic group. For one thing, many factory workers come from small villages, according to Supek, and a "substantial percentage remain 'worker peasants,' " with a high degree of illiteracy. The different cultural groups in Yugoslavia, furthermore, traditionally have been patriarchal hierarchies, according to Sachs, "emphasizing age, male superiority, achievement and education as the basis of social status and authority. The principles of democratic participation and essential equality of all people, which are fundamental to socialist self-management of the workplace and of society, are new to most of Yugoslavia." As Sachs points out, most workers "have been enculturated to respect the authority of those holding 'higher positions,' or those with greater education or expertise, and in practice they defer to such authority figures rather than assert their opinions or rights."

Against this backdrop, it is easier to understand the vagaries of self-management in Yugoslav enterprises. Managers at many firms tend to manipulate decision-making, observers point out, by carefully controlling the kinds of vital technical and financial information which they, and their engineers and financial specialists, dispense to the rank and file workers. The Yugoslav government, says Sachs, urges managers in each firm to present a number of alternative plans to the workers' council for consideration, and then let the council select the one it wants; by manipulating the kinds of alternatives they offer to the workers, managers are able to manipulate the councils' final choice.

Sachs also reports that the managers and "experts" often tend to do most of the talking at meetings, as workers, intimidated by the managers' grasp of technical information and financial statistics, retreat into silence. "The people who have the monopoly on the technical knowledge and who have the everyday managerial functions and authority in the workplace," David Tornquist told participants at the Third International Conference on Self-Management, "have been able to put their decisions through." But since the workers' councils go through the motions of voting, Tornquist added, the managers can absolve themselves of responsibility for bad, or unpopular, decisions. "The manager can tell the council, 'Well, you made the decision, I cannot take responsibility for your vote,'" Tornquist said. Under this dynamic, the workers and their councils can sometimes become little more than rubber stamps. In all fairness to managers, observers say, managers find themselves in a bind: while workers are expected to take an active part in making key decisions, they cannot take an active part if they are not well educated both in the fine points of the business and in the dynamics of group decision-making. Furthermore, the managers find themselves caught partway between the workers and the government: the government pressures them, on the one hand, to increase production and efficiency and surplus (or profits) — yet the workers who elected the managers to office pressure them to fulfill the workers' immediate self-interests. Frequently, these demands conflict.

But while managers and their "expert" staffs often do dominate decision-making in the workers' councils, Garson writes, "they do not do so to the exclusion of substantial lower-level initiative and influence." Various researchers have attempted to quantify in some precise way just how much workers do or don't participate, and the results seem to show that workers are continually asserting themselves with more vigor. Rudi Supek, for instance, quotes studies which show that between 1950 and 1960, the activities of the workers' councils "consistently grew in intensity." Workers' councils met ever more frequently, for more hours per meeting, and they discussed and made decisions on a continually greater number of issues. Garson quotes more recent studies (he calls them "the most systematic attempt to date" to evaluate workers' performance under self-management); according to Garson, the data show that "the representatives of the lower echelons of the firm made a substantial number of proposals and were disproportionately effective in having these proposals accepted." For instance, worker council members from the shop floor made 27 percent of all the proposals concerning the internal finances of the enterprise, while their proposals accounted for 32 percent of all the proposals adopted.

How workers see it

One of the problems which sometimes plagues self-management in the factories, observers say, is that many workers don't perceive that they have power. In 20 different enterprises, Supek discovered, the workers perceived that the directors, management board and technical staff exerted the most power, in that order, while they said that the rank and file and their trade unions ranked near the bottom of the power list. When workers were asked what they would like the power hierarchy to look like, however, they turned the hierarchy on its head — and rated the workers' council first, the rank and file workers fourth, and stuck the director and management board near the bottom.

Still another problem is this: even when the workers' councils do exert power and make key decisions, many rank and file workers don't know it; others don't care. Sach reports that he attended "important sessions of workers' councils" at which workers made key decisions affecting levels of take-home pay—yet the rank and file workers out on the production floor were oblivious to the decisions. At one paprika factory employing 150 workers, Sachs reports, the firm was suffering severe financial problems due to a paprika-saturated market. The workers' council rejected proposals to cut production levels and to fire part-time workers, and instead voted to increase efficiency and cut wages across the board. When Sachs asked rank and file workers a few days later how they felt about the council's decision, Sachs reports, virtually all of them said, in effect, "That is the job of the members of the workers' council. It is not our concern." When Sachs asked workers in another enterprise "about an important meeting of the unit workforce that they had attended two weeks before," he says, "none of them could remember what had been discussed or decided."

Breakdowns in the self-management system, then, are caused both by a management which withholds information and manipulates worker councils to make the decisions it wants, and by workers who are uneducated and unprepared to assert themselves, and therefore submit to management. One of the key problems in Yugoslav self-management, therefore, is lack of information: if managers and their expert

---

Self-management means . . . I

"If one assumes that self-management 'works' only if there is high rank and file participation on all issues, especially important matters such as investment policy," G. David Garson writes, "then it is unlikely any system will meet the implied standard. Not only is it physically impossible to make numerous decisions in some sort of mass-meeting or plebiscite format, but managers and employees alike will ordinarily not wish to trade time for participation in unnecessary meeting — unnecessary in the sense that . . . under normal circumstances a democratic management will make decisions in accordance with anticipated membership preferences.

"A more realistic standard is to say that self-management 'works' when, in cases where the will of management differs from that of the employees, management cannot impose its preference because of constraints associated with participative organization structures."

Garson describes a conflict in one enterprise, a paper factory, which ignited when management proposed a return to more centralized decision-making. Centralized decision-making, management argued, would make the factory more efficient. But the workers insisted on retaining power through their decentralized workers' councils, and the managers backed down.

"The director and department heads, though favoring centralization," writes Garson, "refrained from opposing re-decentralization openly because they were elected for four-year terms by the workers' council and did not wish to antagonize their constituency."

---

staffs shared information openly with rank and file workers, and if worker councils shared information openly with their colleagues on the shop floor, they would help break down one of the major obstacles to

The Yugoslav government has launched campaigns against managers who attempt to dominate decision-making, branding them "class enemies"

Self-management means . . . II

"The purpose of worker management is not to teach all workers to discuss all problems, including those of a scientific nature," Dusan Bilandzic of the University of Zagreb told participants at the Third International Conference on Self-Management. "In practice self-government by the working people does not consist of declaring themselves for or against a technical and economic investment, or a financial study or plan, as if the workers were experts. Self-management means . . . deciding the social, economic, and political implications of such plans. And self-management means dictating the framework, the aims, the social and political goals of the decisions."

---

effective self-management. Official government publications are continually pushing this point: "An important element . . . is securing timely and reliable information, without which there can be no real self-management, no real control of workers over the work of the elected bodies of social self-management," declares one report.

One innovation which could help solve the dilemma of information-sharing, some researchers say, would be for workers' councils to establish their own boards of technical advisers to interpret complex technical and financial information for them — much in the way that major U.S. labor unions have assembled technical staffs which attempt to duplicate and interpret secret management financial records. Observers also say that the Yugoslav trade unions, which until now have played a passive role in the evolving self-management structure, could pay a crucial role by educating the workers.

Transforming the nation

Panelists at the Third International Conference on Self-Management stressed tht the most crucial aspect of self-management in Yugoslavia is not the self-management structure within each enterprise, but the remarkable effort to bring self-management principles to the entire society.

On the local level, for instance, Yugoslavia is governed by about 500 communes (roughly equivalent to an American county) each with an average population of about 40,000 persons. The communal assembly, or legislature, is divided into two chambers — one elected by all adults in the commune in their role as *citizens*, and the other chamber elected by *workers* in business enterprises and institutions. "The communal assembly is thus designed to represent citizens both as consumers and as producers," says Gerry Hunnius.

In addition, separate enterprises cooperate together under "social compacts," coordinating their wage levels, their production levels and even their investments. Representatives from different companies also come together in "communities of interest," regional conferences at which worker representatives discuss, and make proposals on, regional education, health care, and other social service programs.

Observers say it is this transition — moving from self-management in individual enterprises to self-management in the society — which confronts Yugoslavia with both its biggest potential accomplishments and its most troubling problems. "One of the most important issues for the present and future of the Yugoslav economic system is the task of integrating the autonomous self-managed enterprises into a complete economic system of self-management," Hunnius writes. "Self-management must transcend the limits of the enterprises to a much greater degree than has so far been the case.

"The future of self-management in Yugoslavia, writes Hunnius, "is still very much an open question." "Unless appropriate corrective steps are taken soon," to spread self-management throughout the society, Sachs writes, "there is a chance that all that has been achieved in developing self-management in Yugoslavia may be lost."

Sachs stresses, as Garson and other observers do, that the unions must play an increasingly important role to ensure that rank and file workers assert their self-management powers. "If self-management is to succeed the unions in each enterprise must . . . act as a strong and persistent advocate of workers' rights," says Sachs. "The union should carry out a program of self-management education for all workers, including administrators and technical experts . . . along with training for workers in issues relating to the operation of a firm so that everyone would have the knowledge and understanding to participate effectively."

Sachs argues — much as workers at International Group Plans in Washington, D.C. argue — that one of the biggest obstacles to achieving full self-management is educating the managers. Sachs notes that the Yugoslav government has launched various campaigns against technocrats who attempt to dominate decision-making, labeling them as "class enemies"; Sachs argues that such a campaign has made managers even "more insecure and alienated, and hence more secretive . . . Administrators and specialists should not be suffered as necessary evils, but should be treated as workers with particular responsibilities, who like all workers need to be enculturated to the new system."

What gives Yugoslavia's enormous experiment in self-management the most chance of success, observers say, is the fact that self-management is the law of the land. In the United States, managers and workers who advocate democratic decision-making are an exception, almost corporate outcasts; in Yugoslavia, the outcasts are those workers and managers who do not.

"Uninterested apathetic workers are condemned and called 'little citizens,' " writes Paul Blumberg, "and the working class hero today is one who actively participates in workers' management . . . Because the formal structure and ideology permit and even encourage a high degree of participation, all that is required for genuine workers' self-management in a factory is the sheer *determination* of the workers themselves. If they are bold enough, interested enough, self-confident enough, and aggressive enough, they can take power through the machinery of workers' councils, management boards, and economic units," Blumberg writes, "and they can hold power and wield it."

Gerry Hunnius, "Workers Self-Management in Yugoslavia " in *Workers' Control A Reader on Labor & Social Change*, Random House, 1973.

G. David Garson, *On Democratic Administration and Socialist Self-Management: A Comparative Survey Emphasizing the Yugoslav Experience*, Administrative & Policy Studies Series, 1974.

Stephen Sachs, *Implications of Recent Developments in Yugoslav Self-Management*, manuscript, 1975.

Ichak Adizes, *The Role of Management in Democra-* *tic (Communal) Organizational Structures*, paper presented to the Center for the Study of Democratic Institutions.

Adizes, "Economic Change in Yugoslavia," in *East Europe*, 1972.

Paul Blumberg, *Industrial Democracy: The Sociology of Participation*, Schocken, 1968.

Transcripts of the Third International Conference on Self-Management.

WHAT LABOR THINKS

When advocates of self-management, or any system which brings more democracy to the workplace, talk shop, their discussions inevitably lead to what many see as a painful paradox: most leaders of the American labor movement are not spearheading the effort to democratize work, but seemingly have resisted it.

"We have a feeling that if we get into bed with management," Robert Rodden of the International Association of Machinists and Aerospace Workers told participants at the Third International Conference on Self-Management, "there's going to be two people screwing the workers instead of one."

"Rainbow chasing," Thomas Donahue, executive assistant to the president of the AFL-CIO, calls some visions of worker self-management. "We do not seek to be a partner in management—to be most likely the junior partner in success and the senior partner in failure."

"Sooner or later the workers will become

managers themselves, and they'll start acting like managers," warns William Burns, assistant research director of the Amalgamated Meat Cutters in Chicago. "It pits worker against worker."

And to William Winpisinger, the new president of the IAM, "this whole business of workplace democracy (is) an invention of intellectuals, way off the track of American realities. And most of these experiments are doomed to nil. I don't see that they can accomplish things that collective bargaining can't produce," Winpisinger said. "They're a ruse to increase the productivity of the workers."

To advocates of worker self-management, these kinds of views have seemed a frustrating and troubling obstacle to building a movement. For the way self-management advocates see it, worker self-management is the most powerful strategy for workers to protect and advance their best interests.

"We believe that self-management offers solutions to the major social and economic dilemmas which confront our nation today," the Federation for Economic Democracy has written. It lists runaway plants, low wages, hazardous work environments and boring jobs as some of the problems self-management could help solve.

Supporters of self-management feel especially frustrated as they look across the ocean to Europe, where at least half a dozen nations have laws on the books requiring workers on the boards of directors of major corporations, a possible step toward self-management which many labor unions there have supported.

Why does the U.S. labor movement oppose the push toward workplace democracy? Or perhaps a better question: *Does* the U.S. labor movement really oppose it? For while labor leaders have often been suspicious of "workplace democracy" experiments across the nation, it is true, "labor's attitude" toward "this whole business of workplace democracy," as Winpisinger puts it, cannot be summarized so simply.

The many faces of labor

In the first place, the "American labor movement" is not monolithic. The same "movement" encompasses both progressive unions—or unions directed by progressive leaders—such as the American Federation of State, County and Municipal Employees, the United Auto Workers and the Oil, Chemical and Atomic Workers International Union, as well as more traditional, conservative unions such as the United Steelworkers. While some union leaders criticize the notion of giving workers more power over traditional management decision-making, other union leaders endorse it.

"Should unions be interested in workplace democracy?" asks Peter DiCicco, international vice-president of the International Union of Electrical, Radio and Machine Workers. "I can think of no better way of improving working conditions than giving workers control over the workplace."

"The time is now ripe for the second stage" of the union struggle, says UAW vice-president Irving Bluestone—"workers' direct participation in the decision-making process."

It is also important, when talking about "labor's attitude," to remember that leaders and members of the same union are often in sharp disagreement about many issues—including "workplace democracy."

"I find cases where the local officers have said, 'let's set up a cooperative management-labor project,' " Michael Brower, executive director of the Massachusetts Quality of Working Life Center, told participants at the Third International Conference, "and the membership said, 'Hey, what's going on here, are you selling us out?' I also find cases where some of the members are moving forward and saying, 'Hey, this looks like something we ought to get involved in' and the local officers are dragging their feet.

"I caution all of you in this room," Brower told participants at the Conference, "from generalizing about what trade union leadership or trade union membership thinks about these issues, because it is constantly changing."

But there is another reason why it has been so difficult to discuss "labor's attitude" toward "workplace democracy" in a productive way: labor leaders and political activists have seldom clearly defined precisely

Labels have been tossed around so loosely in the "workplace democracy" debate that it is impossible to generalize "what labor thinks"

what sort of workplace structure they are talking about when they criticize—or endorse—"this whole business of workplace democracy." Are they talking about job enrichment, or humanization of work projects, in which a corporate management unilaterally imposes carefully limited powers and freedoms on employees on the shopfloor? Are they talking about labor-management committees, often called "quality of work life" projects, which engage unions and managements in a cooperative process of change?

When union leaders condemn "this whole business of workplace democracy," are they condemning a company such as the Vermont Asbestos Group, whose employees bought a majority of the corporate stock in order to save their jobs? Or are they thinking about a company such as Consumers United Group, where rank and file employees and their elected representatives have voting power over major corporate policies including how to distribute the profits and setting wages?

Labels have been tossed about so loosely in the whole debate about "workplace democracy" that it is impossible to generalize about "what labor thinks." It is more productive to focus on what specific labor leaders feel about specific kinds of experiments. Only then can activists working toward a more democratic workplace understand the possibilities and map out the strategies for the future.

How unions evolved

To understand some of the different perspectives of labor leaders in the debate on various forms of "workplace democracy," it's useful to recall how the American labor movement evolved. While "workers' control" has remained a visible and volatile topic in the European labor movement for many decades, it has never become an issue considered worthy of serious debate in the U.S. labor movement.

Since the late 1700s, there *has* been a sprinkling of political groups on the periphery of the labor movement which advocated worker self-management; his-

Do workers want changes in the workplace?

When some union leaders explain why they don't support "this whole business of workplace democracy," they often emphasize one reason: the rank and file members are not asking for it.

"There's been a flood of articles and thought pieces and studies by journalists and academicians on why U.S. unions ought to be more involved with the issues of quality of work life," the AFL-CIO's Thomas Donahue has said. "All of these assume that there is a surge of worker interest in participating in management . . . and that assumption is false."

"If the members of our union come up to us and say, 'Look, in our next contract we want to have some say about jobs," Robert Rodden said, "believe me, that will be in our next contract. But I do not know of one single case where a worker bargaining committee has said, 'We want to change around our jobs.'"

While these union leaders argue that lack of overt worker demands for more workplace democracy is a sign that the leadership should not promote it, leaders such as the IUE's Peter DiCicco argue precisely the opposite: union leaders have a responsibility to educate their members about workplace democracy, he says, and to lead them toward it.

"Do workers support workplace democracy?" DiCicco asks. "I don't think that would be the proper question, because no one knows what we're talking about. But if we went through the process of explaining what was happening, they'd have great interest.

"Leadership means having new ideas and showing initiative," DiCicco says. "We ought to be in the forefront of the movement, not falling behind and fighting only under the traditional collective bargaining relationship."

torians have recorded the birth—and rapid death from capital starvation—of several hundred worker-owned and controlled firms, usually producer cooperatives, during various periods of the mid- and late 1800s. But practically every enterprise and political group which has practiced or advocated workers control in this country has died within a few years after it was born. By the 1890s, the American labor movement was practically synonomous with the philosophy of the American Federation of Labor, and leaders such as Samuel Gompers.

Gompers and other union leaders argued that, rather than attempt to replace management and control the workplace, workers should form strong trade unions which would concede to management the right to direct the workplace—and then devote their energies to wresting various concessions from management in return. Workers would not exert any direct power over the workplace, according to the trade union philosophy, but they would always have the ultimate threat of shutting down production and pinching management's profits—going on strike—in order to win the concessions they wanted. The system became known as "collective bargaining," and by the 1930s, virtually all of the major unions had joined the collective bargaining movement under the banner of the AFL or CIO.

As the major unions became stronger and more entrenched, so did management's insistence that the unions steer clear of treading on "management prerogatives." During the 1950s and 1960s, numerous management-union contracts included "management rights clauses," which spelled out management's invincible right to control fundamental issues concerning what to produce and how to produce it.

UAW vice-president Irving Bluestone has described the trade-off this way: "Labor contracts, with their hundreds of provisions establishing and protecting the rights of workers, substantially leave to management the 'sole responsibility' to determine the products to be manufactured, the location of plants, the schedules of production, the methods, processes and means of manufacturing, and the administrative decisions governing all financial, marketing, purchasing, pricing matters and the like." Former United Mine Workers president Tony Boyle put it like this: "The UMW will not abridge the rights of mine operators in running the mine. We follow the judgment of the coal operators, right or wrong."

The unions' fundamental role, then—their very reason for existence and their fundamental source of power—has been to organize workers and then represent them in collective bargaining, for certain limited rights and tangible benefits.

When U.S. labor leaders talk about the history of the American labor movement and collective bargaining—how the unions endured often violent battles with management to organize more than 14 million workers, how they boosted U.S. wages to among the highest in the world, how they bargained for and won generous medical and pension benefits and vacation time—they speak with obvious pride.

"(W)e have developed the world's most elaborate, extensive and complex system of collective bargaining," Donahue says. "Consider for a minute that the more than 14 million AFL-CIO members are covered by 150,000 collective bargaining agreements negotiated by tens of thousands of participants in the collective bargaining process . . . We have fought for a clean, safe workplace, for sensible, tolerable limits on discomfort, in short, for humane conditions—respectful of the workers' dignity." Donahue adds, however, "there is a long way to go before labor's goals for collective bargaining are fully realized."

What union leaders say

Against this backdrop, it's easier to understand why many union leaders worry about recent development in the workplace, often referred to as "workplace democracy."

• The first kinds of so-called "workplace democracy" which most union leaders oppose are "humanization of work" and job enrichment.

Numerous corporations such as Proctor & Gamble,

"Workers' control" has never become an issue in the U.S. labor movement considered worthy of serious debate. By the 1930s, most unions were marching for collective bargaining

Texas Instruments, AT&T and General Foods (see case study) began initiating these kinds of worker participation experiments in the late 1960s, as a flurry of social research surveys suggested that worker boredom and alienation were responsible for labor ills.

If you ask union leaders why they oppose humanization of work reforms, they'll probably answer something like this:

They're management attempts to bust the union, or to prevent workers from joining a union in the first place.

By "humanizing" the shopfloor, and making work slightly more interesting, union leaders say, management is trying to lull workers into a feeling that management really cares about them. That way, the workers won't want a union.

To fuel their charges, union leaders point to the fact that most humanization of work projects have been launched unilaterally by management, often in nonunion plants. Management imposed the limited freedoms and powers on the workers, without consulting with them first.

And union leaders point to the fact that humanization of work reforms *have* helped encourage workers to shun unions. Employees from General Foods proudly told participants at the Third International Conference on Self-Management that they've shunned several union organizing attempts. "What do we need unions for?" one worker asked. "They won't give us anything that management hasn't already given us."

Humanization of work reforms have prevented enough union organizing attempts across the nation, in fact, so that one team of management consultants has promoted executive seminars on humanization of work called "Making Unions Unnecessary."

"They're making a bundle, running around the country charging a few hundred dollars for a two-day seminar in luxurious places like Florida," Steve Confer, director of training at the Communications Workers of America, said at the Third International Conference. "And the whole thrust of their presentation is, if you increase the participation of the workers, then you won't have a union."

Humanization of work reforms are gimmicks to speed up production without boosting workers' pay.

In general, union leaders charge, these reforms are designed to satisfy worker discontents with superficial benefits—such as the freedom to rotate jobs or assemble entire products—rather than with more bread and butter benefits.

"Management will grab at any chance to redesign jobs if it means an increase in output without an increase in pay," William Winpisinger has said. "I have nothing against profits but I do not intend to lose sight of the fact that the [corporate] goal of job enrichment is not worker contentment but worker efficiency. Worker efficiency generally means speedups."

To back their argument, union officials point once again toward the Gravy Train factory in the fields outside Topeka. One of the major objectives of the Topeka System, General Foods executives said, was to boost productivity. "An organization which more fully utilizes the human potential of employees can pay off in dollars and cents," one document explained.

It worked: using only 70 employees, the Topeka plant has achieved the level of production which corporate engineers figured would require at least 100. But while they're producing more, the Topeka employees are not receiving special bonuses, profit sharing payments or other direct financial benefits for their superior work.

Union officials point also to the proliferating number of management consultant firms and industry publications which promise executives how shopfloor reforms will boost their productivity and profits. The Work in America Institute, Inc., sends corporations its *Guide to Worker Productivity Experiments in the United States.* One experiment, called "Positive Reinforcement," consists of "simply giving praise and recognition to employees who do a good job." The results: one company, the Institute says, doubled productivity and cut costs by $3 million—all without boosting workers' paychecks.

Whatever benefits workers do gain from humanization of work reforms, they are never guaranteed. Just as management bestows the benefits on the em-

ployees, so management can take them away.

This caveat, union officials argue, has already disappointed workers and created tensions at the General Foods plant. For a new regime of managers is scuttling some of the popular worker freedoms and powers—highly popular among the workers—which an old regime had imposed. "You get right down to the fact that they can do whatever they want," one General Foods employee told participants at the Third International Conference on Self-Management. "They run it. They own it . . . I mean, they didn't even have to let us do this whole thing [humanization of work] in the first place."

- Another workplace reform which many union leaders oppose is "co-determination"—putting union or worker representatives on the corporate board of directors.

On the face of it, it might seem that unions would jump at the chance to have representatives invited into the boardroom. They could become privy to management secrets, inspect the financial records, keep close watch on management's every move. But union leaders describe these fears:

Putting workers or union officials on the board will blur the sharp distinction between employees and employers—the distinction which gives unions and union officials their identities.

"If we're taking part *in* management," said Red Campbell, a United Auto Workers committeeman in a General Motors factory in Pontiac, Michigan, "who in the hell will we be fighting *against*?"

By putting workers on the board and exposing them to the luxuries of power, union leaders fear, they'll quickly get seduced by the management point of view. "It's a little like the pigs in George Orwell's *Animal Farm*," Robert Rodden of the IAM told participants at the Third International Conference on Self-Management. "Do you remember the last line, where the animals look from the pigs to the men, and from the men to the pigs, and they can't tell the difference? We prefer collective bargaining, a strong

grievance procedure, an adversary relationship in which management does its job, which is to manage, and we do our job, which is to represent the workers."

If union representatives join the board of directors, the union will get saddled with blame for management mistakes, while getting little reward for management successes.

"We do not seek to be a partner in management," as the AFL-CIO official Thomas Donahue says, "to be most likely the junior partner in success and the senior partner in failure."

What's the evidence that putting worker and union

The second stage

"In the 35 years of industrial unionism's growth, the concept of workers' rights has taken root and flowered," writes UAW vice president Irving Bluestone. The first stage of the unions' struggle, Bluestone says, was the effort to "improve their standard of living, win better working conditions and achieve a greater measure of dignity and security, as important members of society." Now, "seasoned observers of the labor-management scene recognize that industrial society is on the threshold of what promises to become the second stage on the road toward industrial democracy . . . In *quantitative* terms organized workers in the United States have made commendable progress in winning a larger share of economic well-being . . . But in *qualitative* terms workers have not made the same progress and are still struggling to play a more meaningful role in the broad administrative decisions which affect their welfare, in the enterprise and on the job . . .

"The second stage on the road toward industrial democracy," Bluestone predicts, "will in all likelihood challenge certain of these 'sole responsibility of management' prerogatives."

representatives on the corporate boards will damage the union? It may be true that some corporations which have workers on their board are hoping to bring them into the management fold. *Business Week*, for instance, reports that offers from corporations such as Chrysler United Kingdom Ltd. and Fiat, in Europe, to put workers on their boards, represent a " 'last resort' strategy . . . designed to defuse worker militance by pulling unions under the corporate umbrella."

In the U.S., there is evidence in some corporations that union officials and workers who sit on the board of directors *do* move closer toward the management point of view. At the worker-owned South Bend Lathe, Inc., for instance, one union official whom management placed on the board recently resigned; he said he couldn't do a good job representing his union members and corporate management at the same time. A second union official has remained on the board; he acknowledges that the experience of sitting down with management and "getting a deeper understanding of some of the problems your opponent across the table faces" has "moderated" his views.

The Vermont Asbestos Group, also owned by the workers, shuddered through an explosive controversy recently when worker-representatives and others on the board of directors sided with a management proposal which workers had opposed.

But as case studies of corporations across the country show, merely sitting on a board of directors isn't what makes workers "sell out" and ignore their fellow workers. Instead, it is putting worker representatives on the board *without also* building in mechanisms which let the rank and file make their voices heard.

At both South Bend Lathe and Vermont Asbestos Group, there is no structure which gives workers any input into board deliberations, or even a chance to communicate with their board representatives. As a result, it's easy for the worker representatives on the board to lose touch with the rank and file. But case studies of companies which have workers on the board *and* a dynamic process of give-and-take between board members and the rank and file—IGP and the

plywood co-ops, for example—show that worker representatives in the boardroom can give employees a powerful tool to gain remarkable benefits.

- Many union leaders fear that workers and their union could be weakened if they own their own enterprise.

"Ownership?" Winpisinger asks. "I view that as a catastrophe." For one thing, Winpisinger and other labor leaders say, owning a company puts workers and unions in the same bind as serving on a corporate board. They'll lose their identity. "Pretty soon you'll get workers managing the workers, and then you'll have *management* managing the workers all over again," as Winpisinger envisions it.

Furthermore, some labor leaders argue, by giving workers ownership of an enterprise, they'll develop a competitive ownership mentality: instead of joining together in union brotherhood (and sisterhood) they'll start squabbling over the profits. Labor leaders point to the recent controversy at Vermont Asbestos Group, where workers debated whether or not to divert corporate profits into building a subsidiary, into increasing wages, or into other uses. "As soon as the company's doing really well," one union president warns, "you just wait for the workers to begin fighting each other for the spoils, worker against worker. You bet your ass they will."

Union officials paint just as gloomy a picture if the worker-owners *don't* make a profit. Indeed, Winpisinger says, the companies most likely to be sold to workers are marginal firms, which conglomerates are dumping because they have no economic future. "If a factory's closing down, which usually means it wasn't making enough money for the corporate owners," Winpisinger asks, "how in hell is the union going to make it?"

So far, these union leaders have little evidence to bolster their fears. Workers at VAG did debate bitterly about what to do with their profits, true—but they resolved the controversy with a democratic vote (see case study). There have been similar controversies at worker-owned firms from the Cooperativa

Central to the plywood co-ops, to the International Group Plans insurance company. In all cases, workers resolved their disagreements by open debate, and by democratic votes. The controversies among worker-owners over finances seemed no more wrenching than a heated campaign among workers to elect a new union president.

And the workers who have purchased their own enterprises in recent years have not plunged into bankruptcy, far from it. In most of the recent cases where workers bought a plant which was closing down—VAG, Saratoga Knitting Mill, the Herkimer Library Bureau—the company under worker ownership increased its production and profits.

- What do union leaders say about the worker *self-managed* firms—the plywood co-ops, IGP, the Cooperativa Central—where workers take part in making fundamental corporate decisions?

Most union leaders don't oppose the notion of worker self-management, exactly: they just think it's so unrealistic that it is scarcely worth talking about.

"The concept of workers' control is an exciting one," as Jerry Wurf, president of the American Federation of State, County and Municipal Employees says sardonically, "for soapbox oratory in the streets and rap sessions in the faculty lounge. It's just not realistic to talk about under the social, political and economic system in this country."

Other union leaders view the notion of self-management as a threat. For if rank and file workers are taking part in formulating corporate policies from wages and sick leave to layoffs and investments, what's left for the union to do? There is no union at IGP, and most plywood co-ops don't have unions either. At the Cooperativa Central, most members used to belong to the United Farmworkers, "but now that we all run our own ranch, we don't need them anymore, although we support their struggles at conventional ranches," one farmworker at the co-op says.

But bringing self-management to the workplace does not necessarily mean the union has to go. It depends on whether the union carves out a role for itself, or whether it shrinks away. Researcher Paul Blumberg suggests that unions could play as vital a role in self-managed firms as they do in conventional ones (see "Unions under worker self-management-I").

Unions for workplace democracy

While many union leaders oppose widely different workplace changes, ranging from humanization of work to self-management, increasing numbers of union officials are actively promoting other kinds of workplace reforms which bring greater power and freedom to workers on the shopfloor.

The most common manifestations of this emerging union spirit are the labor-management "quality of work life" projects. These are special committees which bring union, management and worker representatives together at various levels of the corporation or institution, from the shopfloor to the executive suite. The labor-management committees don't advocate worker self-management, nor do they advocate putting worker representatives on the board. They don't advocate worker ownership of the firm. Instead, the most advanced labor-management committees aim to create a new forum which encourages rank and file workers to analyze their own jobs, to raise any issues affecting their work life, and to propose and help design changes in the workplace—issues and changes which would not normally be covered under the collective bargaining contract.

The union-management committees at Harman Industries, and the former committees at the Rushton Mining Co. are two of the nation's most prominent examples of these quality of work life reforms (see case studies). Since 1973, the United Auto Workers and the major auto corporations, especially General Motors, have launched dozens of other labor-management projects at factories across the nation.

These projects come under the umbrella of management-union national Quality of Working Life Committees, established during the 1973 con-

Some leaders don't see workplace democracy projects as a threat to union power, but as a powerful vehicle for boosting union strength

tract negotiations. But there are dozens of other labor-management experiments outside the auto industry. At two recent conferences near Washington, D.C., there were union and management officials and shopfloor workers from more than 25 corporations, public institutions and even city governments which have been experimenting with labor-management quality of work life projects.

Why are growing numbers of unions participating in shopfloor "democracy" projects?

One purely strategic reason, union officials say privately, is self-defense: if the unions shrink from expanding workers' powers and freedoms on the shopfloor, management might take the initiative—and the workers will lose faith in their union.

By actively fighting for more workplace democracy, these union leaders say, unions can grab the initiative from management and earn the respect of their members, especially the more rebellious and militant younger workers, who are widely disenchanted with the union movement.

Michael Brower of the Massachusetts Quality of Working Life Center described the unions' options to participants at the Third International Conference this way: "One choice is for unions to sit back away and say, 'We don't want anything to do with cooperation, we'll fight you all the way'"—and management will fill the vacuum. "The alternative road is for unions to jump in and say, 'Yes. There are good things that can come out of management-union efforts, and we want our share, in fact, we want half the control everywhere we go in.'"

But beyond the purely strategic motivation, growing numbers of union leaders genuinely see the struggle for more democracy in the workplace as the desirable and logical outgrowth of the union struggle during the past 50 years.

They don't see union involvement in "workplace democratization" projects as a threat to union power and worker security—they see it as a powerful vehicle for gaining more union power and strength. "You can't find a collective bargaining unit that doesn't

include improving workplace conditions as a goal for collective bargaining," says Peter DiCicco of the IUE. "And I can think of no better way of improving workplace conditions than giving workers control over the workplace. Experience shows that whenever you give workers some control, it can improve working conditions all the way around."

The UAW's Irving Bluestone agrees. "The projects strengthen the union, not weaken it," he says. They "strengthen the unions in the traditional collective bargaining process, in the adversarial relationships on which unions thrive." Local union leaders involved in labor-management projects often say that the union's own members become more enthusiastic about taking part in union activities, as a result of the projects; they feel as if their union leaders are finally listening to them. And at companies such as Harman Industries, union officials say contract negotiations are much easier—and yield the union more benefits—since the labor-management committees came to town.

Advocates of labor-management projects emphasize that the workplace committees should not replace the traditional adversary process between union and management; they add on an entirely new dimension, in which the union and management can cooperate.

Bluestone puts it this way: "While issues of economic security (wages, fringe benefits) and continuing encroachment on what management terms its sole prerogatives will remain adversary in nature, there is every reason why democratizing the workplace should be undertaken as a joint, cooperative, constructive, non-adversary effort by management and the union. The initial key to achieving this goal may well be open, frank and enlightened discussion between the parties, recognizing that democratizing the workplace and humanizing the job need not be matters of confrontation, but of mutual concern for the worker, the enterprise and the welfare of society."

Labor-management quality of work life projects come in as many different shapes and sizes as the companies and unions which launch them. Following are three widely different labor-management experi-

Unions under worker self-management . . . I

Many union leaders fear that worker self-management would make American unions obsolete. But some self-management advocates argue that unions would be as important in a self-managed enterprise as they are in a traditional corporation. Researcher Paul Blumberg describes the unions' potential role this way:

"The trade union is not superfluous in a factory with a system of workers' management, because the two bodies, though both representing the worker, represent different functions and different interests of the workers. The function of the trade union is to protect the worker as employee; the function of the (worker self-management) council is to protect the worker as producer. Insofar as these functions are distinct, two organizations are justified and neither is redundant; insofar as these functions conflict with one another — as they must at times — there is room for negotiations, for 'labor-management negotiations.'

"For those who believe that it would be a

peculiar spectacle, indeed, for one set of workers' representatives (the trade union) to sit down at a bargaining table with another set of workers' representatives (a workers' council), it would be instructive to turn for a moment from the economic setting to the political setting. In the election of a school board and a city council, we do not think it at all odd for citizens to elect two different sets of representatives for different purposes, and for these representatives to discuss, bargain, and occasionally even clash.

"In such a case we do not wonder how it is possible for citizens to 'disagree with themselves,' and think the idea absurd, but realize it is the natural outcome of the exercise of different functions, activities, assignments, and interests in the community. When Congress and the President clash, both in essence popularly elected, we do not wonder how it is that the voters can disagree with themselves. There is no reason why this analogy cannot carry over into an industrial setting and why it is any more ludicrous to think of workers 'bargaining with themselves' than for citizens to do the same."

ments in "democratizing" the workplace—one in the white collar offices of the *Minneapolis Star-Tribune* newspaper, one in a Nabisco cookie and snack factory, another in a machine parts manufacturing plant.

Minneapolis Star-Tribune

Union representatives at the *Minneapolis Star-Tribune* launched what is the nation's first and only management-union workplace democracy project on a newspaper. During contract negotiations in 1972, members of the Newspaper Guild proposed forming a joint management-labor committee which would discuss any issues not covered by the normal collective bargaining machinery.

"We wanted to give the committee the power of

'advise and consent,'" Newspaper Guild representative John Carmichael told participants at the Third International Conference on Self-Management, "but management wouldn't allow it, so we had to settle for 'advise.'"

The Guild and the newspaper management formalized the role of the management-union committee, however, in the official contract: "It is stipulated that committees . . . shall discuss matters affecting relations between employees and the employer . . . (in) an effort to encourage discussions of subjects not covered by the normal bargaining and grievance machinery."

Members of the Guild elect seven or eight representatives to the management-union committee, each from a separate constituency—for instance, the city desk elects one or two, as do the reporters, and the clerical workers elect one; the management is represented on the committee by the editor, managing editor, city editor and occasionally other editors as well.

The committee has no power to make decisions—"The Guild agrees that all matters which are discussed," says the contract, "will be on a consultative basis, and that in any case the Publisher retains the right to make all final decisions." But Guild representative Carmichael told the conference that the worker-management committee has achieved some important gains for both the workers and the newspaper.

"At first we tended to take on very minor issues, such as 'We need more typewriters or more telephones or more coin changers,'" Carmichael said. "And in fact the paper was responsive; you know, we'd ask for 10 telephones and might get four or five, where before we would have gotten only a couple or none. But since then we've taken up more substantive issues.

"For the past few years the publishers have discussed with us the departmental budgets—how much money the state and city coverage will get, how much money will be spent on travel. And while they never really change things because of what we've said, the *idea* of sitting down on a newspaper and talking about the budget with the employees is revolutionary. The attitude up till now has been, 'It's none of your goddamn business what we do with the money.'

"This year we've been discussing the effects of new technology, such as the computers [newsroom personnel are using computer editing equipment, which is changing editing tasks on newspapers across the nation—Ed.]. The committee suggested, and the management agreed, to bring in our consultants to make radiation measurements to make sure the computer terminals are safe. And the management has changed the lights—the terminals have a harsh glare which hurts the eyes—at our request. This new technology in the newspaper business opens a whole new can of worms, and now we have a place to take those kinds of problems.

Stepping-stones to bigger things

"We've also been talking about such issues as the size of the staff, what to do with the new weekend sections. We spent several meetings discussing what kind of paper we ought to have. Nationally oriented? State oriented? We also examined whether management had met the goals it had set down in writing a few years back, and found in most cases they had *not*. I mean, it's a way to keep them on their toes."

The result so far of these labor-management discussions, Carmichael says, is that "The morale of the employees at the *Minneapolis Star-Tribune* is better. The communications have improved." Better morale, he says, is likely to make the product—the newspaper —better. In the long run, Carmichael says, the employees have a structure which they can use as a "stepping-stone" to taking part in more controversial issues and even actual decision-making.

"We've had discussions with management about moving toward more sophisticated decision-making," Carmichael says. "For instance, we've discussed if there is some way we could become involved in the hiring process. Management has indicated they are in favor of elevating the discussions toward those issues, although we are only in the early stages. But this year the publisher consulted with us about which candiate we'd like to see hired as the new editor. I don't know if we had any influence or not—our choice was selected—but this is unheard of in the newspaper business, asking the employees whom they'd like to hire."

Inside Nabisco

One of the newest labor-management quality of work life projects in the U.S. was launched in January 1977, inside Nabisco, the breakfast cereal and snack manufacturer. Top officials of the Bakery and Confectionery Workers International Union announced during master negotiations that they would like to launch a joint management-union

Unions under worker self-management . . . II

Cornell University researchers Jaroslav Vanek and Christopher Gunn have written a guide to *Starting Self-Managed Businesses*—using a style that helps make the material accessible to people at all educational levels. Here's how Vanek and Gunn envision the evolving role of unions:

"Labor unions have helped to protect workers in the past. Workers would not be where they are today if they hadn't formed unions. These unions will still be helpful as workers learn to manage their own work. But as times change, so will the kinds of help the unions can give us.

We have learned that most self-managed businesses can't make it all alone. They need help from outside. This help must come from other, larger groups which are already strong and can give support. Unions are among those groups. Here are some ways they can help:

• They can help workers learn more about self-management. They can make it easier for workers to teach each other, and to share ideas on the best ways to do a job.

To do this, unions can change the ways of training, apprenticeship, and professional education. Such teaching programs should guide workers to work together—to *cooperate*. The change should start right in the workplace. Here, workers could study real working models and test new ideas. Unions already have training programs where this new kind of learning could start.

• They can help self-managed groups to find startup money. Some of the ways are
  — to help these groups find ways to raise the money themselves
  — to make loans from union strike funds or retirement funds
  — to guarantee loans from banks.

• They can get managers and technicians to help. Usually unions deal with these supervisors only when they bargain for a contract. They can do more—they can try to get these people to share with other workers to find more democratic ways of doing the job.

• They can try to get big businesses to work more closely together—not to control the workers, but to help everyone make jobs more steady and sure.

• They can help find new ways to do the job. The tools and machines and skills the workers

project, and corporate executives agreed. The union and management selected a cookie and cracker plant in Houston for a pilot project, which might eventually spread throughout the rest of Nabisco.

The project is structured like this: At the corporate level, a committee including senior vice presidents from Nabisco World Headquarters and senior officers from the BCWIU International supervise the Houston project, give it top-level encouragement and keep tabs to make sure it is not encroaching on either management or union powers. The project is actually run from day-to-day by a plant level committee, comprised of nine management representatives (including department heads, supervisors and foremen) and nine union representatives (including top union officers and some rank and file representatives, elected by their colleagues in each major department of the factory).

So far, the union-management discussions have been limited to "opening the lines of communication," as one local union officer puts it. Union representatives got permission from the plant manager to shut down production lines one day, so they could conduct a worker survey to find out what issues and use are sometimes called "technologies." They help workers to produce more, faster and with less work. But the best technologies also make the job better for the worker. Too often the search for new ways of work forgets the needs of the worker. The best technology doesn't.

In the future more businesses will turn to self-management. They will work together on a large scale. They will need to plan far ahead to find the best technologies. Unions should be ready to take the lead in this search.

- Most of all, unions should *start* new self-managed businesses. They should start right away. Many plants are moving or closing down, leaving workers without jobs. If unions start new self-managed businesses, they will create new jobs for their members. And they will draw many new members as well.

More and more big businesses are leaving the country or moving to parts of the U.S. where they can pay low non-union wages. Unions can offer another, better way — through self-management."

Jaroslav Vanek and Christopher Gunn,
*The Basic Folder for Starting
Self-Managed Businesses*

changes the rank and file wanted discussed.

Union members have asked for some cosmetic improvements in the factory, and management has agreed. "We asked for curtains and carpeting in the cafeteria, and got the curtains," one union officer says, "and we also suggested, and got some changes in the cafeteria service so the food would be fresher and hotter for some of the later shifts."

The quality of work life project is helping the union, one local officer said, by creating a forum where workers can raise issues and suggestions which previously would have burdened the union leaders,

taking their time away from more substantive matters. "The quality of work program takes pressure off local union officials from going around and saying things (to management) like, 'why don't you paint this bathroom a different color,'" one union officer says. "So now he can concentrate on more nuts and bolts contract issues."

The Scanlon way

Another form of union-management "workplace democracy" project, which is gaining increasing popularity, is the Scanlon Plan. Scanlon Plans establish a union-management committee structure similar to the quality of work life projects, except that a key part of the project involves giving the workers financial bonuses whenever they cut production costs.

The United Auto Workers and management executives have launched Scanlon Plan projects in at least 14 factories in the Dana Corporation, which manufactures machinery for auto, aircraft and marine industries. Dana management officials first proposed bringing a Scanlon project to the corporation's 1,000-worker plant in Edgerton, Wisconsin, vice president M.E. Lantz told participants at the Third International Conference on Self-Management, because a Japanese corporation was selling the same product as Dana but at a 30 percent lower price. Unless the Edgerton plant slashed costs dramatically, Dana executives told the UAW, the plant might have to shut down.

"The point I stress to the workers," Don Rand, UAW's Administrative Assistant to the Secretary Treasurer told Conference participants, "is that it's our company. It's our business. The acute facts of life are that if we want better wages and better benefits and better working conditions, we've got to do a better job. That is, after the basics are hammered out in the collective bargaining, let's find a way to work together, better. This type of cooperative effort," Rand told the Conference, "is very frankly the only method by which we can survive in this tremendously competitive world."

Employees voted to try the Scanlon Plan, union officials say, by 92 percent. Under the plan, 20 "production committees" were created at the shop-floor level throughout the Edgerton plant. Each committee was comprised of two elected hourly workers and one foreman. The production committees can, on their own initiative, make changes and improvements in the production process as long as they cost $200 or less to implement. Proposed changes which cost more are sent for approval to a plant-level screening committee, which includes five top management representatives and seven employees elected from the production committees.

Each side wins

What do union and management get out of the project? When the project was first launched, the management and the union agreed on the base level ratio of how much labor was required to produce each dollar of sales. Every year, the company computes, with union confirmation, the new ratio for that year. If the ratio is less than the base level—if the workers have cut costs—then the workers get 75 percent of the cost savings and management gets 25 percent. Each employee receives his or her bonus as a percentage of wages, which means that the highest paid workers get more than the lower paid workers do.

The results: the Edgerton plant is still in business, thanks to dramatic cost saving improvements, according to both union and management officials. And workers in the plant have received an average of 17 percent higher pay, including bonuses, than they would have received from the standard negotiated hourly pay. "It's more than that," Helen Kramer, a former UAW aide, now with the IAM, told participants at the Third International Conference on Self-Management. "It involves participation by the workers in designing and controlling their own work. *Participation* is the essence of the plan," Kramer says, "not the bonuses."

In spite of the growing popularity of labor-

agement quality of work life projects, they remain a controversial development within the union movement. For instance, some fear that quality of work life projects can drain union energies on "cosmetics."

A union member at Nabisco, for instance, notes that while management executives approved workers' requests for curtains in the cafeteria, hotter food and new uniforms for female production workers, they cut short labor-management discussions when union representatives raised more substantive issues. "Recently we said we wanted to get into gains sharing and we said we wanted to get into discussing a four-day work week," the union representative said. "The plant manager said no."

And some union leaders worry about a host of other problems: the labor-management committees could take on so much responsibility that union officials, such as stewards, could become obsolete. Or, maybe the labor-management projects could work *too* well—and institute so many workplace improvements that employees wouldn't feel the need for a union anymore.

But advocates of the labor-management approach to democratizing the workplace dismiss these fears. The risks are not inherent in the labor-management projects, they say, but are products of the careless and shallow way in which some labor-management projects have been set up. At Nabisco, for example, the union is having problems because the labor-management committee has no power. The plant manager reigns supreme, and can even prohibit discussions if he wants. The Harman project avoided this pitfall by giving its top labor-management committee *authority*—the authority to tackle any discussions, or changes, that participants on the committee want. If members of the committee object to any proposals or topics before them, they must discuss openly and honestly *why* they are opposed—a rule which in itself forces a discussion of the controversy. Eventually, participants say, the Harman committee members usually reach a consensus.

Even more important, advocates say, is this: in

Worker participation projects, no matter how superficial they may seem, contain the seeds of more fundamental changes in the workplace

order for the project to succeed, the labor and management representatives must commit themselves to firm principles. Projects which pursue mainly economic goals, such as increased productivity, or projects which pursue only nebulous goals—Nabisco's project aims vaguely at "improving working conditions"—aren't likely to achieve much for the workers in the long run. But at Harman, the most successful labor-management project, participants have committed themselves to four "principles of human development," as they call them—security, equity, individuation and democracy (see *Harman Industries* case study).

Where are the labor-management projects headed over the next decade? Some observers see the projects continuing on their present course, with worker-management committees initiating changes in the workplace such as redesigning assembly lines, installing new light fixtures, and changing other day-to-day aspects of workers' jobs.

Many advocates of labor-management projects have sought to assure managers and union officials alike that forming union-management committees, which give workers more participation on the shopfloor, will not lead to worker and union demands for power over management.

"There are fears voiced by some managers," Ted Mills, director of the American Center for the Quality of Work Life, has said, "that encouraging increased 'participation' by the workforce means the opening of a Pandora's box, a first step toward encroachment upon management's prerogatives of controlling and directing the means and processes of production . . . . They see spectres of employee 'participation' as the beginning of a process which will end up with workers managing the managers. They refuse to see the vast difference between direct employee involvement in their work, which workers want . . . and representative employee participation in *managing* . . ."

Seeds of change

It is true that no labor-management quality of work life committees have lead to worker demands for "managing" the enterprise. But some observers believe that's where the labor-management projects are headed: Worker participation projects, they say no matter how superficial they appear to be, contain within them the seeds of more fundamental changes in the workplace. Whenever workers analyze their own jobs, whenever workers talk with management representatives about issues which were previously considered taboo, they gain a better understanding of the enterprise and begin to see possibilities for change where none existed before. "We may only be talking about curtains now," as one Nabisco union representative says, "but at least we've put our foot in the door."

At the more substantive projects, workers are already evolving toward discussions which touch on management prerogatives. At the Minneapolis Star-Tribune, as Carmichael says, discussions about buying more typewriters have evolved to discussions about finances and executive hiring practices. At Harman, shopfloor committees started talking about how to improve ventilation; ultimately, they made changes which reach outside the factory doors and affect their families and community (see case study).

Eventually, some observers predict, the labor-management committees will help generate worker demands to take part in management.

"In our system of industrial organization," UAW vice president Irving Bluestone says, "participation by workers in 'managing the enterprise' by shaping decisions as to such matters as product, product design, accounting procedures, purchasing, sales, long-term expansion, capital investment, etc., is a 'scary' subject for management and for workers. Yet at some point the workers will want and should participate in many areas of decision-making because such decisions can drastically affect the welfare, the security of the workers, as well as of the enterprise."

Sources

William Winpisinger, "Dehumanization on the Job—Crisis or Coverup?" speech at Principia College, April 13, 1973.

Winpisinger, "Worker Alienation: Myth or Fact?" speech to Cincinnati IRRA-Personnel Association Dinner, November 19, 1973.

Winpisinger, "Resolving Conflicts in Labor-Management Relations," speech at the Jamestown Labor-Management Committee Conference, October 18, 1975.

Winpisinger, "Participative Management—A Union View," speech at the American Society for Personnel Administration Fourth Annual Workshop, no date.

Irving Bluestone, "The Next Step Toward Industrial Democracy," speech on January 21, 1972.

Bluestone,. "Democratizing the Workplace," speech on June 22, 1972.

Bluestone, "The System of Work—A New Look Needed," speech at Palmer House, Chicago, December 10-12, 1972.

Thomas Donahue, speech at International Conference on Trends in Industrial and Labour Relations, Montreal, May 26, 1976.

Jim Wilson, "Self-Management, Participation and Organized Labor in American History," paper at the Second Conference on Self-Management, June 6-8, 1975.

"The Quality of Work Program: The First Eighteen Months," report by the National Quality of Work Center and the Institute for Social Research.

"The Joy of Work," *Newsweek*, January 12, 1976 (article on the Sullair Corp.).

Transcripts from the Third International Conference on Self-Management.

Personal interviews by the editor with John Carmichael, Pete DiCicco, Don Rand, Thomas Donahue, William Winpisinger, plus management and union representatives at Nabisco-Houston and others.

RE-SOURCES

Editor's note: This list of resources is distilled from the suggestions of various researchers and activists. Special thanks to Randy Barber, Bill Behn, Mark Looney, Michael Maccoby, Sam Salkin, Walter Schenkel, and Kathy Terzi.

Readings

One of the major obstacles to creating self-managed enterprises in the United States is the painful lack of "how-to" books. But the following readings provide excellent beginning guides to the nuts and bolts of establishing worker self-managed and worker-owned enterprises. All of them can be ordered from Strongforce, 2121 Decatur Place NW, Washington, D.C. 20008.

Democracy in the Workplace: Readings on the Implementation of Self-Management in the United States, by the Ithaca Work Group, Strongforce Series, 1977. $5

The How-to-Start Folder for Self-Managed Businesses, by Jaroslav Vanek and Christopher Gunn, Strongforce Series, 1976. 50¢

No Bosses Here: A Manual on Working Collectively, by Boston Vocations for Social Change, 1977. $3

Non-Profit Food Stores, by Nancy Perelli, William Ronco, et al, Strongforce Series, 1977. $3

Five years ago it was hard to find a good book exploring the theories of worker participation, workers' control and self-management. But now the space reserved for these readings on the bookshelf is getting wider. The following are highly recommended:

Workplace Democratization: Its Internal Dynamics, by Paul Bernstein, Kent State University Press, 1976.

Workers' Control, A Reader on Labor & Social Change, Edited by Gerry Hunnius et al, Random House, 1973.

Industrial Democracy: the Sociology of Participation, by Paul Blumberg, Schocken Paperback, 1973.

184

RESOURCES

The Case for Participatory Democracy, edited by George Benello and Dimitrios Roussopoulos, Grossman Publishers, 1971.

Self-Management: Economic Liberation of Man, by Jaroslav Vanek, Penguin Books, 1975.

The General Theory of Labor-Managed Market Economies, by Vanek, Cornell University Press, 1970.

The Labor-Managed Economy: Essays, by Vanek, Cornell University Press, 1977.

Can the Workers Run Industry? by Ken Coates, Sphere Books, 1968.

Workers' Control, by Ken Coates and Tony Topham, Panther Modern Society Series, 1970.

Self-Governing Socialism, a Reader, edited by Bronco Horvat et al, International Arts and Sciences Press, 1975.

Participation and Democratic Theory, by Carole Pateman, Cambridge University Press, 1970.

Strategy for Labor, by Andre Gorz, Beacon Press, 1968.

Democracy and the Work Place, by H.B. Wilson, Black Rose Books, 1974.

The Quality of Working Life, edited by Louis Davis and Albert Charns, The Free Press, 1975.

Late Capitalism, by Ernest Mandel, New Left Books, 1976.

Most of the previous books concentrate on theories of workplace democracy. The following books contain case studies of actual workplace democracy experiments in the U.S.:

Worker-Owned Plywood Companies: An Economic Analysis, by Katrina Berman, Washington State University Press, 1967.

Industrial Democracy and the Worker-Owned Firm: A Case Study of Twenty-One Plywood Companies in the Pacific Northwest, by Carl Bellas, Praeger Publications, 1972.

Industrial Democracy: The Sociology of Participation, by Paul Blumberg, Schocken Paperback, 1973.

Workplace Democratization: Its Internal Dynamics, by Paul Bernstein, Kent State University Press, 1976.

Job Power: Blue and White Collar Democracy, by David Jenkins, Doubleday, 1973.

Jobs, by William Ronco, Beacon Press, 1977.

Food Co-ops, An Alternative to Shopping in Supermarkets, by Ronco, Beacon Press, 1974.

Democratizing the Workplace: From Job Enrichment to Worker Control, by the Workers' Self-Management Group, American Friends Service Committee (You can order this packet of 12 articles for $1 from AFSC, 48 Inman Street, Cambridge, Massachusetts 02139).

RESOURCES

Work in America: Report of the Special Task Force of the Secretary of Health, Education and Welfare, MIT Press, 1973.

Work and the Quality of Work Life, edited by James O'Toole, MIT Press.

Own Your Own Job: Economic Democracy for Working Americans, by Jeremy Rifkin, Bantam Books, 1977.

It's easier to understand where trends in workplace democracy might be *going* if you understand where the U.S. workplace and labor movement have come from. These books provide a general background on the nature of work, the labor movement, and corporate control of the economy:

Strike! by Jeremy Brecher, Straight Arrow, 1972.

The Lean Years: A History of the American Worker, 1920-33, by Irving Bernstein, Houghton Mifflin, 1960.

The Turbulent Years: A History of the American Worker, 1933-41, by Bernstein, 1969.

History of Labor in the United States, by John Commons et al, four volumes, MacMillan, 1966.

The American Idea of Industrial Democracy, 1865-1965, by Milton Derber, Illinois University Press, 1970.

The Advance and Rise of the American Cooperative Enterprise, by Joseph Knapp, Interstate Printers and Publishers, 1973.

The Rise of Workers' Movements, edited by Root and Branch, Fawcett Publications, 1975.

False Promises, The Shaping of the American Working Class Consciousness, by Stanley Aronowitz, McGraw Hill, 1973.

Labor and Monopoly Capital: The Degradation of Work in the Twentieth Century, Monthly Review Press, 1974.

Working, by Studs Terkel, Random House, 1973.

Where Have All the Robots Gone? by Hal Sheppard and Neal Herrick, Free Press Paperback, 1973.

For details about efforts to build workplace democracy in other nations, try the following books:

Worker Self-Management in Industry: The West European Experience, by G. David Garson, Praeger Publishers, 1977.

Industrial Democracy: Yugoslav Style, by I. Adizes, Free Press, 1971.

Yugoslav Workers' Self-Management, edited by M. Broekmeyer, Reidel, 1970.

Workers' Management and Workers' Wages in Yugoslavia, by Howard Wachtel, Cornell University Press, 1973.

The Economics of Workers' Management: A Yugoslav Case Study, by Jaroslav Vanek, Allen & Unwin, 1972.

RESOURCES

Work and Community: The Scott Bader Commonwealth and The Quest for a New Social Order, by Fred Blum, Routledge & Kegan Paul, 1968.

Experiment in Industrial Democracy: A Study of the John Lewis Partnership, by A. Flanders et al, Faber, 1968.

The New Worker Cooperatives, edited by Ken Coates, Spokesman Books, 1976.

The Shop Steward's Guide to the Bullock Report, by Ken Coates and Tony Topham, Spokesman books, 1977.

Workers' Participation in Management in Britain, by R.O. Clarke et al, Heinemann Educational Books, 1972.

Workers' Participation in Industry, by Michael Poole, Routledge & Kegan Paul, 1975.

Participation of Workers in Decisions Within Undertakings, by the International Labour Office, ILO, 1969.

Report on the International Seminar on Workers' Participation in Decisions Within Undertakings, by the International Labour Office, ILO, 1970.

Democracy at Work, by F.E. Emery and E. Thorsrud, Martinus Nijhoff, 1976.

The Land to Those Who Work It: Algeria's Experiment in Workers' Management, by Thomas L. Blair, Doubleday/Anchor, 1970.

Revolutionary Politics and the Cuban Working Class, by Maurice Zeitlin, Princeton University Press, 1967.

People

When you begin to explore new territory, such as creating a process of worker participation or worker self-managament, it's crucial to have a guide. These centers are all working actively on various aspects of workplace democracy—researching, writing, and in some cases even consulting.

American Center for the Quality of Work Life
3301 New Mexico Avenue, NW
Suite 202
Washington, D.C. 20016
(202) 338-2933
The Center specializes in helping unions and managements explore the possibilities of launching labor-management "quality of work life" projects. The Center has helped design a half dozen labor-management projects at workplaces ranging from a major hospital to a multinational timber corporation.

Association for Self-Management
c/o 1414 Spring Road, NW
Washington, D.C. 20010
(202) 723-5101

ASM publishes a newsletter, often an excellent source of tidbits on worker self-management experiments, debates on theories of worker self-management, and references to good articles and

RESOURCES

books in the field. The Association, a loose network of individuals and local chapters, has sponsored four international conferences on self-management.

Boston College Program in Social Economy and Social Policy

Department of Sociology
Boston College
Chestnut Hill, Massachusetts 02167
(617) 969-0100

This new graduate program, leading toward a PhD, says its "main focus will be on humanizing life in economic organizations and developing a concept of self-governance for people who work within them." Drawing on visiting academics and practitioners from all the major disciplines, the program explores theory and practice of worker self-management, codetermination, and community development corporations; the program also explores the relationship between workplace democracy and social-economic policies at the national level.

Center for Community Economic Development

639 Massachusetts Avenue
Room 316
Cambridge, Massachusetts 02139
(617) 547-9695

When it comes to questions about community economic development, emphasizing community and worker control, the Center is the place to go. Its *CCED Newsletter* and numerous pamphlets discuss strategies for using federal funds, designated for Community Development Corporations, to promote community economic democracy.

Center for Economic Studies

457 Kingsley Avenue
Palo Alto, California 94301
(415) 328-1039

Center researchers have published valuable reports on the role of education in preparing people for autocratic work environments—and the crucial need for dramatic changes in the schools to prepare citizens for workplace democracy. Current research projects at the Center are analyzing the growing problem of plant shutdowns, and the potential for converting enterprises into producer cooperatives.

Community Ownership Organizing Project

6529 Telegraph Avenue
Oakland, California 94609
(415) 653-6555

Write to this group for its excellent newsletter, "The Public Works." The Project writes about, promotes, and provides consultation help in launching community- and worker-owned enterprises. For instance, the Project has prepared feasibility studies on a proposed public power corporation in Berkeley, as well as studies on community-controlled cable TV networks. Most, but not all, of its work focuses on California.

RESOURCES

Cornell University New System of Work and Participation Program
New York State School of Industrial and Labor Relations
Ives Hall
Ithaca, New York 14853
(607) 256-4530

The Cornell project, directed by William Foote Whyte, has been conducting detailed research on, and writing about, worker-owned firms in the eastern U.S. The project's researchers have also been compiling a historical file of all producer co-ops launched in the U.S. since 1790. Their goal is to study whether certain political, social and economic conditions in the nation seem to provide fertile soil for worker ownership and self-management. Whyte's project has also been instrumental in drafting the Voluntary Job Preservation and Community Stabilization Act, now before Congress. The researchers are a rich source of information about the realities of forming a worker-owned and managed enterprise.

Cornell University Program on Participation
and Labor-Managed Systems
Department of Economics
490 Uris Hall
Ithaca, New York 14853
(607) 256-4867

The director of this program is Jaroslav Vanek, one of the nation's leading theorists on workers' self-management. This is one of the few universities in the world where you can get a PhD in the economics of participation and labor-managed systems.

Documentation Center on Self-Management
490 Uris Hall
Cornell University
Ithaca, New York 14853
(607) 256-4070

The Documentation Center will provide what no library in the U.S. can provide: a good, and rapidly growing bibliography of articles, books, and unpublished papers—complete with abstracts—on workers' self-management, workers' participation, team work, production cooperatives, and related issues. So far the data base contains 3,000 references. A search by key-word subject areas costs $10, for up to 10 references, plus $3 for each additional three references.

Harvard Project on Technology, Work and Character
1710 Connecticut Avenue NW
Washington, D.C.
(202) 462-3003

The Harvard Project, directed by Michael Maccoby, is one of the nation's only consulting groups—and probably its best—with considerable experience in launching workplace democracy projects. Its expertise is in labor-management projects, in work places ranging from Harman Industries to the U.S. Commerce

RESOURCES

Department. Members of the Project also conduct research on the effects of workplace democracy experiments, and publish articles and books.

Industrial Common-Ownership Movement

31 Hare Street
Woolwich, London SE18 6JN
England
(44)-1-855-4099

ICOM was originally established in 1958 by the founder of the worker-owned and self-managed Scott Bader Commonwealth, to promote worker control of enterprise. Today, ICOM provides technical assistance to firms that wish to convert to democratic ownership and control structures, as well as to worker and community groups attempting to build industrial co-ops from scratch. The organization, which lists several hundred producer co-ops among its members, publishes excellent pamphlets including "How To Form an Industrial Co-operative."

Industrial Cooperative Association, Inc.

2161 Massachusetts Avenue
Cambridge, Massachusetts 02140
(617) 661-6130

ICA is a new and promising nonprofit organization designed to develop worker-owned and self-managed businesses. During its first year of operation, 1978, ICA provided financial backing necessary to launch the Colonial Cooperative Press, a small worker-controlled firm founded on the ashes of a major printing plant that had been shut down by its conglomerate parent. ICA helped draft what is perhaps the nation's best industrial co-op ownership and control model.

ICA also helped raise financing for International Poultry, Inc., a cooperative poultry processing factory controlled by low-income workers in Willimantic, Connecticut.

Institute for Workers' Control

Bertrand Russell House
Gamble Street
Nottingham NG7 4ET
England
(44) 602-74504

Leaders of the Institute—including Walter Kendall, Ken Coates and Tony Topham—churn out prolific numbers of eloquent publications analyzing social-economic problems and arguing the role which workers' control should play in solving them. Although most of their writings have a British focus, they are must reading for anyone exploring the theory and practice of worker democracy.

Lane Economic Development Council

PO Box 1473
Eugene, Oregon 97440
(503) 484-7007

This foundation-funded community development corporation serves a huge rural county in Oregon; it is one of the few CDCs in the nation that promotes worker-community control of

RESOURCES

enterprises. The Council played an important role in establishing a $900,000 government-funded industrial park, expressly intended for community and worker-owned firms.—perhaps the first of its kind in the U.S.

Massachusetts Quality of Working Life Center
14 Beacon Street
Boston, Massachusetts 02108
(617) 227-6266

The Center helps unions and managements in corporations and agencies around the state launch labor-management quality of work life programs.

National Center for Economic Alternatives
2000 P Street NW
Washington, DC 20036
(202) 833-3208

The National Center (formerly the Exploratory Project on Economic Alternatives) publishes a series of excellent reports on various aspects of economic democracy, including the potential role of producer and consumer co-ops; community and worker ownership of enterprises; and strategies toward fighting inflation and achieving full employment. NCEA has gained international attention as the key organizational and financial consultant to the Youngstown, Ohio coalition trying to reopen a massive, shutdown steel mill under community-worker ownership and control.

New School of Democratic Management
589 Howard Street
San Francisco, California 94105
(415) 543-7973

The New School accurately calls itself "the nation's only business school committed to democracy in the workplace and community control of enterprise." Since 1977, the San Francisco-based school has held week-long teaching sessions in Seattle, Washington; Helena, Montana; Minneapolis, Minnesota; and Austin, Texas. Each session has drawn about 100 participants from worker-owned and controlled enterprises across the U.S. Classes, taught by outstanding professors, researchers and activists, range from techniques of bookkeeping and marketing to democratic decision-making; from computer services and fundraising to how to conduct a meeting. Future teaching sessions in other cities across the country are already being planned.

North American Students of Cooperation
Co-op
PO Box 7293
Ann Arbor, Michigan 48107

NASCO is the national umbrella organization for student co-ops across the nation, most of them food stores and housing cooperatives. But its work is important to all workers and community self-managed organizations. NASCO's *CO-OP* magazine has excellent in-depth articles exploring worker and community control issues, co-op politics and economics, and related issues

RESOURCES

(bimonthly, $10.50 per year). The group also provides technical assistance to co-ops—such as its annual Cooperative Educating and Training Institute in Ann Arbor, three days of intensive workshops for co-op workers from across North America.

Peoples Business Commission
1346 Connecticut Avenue NW
Washington, D.C. 20036
(202) 466-2823

The Peoples Business Commission, an outgrowth of the People's Bicentennial Commission, says it is dedicated to "challenging the abuses of corporate power" and "mobilizing public support for democratic alternatives" to the current economic system. PBC produces a wealth of books and pamphlets on the subject, and also provides good speakers for everything from high schools to TV talk shows to enormous political rallies. One of PBC's major projects is researching, and publicizing, how unions could use their pension funds to promote social change.

Project Work
490 Riverside Drive
Room 517
New York, New York 10027
(212) 866-2221

Just getting off the ground with foundation funding, Project Work will coordinate educational activities among New York City's worker self-managed businesses. It aims to become the same sort of resource center in New York as Strongforce has become in Washington, D.C.

Quality of Work Program
Survey Research Center
Institute for Social Research
University of Michigan
Ann Arbor, Michigan 48106
(313) 764-9397

Researchers on the program's staff have conducted some of the major studies on worker boredom and alienation in the U.S. They also conduct studies exploring how various workplace reforms, from autonomous teams to flexible hours, affect work and employee attitudes in specific companies. The Program recently conducted a major federal-funded survey on worker-owned enterprises in the United States.

Southside Community Enterprises
2550 Pillsbury Avenue South
Minneapolis, Minnesota 55404
(612) 827-5381

This city-funded community development corporation has drafted a fascinating plan for promoting community- and worker-controlled enterprises in the economically depressed Minneapolis southside. SCE has organized a number of workshops and conferences on community and worker control, and it has provided financial and technical assistance to some of the city's small worker-owned firms.

Strongforce
2121 Decatur Place NW
Washington, D.C. 20008
(202) 234-6883

Strongforce has become one of the better known educational and financial resources in the movement for worker and community control of enterprises. Its series of booklets on self-managed enterprises fill an important gap in the literature (see *Readings*). Using funds from a federal grant, Strongforce has provided technical assistance to worker collectives in Washington, D.C.

Technica Incorporado
53 Russell Road
Salinas, California 93901
(408) 443-1676

Technica is the remarkable training school established by the Cooperativa Central to help other farmworkers launch their own agricultural co-ops. Besides giving training in the classroom and in the field, Technica is preparing some "how to" guides to setting up and managing profitable worker cooperatives.

Workers' Self-Management Group
American Friends Service Community
48 Inman Street
Cambridge, Massachusetts 02139
(617) 864-3150

Besides publishing the useful *Democratizing the Workplace* packet (see Readings), this group has been holding workshops and conferences for worker self-managed enterprises in New England. It also provides technical assistance to worker self-managed firms.

A bill toward workers' control

Two of the major obstacles which confront workers and communities who want to save viable companies that are closing down are money and know-how—rather, the dire lack of them. In the cases where workers and worker-community groups have been able to piece together a financial package to save an enterprise, it has usually been a Scotch-tape affair: a little worker savings here, some local bank loans there, and infrequently some aid from the U.S. Economic Development Administration. The case studies don't reveal the numerous communities in which efforts to save a shutdown plant failed —or never even got off the ground, simply because the prospects of raising the necessary cash were so hopeless.

Even when workers and worker-community groups manage to buy the enterprise, the long-term problems begin: they do not have any experience or training to prepare them in their new roles as worker-owners, to teach them how to establish a sound structure which will allow increasing worker participation in decision-making.

But now there's a bill before the U.S. House of Representatives which would go a long way toward dismantling both obstacles. The bill—called the "Voluntary Job Preservation and Community Stabilization Act" would pour almost $1 billion over the next seven years into "facilitating employee, or employee-community, ownership of concerns that would otherwise close down or move out of the community." Worker and worker-community ownership of corporations, the bill declares, would help prevent unemployment "by strengthening local initiative and responsibility, and by helping individuals and communities to use their own

resources to solve this problem." The bill, introduced by Peter Kostmayer (D-Penn.), Stanley Lundine (D-N.Y.) and Matthew McHugh (D-N.Y.), includes the following highlights:

- The U.S. Economic Development Administration would "conduct a continuing investigation" across the nation "to identify concerns which are in danger of ceasing operation" or migrating to another location, causing "substantial unemployment and economic dislocation to the community."

The government would be required to alert workers and communities affected, and to inform them about the possibilities that they could buy the enterprise. Today, the government does not keep systematic records of corporations which are about to shut down—and when the government *does* learn that a company is going to shut its doors, Labor Department officials say, they regard the news as "proprietary information" and keep the information secret. In many cases where plants have shut down, such as the Vermont Asbestos Group, the workers didn't learn they were about to lose their jobs until they read it in the newspapers.

- Workers and community groups which are interested in buying their plant can apply to the government for special long-term (maximum 10-year) loans. The government can lend money both to the corporation itself and to individuals, to help them buy stocks. Within 60 days after the employee or employee-community groups apply for aid, the Department of Commerce "shall conduct a feasibility study" to determine if the corporation is viable.

This clause would be invaluable to worker-community groups, which often are unable to raise cash—simply because they can't even afford to finance the kind of feasibility study which financial lending institutions demand. According to the bill, the government "shall consult with the organization" of worker and community members before choosing a consultant to conduct the feasibility study "to insure the appropriate participation of the organization in the feasibility study." This would guarantee that the local citizens wouldn't be upstaged by technocrats, but would be involved in buying their own enterprise at every step of the way.

• Worker and worker-community groups which apply for government assistance must first certify that they have considered, and deliberated on, "all options relating to the form of ownership and control available." This means, architects of the bill explain, that the workers and community would have to learn about the various kinds of corporate ownership and control structures possible, from co-ops with one-worker, one-vote, to ESOPs.

The reason: the bill's sponsors want to make sure that workers and community groups will choose their own unique form of ownership and control "based upon an *informed* choice among the various options that are possible," explains Cornell University researcher William Foote Whyte, who helped draft the legislation. For as the case studies of worker and worker-community owned companies suggest, workers and communities in the throes of trying to save their enterprises "concentrate all their attention upon the financial and technical problems of saving the jobs and give little thought to the form of

ownership and control under which the employees are to live and work for the life of the new organization." As a result, the new enterprise doesn't operate much differently than the conglomerate-owned firm did. Architects of the bill hope to encourage workers and communities to create a more democratic ownership and control structure. "We can't legislate participation," says a top aide to Kostmayer, "but we can explain how other community-worker owned corporations have worked, and then let the people make up their own minds."

• Workers and community groups applying for government help would have to certify that—whatever ownership and control structures they've chosen—they have built in a process which allows "the inclusion of new members in ownership and participation."

The purpose of this clause, architects of the bill explain, is to prevent "collective selfishness." For instance, many plywood co-ops have refused to let new members join the co-op; instead, they expand the workforce with hourly workers. This creates a hierarchy: on top, members who have voting rights and get a share of the profits, and on the bottom, "second class" workers who have no rights and get paid by the hour.

The bill also requires the workers and community groups to guarantee that the new corporation will have the right of first refusal to buy back shares of stock, from any workers who are quitting. That way, the new worker and worker-community owned firm can't be sold out from under the workers' feet. At the Vermont Asbestos Group, for instance, a private investor has been trying to buy a controlling percentage of the workers' stocks, in order to take over the worker and community-owned mine.

Workers who want to preserve their community enterprise really have no way to stop fellow workers who want to sell out.

• Once the workers' and community's application for assistance is approved, they'll get more than money from the government; they'll get training and advice about financial, engineering, marketing and legal aspects of the new enterprise, too. Just as important: the workers and community members will get *organizational* advice, with special emphasis on "The design of the work environment after the transfer, including worker motivation and productivity, job satisfaction, and the improvement in the quality of working life through increased employee participation in decisionmaking."

Each of the companies which has experimented with worker participation in decision-making—from Consumers United Group to McCaysville Industries to the plywood co-ops—has been like a pioneer grappling to set up a workable structure on its own. None of them have had the benefit of expert consultants to help them—and indeed, there aren't many consultants in the U.S. who know how. One of the most important side effects of the bill would be that the government would have to provide these consultants—and *that* would probably mean financing special schools and training centers across the country which could turn out experts in the techniques of worker participation and democratic self-management.

What are the chances the bill will get passed? So far, it's not possible to predict. But the bill has already attracted more than 40 cosponsors in the House—a sign that the notion of worker and community control of industry is making important inroads into the political establishment.